Booksharing

Booksharing:

101 Programs to Use With Preschoolers

Margaret Read MacDonald

with illustrations by
Julie Liana MacDonald

Library Professional Publications
Hamden, Connecticut

C. 2

© 1988 Margaret Read MacDonald.
All rights reserved
First published as a Library Professional Publication,
an imprint of the Shoe String Press, Inc.,
Hamden, Connecticut 06514
Printed in the United States of America

Library of Congress Cataloging in Publication Data
MacDonald, Margaret Read, 1940–
    Booksharing: 101 programs to use with preschoolers.

    Bibliography: p.
    Includes index.
    1. Public libraries—Services to preschool children.
2. Libraries, Children's—Activity programs.
3. Children—Books and reading 4. Reading (Preschool)
I. Title.
Z718.1.M24   1988   027.52'776251   87-35777
ISBN 0-208-02159-0 (hardcover)
ISBN 0-208-02314-3 (paperback)

First paperback edition printed 1991

Dedicated to the Children's Librarians of the King County Library System for their incredible creativity and exuberance in sharing programming ideas.

Because of the fine cross-fertilization of ideas which take place in this system, this book must have been influenced by each of you. Thanks to Director Herb Mutschler and Children's Coordinator Bob Polishuk for creating an atmosphere and a monthly time in which librarians can meet and share. And thanks to the following children's librarians:

Ruth Bacharach
Maureen Bala
Michaelan Beytebiere
Louise Blaine
Barbara Blue
Carole Burkhart
Kay Carlisle
Nell Colburn
Myrle Dougherty
Margaret Ellsworth
Linda Ernst
Dorothy Ferguson
Carole Fick
Ellen Fowler

Gretchen Furber
Bonnie Gerken
Susan Golden
Beth Gregg
Cheryl Hadley
Marilyn Hanna
Harriet Herschel
Kathy Huber
Jan Ian
Pat Jackson
Elizabeth Love
Mariko Martin
Dorothy Matsui
Sue Mooseker

Sandra Ogren
Scooter Poore
Sally Porter-Smith
Linda Reed
Sherry Roselius
Anne Roush
Pat Shaw
Laurel Steiner
Lisa Stock
Rebecca Teeters
Roz Thompson
Lois Van Dress
Joyce Wagar
Suzanne Woodford

Table of Contents

Acknowledgments   xiii
About These Programs   1

Science Beginnings

Habitats
1. Habitat: The Field   15
2. Habitat: The Tree   16
3. Habitat: The Garden   17
4. Habitat: The Sea   20
5. Habitat: The Pond   21

Exploring Your Backyard
6. Down in the Grass: A Bug's Eye View of the World   23
7. A Seed Grows   25
8. Meet a Worm   26
9. A Mushroom is Growing   28
10. Lots of Rot   29

How Things Work
11. But Will It Fly? Aerodynamics   30
12. Wind Power   32
13. Tools Work For Us!   33
14. Wheels and Gears   35

Young Scientists
15. Classifying Chairs   36
16. Take a Closer Look!   38

Geological Wonders
17. Dinosaurs   39
18. Your Own Special Rock   40
19. Volcanoes Erupt!   41

Exploring Our Senses
20. Hear It!   42
21. Taste It!   45
22. Touch It!   46
23. See It!   48
24. Smell It!   50

Basic Concepts

25. Number Rhumba 52
26. Color Me Red! 54
27. Is It Fast? Is It Slow? 56
28. What Then? A Sequencing Storytime 57

Through the Year: Seasons

Fall (See also: Halloween)

29. All Falling Down 63
30. Apple Day 64
31. Harvest Moon 66
32. Owls in the Night 67
33. Black Cats 69

Winter (See also: Thanksgiving, Hanukkah, Christmas)

34. The Snowy Day 72
35. Snow Bears 73

Spring (See also: Easter, Wind Power)

36. It's Spring 75
37. Feathered Babies 76
38. Spring Kittens 78
39. Spring Hats 80
40. The Rainy Day 81

Summer

41. Sun! 83
42. Shadow Play 84

Celebrations

Valentine's Day

43. Be My Friend 89
44. Mailman, Mailman, Bring Me a Letter! 90

St. Patrick's Day

45. St. Patrick's Day Parade 92

April Fool's Day

46. Feeling Foolish 93

Easter

47. Easter Rabbits (See also: It's Spring, Feathered Babies, Spring Hats) 95

May Day (See: Music Time: May Day)
Arbor Day (See: Habitat: The Tree, Apple Day)
Fourth of July
    48. Fourth of July Parade   97
Halloween (See also: Black Cats,
        Owls in the Night)
    49. Pumpkin Magic   99
    50. Ghosts and Witches   100
    51. Trick or Treat   102
Thanksgiving (See also: Feeling Glad)
    52. Thanksgiving Turkeys   103
Hanukkah
    53. Happy Hanukkah   105
Christmas
    54. Christmas Lullabies   107
    55. Christmas Bells   108
    56. Here Comes Santa Claus!   110
Birthdays
    57. Happy Birthday to Me!   112

Getting to Know Yourself

Feelings (See also: Making Faces, Copy Cats,
        Exploring Our Senses, Feeling Foolish)
    58. Feeling Glad   117
    59. Feeling Mad   118
    60. The Don't Be Scared Storytime   120
    61. The Caring Day   121
    62. Just Me!   123
    63. The New Baby   124
About You
    64. Making Faces   126
    65. Sleepy Storytime   127
    66. New Shoes   130
    67. Button, Button   131
    68. My House, My Home   133

Using Your Imagination

Adventuring
    69. Here Comes the Train!   139

70. Take Me Ridin' In Your Car!   140
71. On the High Seas!   142

Animal Antics (See also: Music Time, Frog Songs, Spring Kittens, Black Cats, Owls in the Night, Snow Bears, Feathered Babies)

72. Happy Lions   143
73. Elephants, Babies, and Elephant Babies   145
74. Crocodiles and Alligators   147
75. Mice Are Nice   149
76. Portly Pigs   150
77. Problem Pups   151

Dreams and Nonsense

78. Freaky Food   153
79. Foolish Furniture   155
80. Dream Time   157
81. Teddy Bears Go Dancing   158
82. Copy Cats   159
83. Rhyme, Rhyme, Rhyme   160
84. Wonderful Words   162
85. Monster Bash!   163
86. A Visit to the King and Queen   164
87. Blueberry, Strawberry, Jamberry!   165

Ethnic Programs

European Travelers (See also: St. Patrick's Day Parade)

88. Highland Fling   169
89. Russian Winter   170
90. Voici Paris!   172

Art Concepts Series

Focus on Art

91. Print It!   177
92. Looking at a Line   179
93. Paste a Collage!   181
94. Mold It!   183

Music Time

95. A Little Schubert   189
96. Frog Songs   189
97. Barnyard Dance   191
98. Chicken Soup   192
99. Drummer Hoff   193
100. Dancing Dolls   193
101. May Day   194

Bibliography   197
Index of Films   235
Appendix: Musical Notations for Songs   237
Subject Index   253

Acknowledgments

Thanks to my editor Virginia Mathews for insisting I write this book and to the staff of the Bothell Public Library for putting up with piles of pictures books, hoarded titles, and a children's librarian distracted at times. To Head Librarian Mary Ann Chatman and her staff: Belle Britton, Sandra Dechant, Mary Lane Stain, Eleanor Topham, Christy Watkins, Barbara Whitney, and Su Vathanaprida, thanks.

To Shirley Buckingham for typing the manuscript. One of life's blessings is a typist who transcribes nearly illegible notes, corrects spelling and punctuation errors, and straightens out garbled syntax!

And to Julie MacDonald for contributing drawings for these programs. Julie was twelve at the time.

For specific elements that I use in these programs credit is due to: Elaine Read Buchanan for "Mr. Moon" camp song; Floating Eagle Feather for the Irish Benediction; Gretchen Furber for the button card threading idea and button covered felt jacket; Peggy Hart for "Black Cat" poem activity; Kaysie Mendonca for "Peanut Butter" camp song; June Pinnell for "Blue Danube"/*Dawn* idea; Patty Drew for the hibernating bear activity; Jane Stone Veal Read for "Tiny Little Pussywillow" fingerplay; Marion Taylor for *Bears in the Night* activity; Tacoma Public Library Children's Specialists for pussywillow craft; Joyce Wagar for "I Wrote a Letter to My Love" game; Suzanne Woodford for "Number Rhumba" idea and "I'm a Little Tire" action poem; Marie Nelson for Easter Egg Story.

The songs used in these storytimes have been altered through use but were learned originally from Linda Crisalli, Martha Nishitani, Helen and Richard Scholz, and assorted other pre-school and Yamaha music teachers who taught my children and myself how to make music. Thanks to Martha Nishitani for permission to reprint her "Happy Peter Pink Ears" song.

About These Programs

My Use of These Programs:

This is a collection of storytime programs that I have put together in the course of my work as a children's librarian and storyteller. They have worked well for me and for the children with whom I have interacted. I expect, however, that most of you will use them as guides and suggestions rather than reproduce them just as they are. Your storytime programs will reflect your own personality, and you may choose to use some of your favorite books, songs, poems and activities to mix with mine. You will find that it is easy to create around these ideas programs tailored to fit your style.

For my storytimes, I offer four sessions a week. Two of these are for ages two-and-a-half to three-and-a-half. These are advertised as "sharing times," and thought of as a time for parent and child to enjoy together. The parents/grandparents sit on the floor with their children in their laps. Younger siblings may be brought along, too, since many parents of three-year-olds also have a younger child. This makes the noise and movement level in the room fairly high at times. I just block it out and keep going unless it begins to fracture the group's attention.

There is one session offered each week for two-and-a-half to five-year-olds, in which parent participation is required. This session allows parents with a five-year-old and a three-year-old to attend just one session. Another session is offered for just the four- and five-year-olds. Parents are welcome to stay and watch this session but they do not participate.

The *same* program is used for all four storytimes, but it is adapted stylistically to the age group being dealt with. With the two-and-a-half to three-and-a-half group, much group participation is encouraged, key phrases are repeated, and miming of actions from the story are called for. If the group is especially wiggly, one book may be cut from the second half of the program. With this group, quite a bit of time is spent on the singing and stretching activities at mid-storytime. For the four- and five-year-olds the storytime becomes much more of a dialogue between the leader and the children. We spend a lot of time talking—about the

1

story, about ourselves. For this group, a longer book is often added, and the creative dramatics become more detailed. The very simple art projects designed for the younger group become elaborate and quite exotic in the hands of the fours and fives.

Those of you who work with only one of these age groups—the twos and threes or the fours and fives—may want to tailor the suggested programs to fit your age requirements. For those who, like myself, have to teach varying age groups each week with little preparation, these programs may work well as they stand, with stylistic adjustments of the type suggested above.

Start With the Book

A major concern in preparing this collection is that my programs not fall into the trap of being "built around a theme." By this I mean *starting with a theme* and then looking for books to fit it. In my opinion this is going at it backwards, and it is a mistake. We need to think of the books *first*. The aim of the storytime is to share fine books with children; the books that are so wonderful that no child should miss them must be featured in our programs again and again. Of course themes make for an attractive program. They give a sense of substance and please parents, and all of my programs are, in fact, thematic. But we build programs and find the theme by starting with an excellent book and looking for material that would enhance its use in a program. To complete this collection of programs, I created my own personal list of "books that *must* be shared," then worked on storytime ideas until I made sure that most of my *musts* were featured.

The Aim of the Preschool Story Program

Our intent with the storytime or story program is to bring children into a joyous connection with books and ideas. We want the child to learn to concentrate on the book, its illustrations and its language. We want children to learn to draw different levels of meaning from these, and to move from these meanings on into the joy of creating on their own. Therefore, we present the book, then follow it with activities which give participants a space in which to create their own images around the ideas presented through the book. Though I speak of a "book" here, the idea-filled object could be a movie, a recording, or another medium, because the *ideas* and their artistic representation are what is important, not the format.

The picture book, however, is a most useful format for the presentation of art, words, and the ideas they symbolize to children.

We want to encourage young children to learn to play with ideas, abstract images, and emotions. "Play" might be defined, in this context, as a state in which one "creates without fear of consequences." This creation can be through physical movement, artistic representation, vocalization—any expression possible.

Here are some of the elements which might be incorporated into a preschool story program to stimulate creative response.

Include Parents in the Story Program

I would like to make a plea here for the inclusion of parents as participants in preschool programs. Most libraries do offer a toddler session for twos which includes both parent and child. But I suggest that the parent-child connection is a valuable one for older preschoolers as well. Here are some important benefits of such a program.

1. The parent learns. The parents learn fingerplays, singing games, craft ideas. The parent is exposed to the best in children's literature. The parent notes ways to interpret children's books.
2. The parent continues the literary and educational experiences begun in class. At home the fingerplays and songs are repeated, the storytime topic is discussed, the books are reread, and the storytime is remembered.
3. The parent receives social and intellectual stimulation. The importance of this as a beneficial activity for the *parents* during these years of homebound preschool rearing should not be underestimated.
4. The child is nurtured by a parent for a comfortable forty-five minutes with no fear of interference. The phone cannot ring, an older sibling cannot take away the parent's attention. The parent "belongs" to the child for the duration of the storytime. The importance of *this* to the child should not be underestimated.
5. The parent becomes your accomplice in teaching during the storytime. The parent helps keep the child's attention directed toward the book, helps clarify difficult concepts on a one-to-one basis. And of course helps with the singing games and crafts. Crafts become simple with an adult for each child.

6. The child sees the parent in a playful, creative role. Parents can take part in the creative dramatics activities, revealing a playful, creative side of their own natures which may not be so apparent in all parent-child relationships.

How do you facilitate such a parent–child format? First of all you need to limit the size of your storytime. Fifteen parent–child groups are probably the maximum number you can handle. Most parents will bring more than one child. At least one-third of your class will have babies or younger siblings that need to come along. I find these babies and toddlers most often watch quietly from their carriers or from a parent's lap. The occasional crying baby must be removed, of course. And I do not tolerate *toddling* toddlers. So the occasional child who just cannot sit on a parent's lap during the story is taken for a walk during the story segments.

This kind of storytime works best with everyone sitting on the floor in a semi-circle. It is important that the children stay on their parent's lap or cuddled near them. This keeps the parent–child functioning as an interested unit and participating in the story-time as a whole. If the children move away from the parents, both parent and child begin to interact with peers and soon no one is paying attention to the storytime activity. Parents are worse offenders at this than are the children. You need to be firm with the adults about "no talking during the picture book reading." Craft period offers a nice relaxed time for parents to chat over their children's heads while helping with the craft tables.

All the storytimes in this collection were designed for a parent–child format. When I came to my work at the Bothell Library, I had just completed five years as a preschool mom. I remembered that when I first moved to the Seattle area, my only contact with other adults was through the parent–child toddler groups and music classes that we eagerly trekked to each week. I didn't have the heart to tell parents to leave their children at the library door and come back later while *we* had all the fun.

Elements of the Preschool Program

Poetry

Every storytime should contain a bit of poetry. Children respond naturally to poetic language. Let them chant it with you, act it out. An especially enjoyable activity for family groups is the poetry roundelay. Pass out a poem to each family and let the children devise a way to act the poem for presentation to the class.

Most of the poems I suggest are available in more than one anthology, but since *The Random House Book of Poetry*, edited by Jack Prelutsky, contains so many of my favorites, I have used that as my primary source.

Music in the Storytime

I always include music in my story programs. Quiet song is a great means of relaxing and bonding a group. Energetic action songs are excellent for releasing the pent-up energy that has been contained during story listening. Here are some suggestions for using music in the story programs.

• Use Music to Start the Program

Play a recording to set the mood of the room as the children enter. Use a song to bring the children together as a group as your storytime opens. Beginning to sing even before all are gathered serves as a magnet to pull them into the group. Or, you can assemble your group first and sing your hellos together. Choose a song that pleases you and arrange the tune to suit yourself. It should be a "hum in the shower" tune that sticks in your head easily. My own favorites are given in "Opening and Closing Songs." Details about these are found in the appendix.

• Use Songs to Release Energy

Move the children to a standing circle at some point mid-storytime. I usually do two or three stories, move into circle singing activities, and then return for a final story or two. Energy-releasing songs should have lots of participation and lots of movement. It might be fun to learn a dancing song, such as "Old Brass Wagon" and use that song every week in addition to your thematic songs which change weekly. Repetition of old favorites gives a sense of pleasure and confidence to any group.

• Use Song to Quiet the Group After Wild Activity

As you return to your story circle after an exciting creative dramatics activity or game, you may find it works well to start singing quietly, letting the children join in as they take their places. I often use this technique at the end of storytime as children slowly finish their craft or other project and drift back to the circle for our closing songs.

• Use Song to Close the Storytime

Coming together as a group to sing familiar closing songs gives a sense of completion to the event. It also presents the opportunity to make eye contact with each child as you sing goodbye. During the story time this kind of personal attention is not always possible, but the opening and closing songs should be material you know so well that you can just relax and smile your "hellos" and "goodbyes" to each child in the room. See the appendix for my favorite closing songs.

• Recordings

Recordings can add texture and mood to a storytime. They can provide a background for craft work or the stories themselves, or actively accompany creative movement and dramatics. Good music should be a part of the artistic and aesthetic experience we present to young children in libraries and other learning sites. Another good reason to add audio recordings—disk or tape—to your storytime is to introduce them to the parents who are present.

Several excellent records to accompany and stimulate creative movement and dramatics are available. For anyone who feels timid about initiating these activities, recordings such as those by Ann Lief Barlin and Marcia Berman may be of help. *They* tell the children what to do; you just follow along. If singing is difficult for you, you may find that recordings help you to sing with the children. Usually, the leader on the recording tells the children how to respond and leads the singing. Again, all you have to do is join in with the kids.

• Rhythm Instruments

I reserve use of rhythm instruments for a special "music time" series each spring. The series always attracts a few new parents who have not bothered to bring their children to regular storytimes during the winter. These programs are detailed in the "Music Time" program section of this book.

Art in the Storytime

An art activity at the end of the storytime period can enhance the experience the child has encountered with books, music, and visuals. The tie between the creative handling of objects and materials and the ideas of the story program must be made very clear. In planning your art/craft activities, this connection must be maintained. Art educators criticize workers with preschool children for the tendency to hand the children coloring sheets or pre-cut materials to paste together. We must make sure we emphasize activities that will allow the child art play that is as free and creative as possible. Bev Bos makes a good case for letting children experiment with interesting art materials and helps you overcome the "craft syndrome" in which adults constantly "tell them what to do." Be sure to read her *Don't Move the Muffin Tins: A Hands-Off Guide to Art for the Young Child* (Roseville, CA: Turn the Page Press, 1978). This book will be of real help to you.

There is much a child can learn about art and about creating through the process of constructing craft objects. Such objects reinforce concepts and illuminate meanings that books have introduced. Despite the current scorn for "crafts," we need not throw the baby out with the bath water.

The children's learning from their art activities can be enhanced by your commentary as they work. For example, while they are making a baby chick for the spring storytimes, comment on the softness of the cotton balls, the sharpness of the beaks. Talk about the colors, the textures and shapes as you work. You may not think there is a lot of creativity involved in pasting eyes and beaks onto a cotton ball, but the experience can be an imaginative and very meaningful one for a young child.

Your overall aim in planning art activities to include in the storytime sessions should be to allow the child experience with a variety of materials and contact with various artistic concepts. If you keep this goal in mind while planning projects and working with the children, you can find ways to make the "recognizable object to take home" a worthwhile artistic experience. I still have bright memories of the paper bluebird on a string that I took home from Summer Bible School when I was five, and also the bright blue spool with a pipe cleaner through it that was a lawn mower. I don't know whether making these little objects enhanced my creativity or not, but they certainly captured my imagination!

Discussion with parents about your goals for the art/craft segment of the storytime can be helpful. Two of the most difficult problems in executing art/craft activities are finding projects simple enough for the youngest children to undertake, and keeping the mothers' hands off of the children's projects while they work!

Science in the Storytime

Young children want to know. They are fascinated with new ideas and are eager to learn anything you can tell them about the world around them. There are many excellent books available which present scientific concepts accurately and interestingly for young children. Plan to include some science programs in each year's storytime schedule. Summer is an especially good time for these programs as you can usually get outdoors for mini field trips.

This book includes suggestions for several science-based programs. A brief science element can be added to many other programs as well. For example, mention science elements in the program dealing with the seasons, and in the "Animal Antics" programs. If you add a bit of scientific information to a basically fantasy program, however, be sure to make a clear demarcation between what is real and what is not; between the factual book and the fantasy theme.

Films in the Storytime

Films are an art form just as significant as books. It is important to introduce children to stimulating ideas, flowing language, and lovely and interesting images in any format where these may be encountered.

There are many short films available that should be seen by children. These can be successfully programmed into your storytime sessions, but it takes some thought. I like to assemble a series of story and film programs to offer once a year, usually at the same time each year so that I can tell parents when to watch for it.

Showing a film now and then in the regular storytime series is fine, but it leads soon to the "When is the movie?" syndrome. The screen *is* magic to children. If they show disappointment that there is no film today, you may find yourself feeling a bit disgruntled because they seem to prefer a film to the program you have just worked so hard to prepare.

The preschool film series is very popular in public libraries, but I have never been truly satisfied with most of these programs, including the ones I plan myself. An entire program of films is usually screened without much introduction. The children settle into a TV viewing mode and are thus not prepared to be talked to or to participate very much. This makes it difficult to frame the movies intelligently in a way that might help the children to better understand and appreciate what they are seeing. Still, film programs offer a way for the librarian to get a break from the rigors of weekly story planning. This is even a program which other staff members may be left to execute during your absence, if necessary.

Despite my qualms about the preschool film programs, I continue to do them. One good reason for continuing them, quite apart from the direct benefits to the children, is that they bring in a group of parents who never darken the door of a regular preschool storytime. I always break up the movie showing after the third film for some fingerplay and stretching. This serves to relieve sitting tension and also to acquaint the parents with the fact that their children might enjoy activities other than watching a screen of some kind. Other kinds of upcoming storytime series can be plugged at this time, and once in a while the promotion effort has some effect.

Though I continue to do programs consisting of nothing but film, I much prefer a setting which mixes film and books in happy conjunctions. A series of storytimes which include films—one film to each storytime session—seems to me to be the best arrangement. In this setting, talking about the movie, before and after it is shown, and relating it to books, other media, ideas, and activities, is possible. This makes the experience a much more memorable one for the children.

Several programs designed to feature selected films are included in this book. Make the film an intrinsic part of the total storytime program. Set the group up for active, responsive viewing and fight the "turn off the lights and phase out" trap that media can present.

Most of the films suggested here are short, artistic pieces. I have not included many picture book-based films because these can easily be plugged into almost any storytime if you have easy access to them. These can add an enjoyable dimension to the storytime, but keep in mind that there is no substitute for the book itself. Always read the book first, then screen the film. The children will not find this repetitious. They will enjoy both events. For a list of films included in programs here, see the Index of Films.

Creative Dramatics in the Storytime

Creative dramatics activities seem to flow naturally from many of the stories you will be reading aloud. Letting the children get up and act out the story they have just heard allows them to experience the plot and characters in a physical way. It gives them some experience with role playing, and provides a good stretch in the process.

This kind of "acting out the story" activity needs no special preparation. Just assign roles from among the story's characters, and let the actors walk through the story as you retell it. Four and five-year-olds will want to say all of their parts; twos and threes may need to have you speak for them while they concentrate on the actions.

More elaborate creative dramatics activities may be included in the storytime if you like and make good stretching activities between stories.

Puppets in the Storytime

• Using a Puppet Friend

Many preschool workers like to use a puppet friend to introduce their material and talk with the children. This is a matter of personal taste. If the idea sounds appealing, you can give it a try. You can purchase a fluffy, hand puppet with an engaging appearance. Be sure that the puppet is comfortable to wear and has a wide range of possible movement. Tuck the puppet into a basket, bring it out at storytime, and you are in business. Most librarians, and others working with young children, simply improvise the puppet's chatter as they go along. After a few tries the puppet learns to prattle on quite effortlessly. This technique requires little preparation once you get the hang of it, and many find it enhances their storytime. It may be especially good for shy people who don't really enjoy performing. I confess I am not one of them—I like to do my own talking and performing!

• Puppet Shows

If a puppet show is to be performed for your audience, it should be artistically conceived and executed. Too much puppetry for children is of the pop-up-and-jiggle variety. Most children's librarians or other workers with young children would not dream of writing and illustrating their own books for storytime, but they think nothing of hacking together a dramatic production. *Everything* we present to children should be well crafted and artistically and professionally presented.

If you plan to include puppetry in your storytime programs, do take some classes in the art and learn how to manipulate the puppets with skill. Be aware of the visual impact of puppets and sets. We are not all artists, but enlist help if the visual arts are not your forte. Above all, scripts should be well written. If you are working from a picture book or short story which is well written, stick to the author's words. Listen to the sound of your production. This does not mean there cannot be some ad libbing and audience participation, but they work well only if there is a good structure to add them to. Work for an artistic whole. Puppetry is *artistry*, not just *bounce*.

Puppetry for preschoolers can be very simple and still be effective. Puppets may be worked over a box on your lap, on a table top, or behind a small tabletop screen. I prefer to work in full view of the children. This enables me to control the group visually if necessary and keeps the puppetry more intimate, less theatrical.

You might like to experiment with object puppetry. This art form is gaining use abroad and consists of telling a story while moving small characters or objects around on a board or tabletop.

• Penny Theatre

This form of children's theatre has been raised to a high level of artistry by library systems in Maryland. A complete wooden tabletop theatre is built with lights, sets, curtains. The puppets are tiny figures or objects, usually made of paper, and pushed out on the end of a rod. The Weston Woods picture book tapes make excellent sound tracks for these productions, and old picture books can be cut up and pasted on cardboard to form the puppets. The performances are magical. They require a considerable amount of production time, and can be viewed by only a small group at each showing, but in a darkened room the small lighted stage makes an elegant production for special occasions.

Flannel Boards in the Storytime

Flannel boards are useful when you wish to present a book whose illustrations are too small to be seen by your entire group. Sometimes they can be enlarged to flannel board size and thus made more accessible. Flannel boards are often used as a follow-up activity after reading a book. The felt pieces are passed out and children come up and put them on the flannel board as the story is retold.

In deciding whether or not to prepare a flannel board set of figures for a book, ask yourself if this presentation will enhance the book or actually come between the book and the listener. As always, your main objective should be to share the joy of the book with the audience.

Fancy Dressing

Storytimes vary from simple programs consisting of a handful of picture books just enjoyed for themselves without elaboration, to staged performances with puppet shows, craft creations to take home, special treats, thematic name tags, and printed, take-home instructions with follow-up activities. The amount of "fancy dress-ing" you wish to give your storytime will depend on how much time you have to devote to this. Do not feel that a fancy program is necessarily a better program, because a program should be judged by what it.does for the children, not how elaborate it looks. Did the child experience the delight of hearing extraordinary words beautifully spoken? Did the child feel a moment of empathy with other children and with characters in the books? Was there a spark of excitement over some new idea? Did the child have a chance to sing out loud, to play with attractive art materials, to move his or her body with joy?

If such things were accomplished, the storytime was a success. So do what you can to make your storytimes festive and special, but bear in mind that the real gift of the storytime is in the intangibles. Sure, mothers will be impressed if the child comes home with crafties and freebies; movies and puppets will make them believe you are really a library/preschool with *everything*. But the real artifact of your storytime is one that cannot be seen. It is the small bit of joy you left inside each child.

Science Beginnings

Preschoolers are extremely curious about everything around them, and yet at this age adults often refuse to give them complete scientific answers, assuming that they are too young to understand. This withholding of knowledge from children seems to be prevalent throughout our educational system. Not surprisingly, by the time the children are old enough to "understand" scientific principles they no longer want to know. Tell them every thing you can find out as soon as they ask. Keep telling them the answers to their questions until they *do* understand. The problem, of course, is that most adults don't *know* the answers to the children's questions. And too often, science handbooks for teachers of young children tell *how* to get exotic effects with experiments, but don't tell you *why* this happened.

Before attempting any of these science programs, get yourself a few good reference books on the topic and bone up. You probably know more about *color* than the preschoolers, but do you really know enough? Even if you don't use many of the assorted bits of information you acquire in your research, your storytime programs will reflect the fact that your understanding is deeper than the tip-of-the-iceberg information you are presenting to the children at the moment.

Habitats

1. Habitat: The Field

Opening Songs.

Read: *Once We Went on a Picnic* by Aileen Fisher; illus. by Tony Chen (New York: Crowell, 1975). Exploration on a picnic.

Read: *Inch by Inch* by Leo Lionni (New York: Astor-Honor, 1960). Travels of an inchworm.

Make a circle and sing: "Little Arrabella Miller." See Appendix for tune.

> Little Arrabella Miller
> Found a baby caterpillar.
> First it crawled upon her brother.
> Then it crawled upon her mother.

They said "Arrabella Miller!
Take away that caterpillar!"

Listen and look: *Poppies Afield*, A Little Nature Book by Bill
Martin, Jr., illus. by Ray Barber. Read by Bill Martin, Jr.;
guitar by Al Caiola (Chicago: Encyclopaedia Britannica Educational Corp., 1975). Life cycle of a poppy.

Read: *The Life Cycle of a Dandelion* by Paula Z. Hogan; illus.
by Yoshi Miyake (Milwaukee: Raintree, 1979).

Show a dandelion and pull it apart.

Act out a day in the life of a dandelion: Turn with the sun,
open and close at morning and evening.

Talk about: The things that have their homes in a field. Insects,
worms, snakes, mice, dandelions, grasses, etc.

Take a walk: Visit a nearby field and see what lives there. Pick
a selection of weeds to bring back to the story room.

Make a mosaic using the weeds you found on your walk. Use
glue to paste them on stiff paper.

Closing songs.

See also related programs: "Habitat: The Garden," Program
3; "Down in the Grass," Program 6.

More books to read:
Please Pass the Grass by Leone Adelson; illus. by Roger
Duvoisin (New York: McKay, 1960). A grassy romp.

Sarah's Questions by Harriet Ziefert (New York: Lothrop,
Lee & Shepard, 1986). Sarah asks questions about the world
around her.

Follow-up activities for home or school:
Take a walk through two or more fields. Notice what things
are the same, how the fields are different. Sit down and
examine one small square of field carefully. What is living
there?

2. Habitat: The Tree

Opening songs.

Read: *The Apple and the Moth* by Ielo and Enzo Mari (New
York: Pantheon, 1969). A year in the life of tree and moth.

Read: *Once There Was a Tree: The Story of the Tree, a Changing
Home for Plants and Animals* by Phyllis S. Busch; photos by
Arline Strong (Cleveland: World, 1968). Show photos and
abbreviate text to discuss the tree as habitat.

Read: *Oak & Company* by Richard Mabey; illus. by Clare Roberts (New York: Greenwillow, 1983). The life and death of a two hundred year-old oak. Text could be condensed or read aloud to older children. Illustrations alone are evocative and could accompany discussion of the tree as habitat.

Read: *A Tree is Nice* by Janice May Udry; illus. by Marc Simont (New York: Harper & Row, 1956). People and animals enjoy trees.

Take a walk to visit a tree: Notice the different habitats the tree offers. Note roots, trunk, lower branches, canopy. How would it feel to live in those various places?

Make a collage: Bring back leaves, twigs, seeds from one tree. Make a collage of objects that can be used to identify that tree. Have an adult label the collage with the tree's name.

Closing songs: "Goodbye to the Elm." Sing to the tree you visited. See also related programs: "Apple Day," Program 30; "All Falling Down," Program 29.

More books to read:

Forest Log by James R. Newton; illus. by Irene Brady (New York: Crowell, 1980). Life in a decaying log.

The Tremendous Tree Book by May Garelick and Barbara Brenner; illus. by Fred Brenner (New York: Four Winds, 1979). Lots of tree facts in bright picture book format.

The Village Tree by Taro Yashima (New York: Viking, 1953). A large tree in the life of children in a Japanese village.

To inform yourself, read:

The View from the Oak: The Private World of Other Creatures by Herbert Kohl; illus. by Roger Bayless (San Francisco/New York: Sierra Club/Scribner, 1977). The forms of life that live in an oak.

Follow-up activities for home or school:

Visit several different species of tree. How does the environment each provides differ from the others? Which tree would you choose as a home?

Learn to identify several trees. Look at their bark, leaves, seeds or flowers, shape.

What is a tree's habitat? Where do various trees like to grow?

3. Habitat: The Garden

Opening Songs.

Look at a bouquet. Examine individual flowers. Look for any living thing on the flowers.

Read: *The Lady and the Spider* by Faith McNulty; illus. by Bob Marstall (New York: Harper & Row, 1986). A spider on a lettuce leaf.

Look and listen: *Messenger Bee*, A Little Nature Book by Bill Martin, Jr; illus. by Colette Portal. Read by Bill Martin, Jr.; guitar by Al Caiola (Chicago: Encyclopaedia Britannica Educational Corp., 1975). Life of the messenger bee.

Say a poem:

> What do you suppose?
> A bee sat on my nose.
> Then what do you think?
> He gave me a wink
> And said "I beg your pardon.
> I thought you were a garden!"

Repeat this several times as a group, using motions.

Fingerplay:

> Old Bumblebee came out of the barn,
> Bundle of switches under his arm.
> "BZZZZZ ZZZZ ZZZZZ ZZTT!"

Bring hand from behind back making erratic bee flight motions during the poem—end with a tickle in the ribs for someone on "ZZZTT!"

A ring of poems: Give each child or family group a flower poem and a picture of the flower (clip up old seed catalogues for photos). Let each group hold up the picture and present its poem—the parent reads while the children hold the picture or act out the poem. Older children without parents present come to the front and act out the poem or hold the picture while *you* read *their* poem. If possible let the children take their poem copy home to share with family.

Flower poem suggestions:

From *Time for Poetry* by May Hill Arbuthnot (Chicago: Scott, Foresman, 1952). "Daffodils" by Christina Georgina Rosetti; "Crocuses" by Josa; "The Little Rose Tree" by Rachel Field. From *Shoots of Green: Poems for Young Gardeners* by Ella Bramblett; illus. by Ingrid Fetz (New York: Crowell, 1968). "Names" by Dorothy Aldis; "Daffy-Down-Dilly" by Mother Goose; "The Crocus" by Walter Crane; "Dandelion" by Hilda Conkling; "Snail" by Langston Hughes; "Window-

Boxes" by Eleanor Farjeon; "Three Don'ts" by Ivy O. East-
wick.
Make a circle, sing and act out: "The Boy and the Bee Song."
See Appendix for tune.

> There was a bee-ay-ee-ay-ee
> Sat on a wall-ay-all-ay-all
> He went a Buzz-ay-uzz-ay-uzz
> And that was all-ay-all-ay-all.
> There was a boy-ay-oy-ay-oy
> Sat on that bee-ay-eee-ay-ee
> Someone went Kai-yai-yai-yai-yai!
> And that was he-ay-ee-ay-ee.

Sing and act out: "I'm Bringing Home a Baby Bumblebee."
See Appendix for tune.

> I'm bringing home a baby bumble bee.
> Won't my mommy be so proud of me.
> I'm bringing home a baby bumble bee. . . .
> OUCH! He stung me!

Cup hands as if baby bumblebee is inside, let loose and
jump on OUCH! I begin this with a dramatic playing out of
the catching of the bumblebee. For another variant, see *Sally
Go Round the Sun* by Edith Fowke (Garden City, NY: Dou-
bleday, 1969), p. 135.
Read: *The Reason for a Flower* by Ruth Heller (New York:
Grosset & Dunlop, 1983). Flower details in gorgeous illustration.
Talk about: Other living things you might find in a garden.
Take a walk: Look at a garden. A simple flower bed will do.
Look closely and find living things that make their homes in
the garden. Pick a flower to bring back to class. Make sure
any insects who live on the flower are replaced in the garden.
Back at the story room take the flower apart. Look at its
stamens, pistil, petals, sepals, stem. Make a flower parts
picture: Let each child take a flower apart and paste the
parts on a paper. To avoid decimating the garden you visit,
you may want to provide a supply of flowers from a nearby
field for this activity.
Closing songs: Sing your goodbyes pointing to each part of the
flower naming it. "Goodbye to the stamens, etc."
See also related programs: "Down in the Grass," Program 6;

"A Seed Grows," Program 7; "Habitat: The Field," Program 1; "May Day," Program 101.

More books to read:

Miss Rumphius by Barbara Cooney (New York: Viking, 1982). Miss Rumphius finds her mission in planting lupines.

The Rose in My Garden by Arnold Lobel; illus. by Anita Lobel (New York: Greenwillow, 1984). A cumulative rhyme of the many flowers in a garden.

Teddy Bear Gardener by Phoebe and Joan Worthington (New York: Viking, 1983). A teddy bear who makes a living as a gardener.

This Year's Garden by Cynthia Rylant; illus. by Mary Szilagy (Scarsdale, NY: Bradbury, 1984). The garden's seasonal cycle.

Follow-up activities for home or school:

Examine each of several small flower plots around your home, school, or neighborhood. How do they differ? What sorts of life can you find in each?

Bring a bouquet of flowers to the home or classroom on several occasions. Learn the names of the flowers. Notice how the stamens, pistil, and other parts are arranged in each flower.

4. Habitat: The Sea

Read: *I Saw the Sea Come In* by Alvin Tresselt; illus. by Roger Duvoisin (New York: Lothrop, Lee & Shepard, 1959). A walk by the sea.

Read: *Blue Sea* by Robert Kalan; illus. by Donald Crews (New York: Greenwillow, 1979). Small fish eaten by bigger fish.

Read: *Swimmy* by Leo Lionni (New York: Pantheon, 1963). Small fish band together to chase off big fish.

Sing: "All the fish are swimming in the water." See Appendix for tune.

> All the fish are swimming in the water
> Swimming in the water

Swimming in the water
All the fish are swimming in the water
This fine sunny, sunny day.

For another version, see *More Songs to Grow On: a New Collection of Folk Songs for Children* by Beatrice Landeck (Edward B. Marks, 1954).
Act out a haiku:

Even the ocean
Rising and falling
Rising and falling
Green like the trees

Read: *Houses From the Sea* by Alice E. Goudey; illus. Adrienne Adams (New York: Scribner's, 1959).
Show: a collection of shells that the children can handle. If possible give each child a small shell to take home.
Make a collage: Green and yellow cellophane strips make lovely seaweed. Give the children pre-cut "Swimmys" to add to their scene.
See also related program: "On the High Seas," Program 71.
More books to share:
Down to the Beach by May Garelick; illus. by Barbara Cooney (New York: Four Winds, 1973). Mood book tells of the things we see at the beach.
Jellyfish and Other Sea Creatures by Oxford Scientific Films; illus. Peter Parks (New York: Putnam's, 1982).
Pagoo by Holling C. Holling (New York: Houghton Mifflin, 1957). Lengthy novelette to read to older children. Life history of a hermit crab.
Follow-up activities for school or home:
Visit a beach (if you are far from the ocean, a lake beach or river shore may yield interesting inhabitants to study).

5. Habitat: The Pond

Opening songs.
Read: *Under the Green Willow* by Elizabeth Coatsworth; illus. by Janina Domanska (New York: MacMillan, 1971). Life under the pond.
Poem: "The Little Turtle" by Vachel Lindsay from *A New Treasury of Children's Poetry* by Joanna Cole (Garden City,

NY: Doubleday, 1984), p. 23. Act out poem. ". . . he swam in a puddle, he climbed on the rocks."

Read: Frog and duck poems from *In a Spring Garden* by Richard Lewis; illus. by Jack Keats (New York: Dial, 1965).

Fingerplay:

> Here's Mr. Bullfrog
> Sitting on a rock
> Along come the children
> and bullfrog jumps KERPLOP!

Read: *In the Pond* by Ermano Christini and Luigi Puricelli (Picture Book Studio, 1984). Clear pictures of life in a pond. Show them slowly and let the children name things they see.

Form a circle and sing: "All the Frogs are Jumping in the Water." See Appendix for tune to "All the Fish are Swimming in the Water." Improvise verses—"All the ducks are diving in the water," etc.

Sing: "Glack Goong Went the Little Green Frog." See Appendix for tune, Program 96.

> Glack Goong went the little green frog one day
> Glack Goong went the little green frog one day
> Glack Goong went the little green frog one day
> And his eyes went glack, glack, goong.

Look and listen: *Frogs in a Pond*. A Little Nature Book by Bill Martin, Jr.; illus. by Colette Portal; read by Bill Martin, Jr.; guitar by Al Caiola (Chicago: Encyclopaedia Britannica Educational Corp., 1975).

Film: *A Boy, A Dog, and a Frog*. John Sturner and Gary Templeton (Phoenix, 1980) 9 min. Live action. Adaptation of *A Boy, A Dog, and a Frog* by Mercer Mayer (New York: Dial, 1967).

Closing songs.

See also related programs: "Frog Songs," Program 96.

More books to read:

Between Cattails by Terry Tempest Williams; illus. by Peter Parnall (New York: Scribner's, 1985). Strikingly illustrated life of a marsh.

Common Frog by Oxford Scientific Films; photos by George Bernard (New York: Putnam, 1979). Fine color photos of frog life.

A Frog's Body by Joanna Cole; photographs by Jerome Wexler (New York: Morrow, 1980). Details of a frog's body.

Life Cycle of a Frog by Paula Hogan; illus. by Geri K. Strigenz (Milwaukee: Raintree, 1979). Good illustrations and brief text.

Pond Life: Watching Animals Grow Up by Herbert H. Wong and Matthew F. Vessel; illus. by Harold Berson (Reading, MA: Addison-Wesley, 1970). Baby animals in pond; simple text.

Rr——aah by Eros Keith (New York: Bradbury, 1969). Lively frog.

Follow-up activities for home or school:

Visit a pond and observe its life. Think about what might be going on *under* the water.

Make a pond picture. Paste a blue construction paper pond on paper, add pictures of fish, frogs, ducks, etc. Perhaps add drinking animals around edges. Cut photos from old natural science magazines. For a group, you might use book illustrations. Photocopy several good illustrations of frogs, turtles, etc. Paste all together onto a master sheet. Run several copies of this, then cut into individual pictures for children to use.

Exploring Your Backyard

6. Down in The Grass: A Bug's Eye View of the World

Opening songs

Talk about: How it would feel to be a bug down in the grass.

Read: Selected poems from *Inside a Turtle's Shell* by Joanne Ryder; illus. by Susan Bonners (New York: Macmillan, 1985), or *Nibble, Nibble* by Margaret Wise Brown; illus. by Leonard Weisgard (New York: Addison-Wesley, 1945).

Read: *The Snail's Spell* by Joanne Ryder; illus. by Lynne Cherry (New York: Warne, 1982). A child becomes a snail.

Act out: *The Snail's Spell.* We all become smaller and smaller and turn into snails, glide, eat, sleep, turn back into humans again.

Poem: "Slugs" by John Kitching from *A First Poetry Book* compiled by John Foster (London: Oxford University Press, 1979), p. 73.

Read: *In My Garden* by Joan Lesikin (Englewood Cliffs, NJ: Prentice-Hall, 1978). A garter snake and a box turtle go down the road looking for a home.

Action chain: Form a circle and tiptoe through the tall grass chanting:

> Walking through the tall grass
> What do I see?
> A little black ant
> Is crawling over me.

Let the children supply the names of creatures they will meet as they pass through the tall grass. They could imagine themselves as insect-size creatures for this adventure. "A tiny grey mouse is squeaking at me"; "a wriggly brown earthworm is squirming past me," etc.

Film: *Why'd the Beetle Cross the Road?* by Jan Skrentny (Pyramid, 1984) 8 min. An upbeat beetle's eye view of life. Some of its humor is best appreciated by more mature audiences, but small children enjoy the beetle's point of view.

Nature walk: Go outside to see what you can find down in the grass. Take one small spot and look closely.

Closing songs: Goodbye to the snail, beetle, etc.

See also related programs: "Habitat: The Garden," Program 3; "Habitat: The Field," Program 1; "Meet a Worm," Program 8.

More books to share:

It's Easy to Have a Snail Visit You by Caroline O'Hagan; illus. by Judith Allan (New York: Lothrop, 1980). How to keep a snail.

Snail in the Woods by Joanne Ryder, assisted by Harold Feinberg; illus. by Jo Polseno (New York: Harper, 1979). Easy to read book of snail's life story.

What Do You See? by Janina Domanska (New York: Macmillan, 1974). How the world looks to a frog, a spider, and other creatures.

Follow-up activities for school or home:

Repeat the close look at a spot of yard, field, garden.

Take time to watch the inhabitants for a while.

Look for and watch the small creatures that live under leaves and down in the grass in your yard.

7. A Seed Grows

Opening songs.

Read: *Titch* by Pat Hutchins (New York: Macmillan, 1971). Smallest one grows a plant.

Read: *The Carrot Seed* by Ruth Krauss; illus. by Crockett Johnson (New York: Harper, 1945). A carrot seed comes up though a doubting family swears it won't.

Fingerplay:

> This is my garden, I'll rake it with care,
> Then some seeds I'll plant right there.
> The sun will shine, the rain will fall,
> My garden will blossom,
> And grow straight and tall.

Sing: To tune of "Here We Go 'Round the Mulberry Bush."

> We are going to plant a bean,
> plant a bean, plant a bean.
> We are going to plant a bean
> In our new spring garden.

Add more verses. "First we plant it in the dirt"; "Now the spring rain will fall", etc. Last of all, "Then we'll pick our beans and EAT them!—in our SUMMER garden."

Read: *The Life Cycle of a Dandelion* by Paula Z. Hogan; illus. by Yoshi Miyake (Milwaukee: Raintree, 1979).

Act out: The life cycle of a dandelion. Be a seed, grow into a full grown plant, spread your seeds, etc.

Listen and look: *Germination*, A Little Nature Book by Bill Martin, Jr.; illus. by Colette Portal; guitar by Al Caiola (Chicago: Encyclopaedia Britannica Educational Corp., 1975). A bean grows.

Plant seeds: Plant grass seeds in styrofoam cups. You will need a package of grass seed, a package of potting soil, and styrofoam cups. Have the children draw faces on the cups with indelible pens or crayons. Then put in the soil and let the children plant the seeds. Don't plant them too deep. Keep in a sunny spot and water. They should grow green "hair" within a couple of weeks. Do this the first week of a summer storytime series and watch the "hair" grow. Or let the children take their projects home to care for them there.

Closing songs: "Goodbye to the Seeds."

See also related programs: "Habitat: The Garden," Program 3.
More books to share:
> *The Amazing Dandelion* by Milicent E. Selsam and Jerome Wexler (New York: Morrow, 1977). Excellent close-up photography and clear text detail the parts of a dandelion.
> *Dandelions* by Eiichi Asayama; illus. by Ryo Ooshita (East Sussex, England: Wayland, 1976). Simple facts about dandelions. Clear, large illustrations, brightly colored.
> *Rabbit Seeds* by Bijou LeTord (New York: Four Winds, 1984). Rabbit plants a garden.
> *Seeds by Wind and Water* by Helene J. Jordon (New York: Crowell, 1962). A "Let's Read and Find Out" Series book. How seeds travel.
> *The Tiny Seed* by Eric Carle (New York: Crowell, 1970). Journey of a seed.

Follow-up activities for home or school:
> Plant a seed or a bulb and watch it grow.
> Take a walk and look for seeds.
> Notice the various seeds we eat—sunflower seeds, walnuts, sesame seeds, etc.
> Look for seeds in the fruits we eat—apples, oranges, etc.
> Make a seed collage.

8. Meet a Worm

Opening songs
Talk about: The earthworm's body and habits. Bring an earthworm to pass around.
Read: *It's Easy to Have a Worm Visit You* by Caroline O'Hagan, illus. by Judith Allan (New York: Lothrop. 1980).
Show: Diagram of inside of worm from *Worms* by Lois and Louis Darling (New York: Morrow, 1972), pp. 20–21.
Listen to: "Lots of Worms" from *Spin, Spider, Spin* by Patty Zeitlin and Marcia Berman (Activity Records, 1974). Pass the worm around while listening to song. All join in on chorus.
Read: *The Earthworm and the Underground*, A Little Woodland Book by Bill Martin, Jr.; illus. Ted Rand (Chicago: Encyclopaedia Britannica Corp., 1979). The earthworm's underground lifestyle.
Activity: Make a tunnel with large boxes. Sing "Wiggly Wiggly

Worm" as children travel through to tune of "Farmer in the Dell:"

> The wiggly wiggly worms,
> The wiggly wiggly worms,
> The wiggly wiggly worms
> Are crawling underground.

Talk about crawling underground. It would be dark. You would be surrounded by earth.

Activity: Earthworms are segmented. They can expand and contract. Just for fun make a straw-paper worm and watch it expand. This doesn't really have a lot to do with worms but it's *fun*. Adults need to help remove the paper covers from the straws. Take a straw, such as MacDonald's often provides, rip off one end of the cover and slide the covering down the straw while pressing firmly to the sides of the straw. This will accordion pleat the paper covering. Remove this and lay it on the table. It looks like a white worm. Pick up one drop of water with your straw, dip the straw in the water, then put your finger over the open end of the straw. Drop this water droplet onto the "worm's" back by holding the lower end of the straw over the worm and removing your finger from the straw's tip. The worm will expand as it absorbs water.

Craft: Make an accordion-fold worm. Give kids worm strips. Have parents turn the paper for smaller children as they press in the folds. Older kids can be taught to accordion fold. Glue on paper-punch holes for eyes, or use stick-on round labels, or page reinforcers depending on the size of your worm.

See also related programs: "Down in the Grass," Program 6.

More books to share:

Worms by Lois and Louis Darling (New York: Morrow, 1972). Excellent scientific illustrations of earthworms and others. Reasonably brief text can be shared with mature preschoolers.

Follow-up activities for home or school:

Follow instructions in *It's Easy to Have a Worm Visit You* and care for a pet worm.

Find five different kinds of worm. How are they different? How are they alike?

9. A Mushroom is Growing

Opening songs.

Pass around a few mushrooms from the supermarket for smell, touch examination.

Read: *Mushroom in the Rain* by Mirra Ginsburg; illus. Jose Aruego and and Ariane Dewey (New York: Macmillan, 1974). A mushroom grows and grows as it rains, expanding to shelter ant, butterfly, mouse, sparrow, and rabbit as each seeks cover.

Act out: *Mushroom in the Rain*. A table or a parent with outspread arms can serve as a mushroom. Assign multiple ants, mice, etc. so everyone can take part.

Listen and Look: *A Mushroom is Growing*, A Little Nature Book by Bill Martin, Jr.; illus. Colette Portal; guitar by Al Caiola (Chicago: Encyclopaedia Britannica Educational Corp., 1975). A mushroom grows, releases spores, dies, is replaced by new growth from mycelium.

Act out: The life cycle of mushroom. Grow, die, put out mycelium, and grow again. Use the tape as background music for the activity.

Poem: "The Elf and the Dormouse" by Oliver Herford from *The Random House Book of Poetry for Children* by Jack Prelutsky (New York: Random House, 1983), p. 206. This works well as a puppet poem. Buy a mushroom from the artificial fruit display at your department store. Make a two-finger dormouse puppet from a piece of grey felt. Two pipe cleaners and a snippet of green felt can be made into a tiny pipe cleaner elf figure with green smock and cap. See program 45 follow-up activities for instructions. I hold this puppet by his back as I make him fly through the air. The two-finger dormouse puppet holds the mushroom while it sleeps under it, until the elf picks it and flies off. The puppet poem is performed in mid-air without benefit of stage. Keep it simple.

Craft: Decorate mushrooms. Pass out pre-cut mushrooms for the children to decorate. Staple foot-long blades of green construction paper to your bulletin board and let the children hide their mushroom among the grass. Save a few out for the children to take home, staple the others to the bulletin board.

See also related program: "Lots of Rot," Program 10.

More books to share:

Mushrooms by Milicent E. Selsam, photographs by Jerome Wexler (New York: Morrow, 1986). Clear, black and white photographs of the growing mushroom and of commercial mushroom-growing.

Follow-up activities for school or home:

Watch for mushrooms in your yard; observe other fungi too. Take apart a mushroom and examine the parts.

Have mushrooms for dinner. Warn *never* to eat a mushroom unless an adult has prepared it for you. Some are deadly poisonous.

10. Lots of Rot

Opening songs.

Read: *The Compost Heap* by Harlow F. Rockwell (New York: Doubleday, 1974). Making a compost heap.

Show: Plant matter in various stages of decomposition, including soil.

Look and listen: *A Mushroom is Growing*, A Little Nature Book by Bill Martin, Jr.; illus. by Colette Portal, read by Bill Martin, Jr.; guitar by Al Caiola (Chicago: Encyclopaedia Britannica Educational Corp., 1975). Life cycle of the mushroom.

Act out: Sprout, grow, die, put out mycelium, sprout, grow, die down.

Read: *Forest Log* by James R. Newton; illus. by Irene Brady (New York: Crowell, 1980). A tree dies and becomes nurse log for much life. Cut the text slightly for youngest groups.

Show: Grow molds beforehand and show them. See *Lots of Rot* by Vicki Cobb; illus. by Brian Schatell (New York: Lippincott, 1981) for ideas for your discussion.

Make a rot pot: Put in stale bread, an orange peel, a potato slice, etc. Take it home and watch it for several weeks to see how it molds or rots.

Closing songs.

See also related programs: "Meet a Worm," Program 8; "A
Mushroom is Growing" Program, 9.

More books to share:

Lifetimes: The Beautiful Way to Explain Death to Children by
Bryan Mellonie and Robert Ingpen (New York: Bantam,
1983). Picture book expressing the inevitability of death for
all creatures by discussing life spans.

The Tenth Good Thing About Barney by Judith Viorst; illus.
by Erik Blegvad (New York: Atheneum, 1971). Dead pet cat
Barney has many good qualities to remember, the tenth is
that he now can grow flowers.

What We Find When We Look at Molds by William D. Gray;
illus. by Howard Berelson (New York: McGraw-Hill, 1970).
Clear illustrations and good informative writing to help
adults gain enough knowledge to inform children.

Follow-up activities for home or school:

Put a piece of fruit on a plate and watch it for several weeks
as it decomposes.

Grow some mold of your own on bread or leftover food.

How Things Work

11.   But Will It Fly? Aerodynamics

Opening songs.

Poem: "Up in the Air" by James S. Tippett from *Surprises* by
Lee Bennett Hopkins; illus. by Megan Lloyd (New York:
Harper & Row, 1984), p. 35.

Talk about: Aerodynamics. Begin the storytime by dropping
sheets of paper on the floor. Hold them overhead and let
them flutter down. Observe how they float. Try different
kinds of paper, heavier objects such as a book. Is the air
holding the paper sheets up? Let the children experiment
with this too.

Read: *Gilberto and the Wind* by Marie Hall Ets (New York:
Viking, 1963). Gilberto plays with the wind.

Talk about: Other things the wind and air can move.

Demonstration: Bring to class several different models of toy
or paper airplanes. Fly them across the room and see how

each flies. Some will crash, some sail, some loop the loop. Be sure to include at least one crasher. If you feel ambitious, try folding several different paper airplanes to use in this demonstration. An excellent source is *The Great International Paper Airplane Book* by Jerry Mander, George Dippel, and Howard Gossage (New York: Simon & Schuster, 1967).

Read: *The Glorious Flight Across the English Channel with Louis Bleriot* by Alice and Martin Provensen (New York: Viking, 1983). Bleriot tries again and again to make a plane that will fly.

Craft: Fold paper airplanes.

Activity: Race your airplanes across the room or better yet go outside. See whose can fly the farthest.

Closing songs: "Goodbye to the Airplanes."

More books to share:

Airport by Byron Barton (New York: Crowell, 1982). Very simple illustrated text.

Flying by Donald Crews (New York: Greenwillow, 1986). Simple illustrations, three or four word texts. A plane takes off, flies over the countryside, lands.

In the Air by Julie Fitzpatrick (Morristown, NJ: Silver Burdett, 1984). Simple science experiments.

The Little Airplane by Lois Lenski (New York: Walck, 1938). Pilot Small goes flying.

Richard Scarry's Great Big Air Book by Richard Scarry (New York: Random House, 1971). Lots of tiny pictures.

Follow-up activities for home or school:

Continue to experiment with the flight patterns of various airplanes. Fold paper airplanes using a variety of patterns and compare their flight performance.

Observe the flight of leaves and seeds in fall.

Visit an airfield where you can watch gliders in flight.

For experiment and craft ideas, see *Amazing Air* by Henry Smith (New York: Lothrop, Lee & Shepard, 1982).

Watch *Pedro* Walt Disney, 1943 8 min. The story of a Chilean mailplane who must fight the downdrafts of the Andes.

12. Wind Power

Opening songs.

Read: *Gilberto and the Wind* by Marie Hall Ets (New York: Viking, 1963). Gilberto plays with the wind.

Read: *Follow the Wind* by Alvin Tresselt; illus. by Roger Duvoisin (New York: Lothrop, 1950). The wind moves many things as it travels across land and sea.

Talk about: The things wind might be able to move.

Sing:"I Wish I Were a Windmill." See Appendix for tune.

> I wish I were a windmill,
> A windmill, a windmill.
> And if I were a windmill
> I'd move in the wind like this.

Act Out: Make a standing circle if there is space, so you can watch each other's inventions. Sing of the many things which move in the wind—leaves, bubbles, clouds, trees, etc.

Read: *Who Took the Farmer's Hat?* by Joan L. Nodset; illus. by Fritz Seibel (New York: Harper & Row, 1963). The wind whisks many objects away.

Act out: Stand and recite Christina Rossetti's "Who Has Seen the Wind?" Point to the group on "you" and to yourself on "I."Become a tree and let your "leaves hang trembling" and then "bow down your heads." Keep it soft and gentle. Do it more than once. For poem text see, "Who Has Seen the Wind?" by Christina Georgina Rossetti from *The Random House Book of Poetry for Children* by Jack Prelutsky; illus. by Arnold Lobel (New York: Random House, 1983).

Read: *The North Wind and the Sun* by Jean de la Fontaine; illus. by Brian Wildsmith (New York: Watts, 1963). The North Wind blows up a storm but the gentle Sun wins the contest.

Act out: *The North Wind and the Sun.* Let half of the group become the North Wind and BLOW. The other half become the Sun and beam and hum benevolently, perhaps with arms overhead in round shapes. One hardy extrovert rides up and down between the two groups while the storyteller recounts the tale.

Go outside and feel the wind: If possible hold the entire

storytime outside. If not, take a short walk to notice the wind in the tops of trees, feel the wind on your face and hands.

Blow bubbles and watch the wind carry them!

Closing songs.

See also related programs: "But Will It Fly?" Program 11; "All Falling Down" Program 29.

More books to share:

Attic of the Wind by Doris H. Lund; illus. Ati Forberg (New York: Parents, 1966). All of the things carried away by the wind must be stored somewhere.

I See the Wind by Kazue Mizumura (New York: Crowell, 1966).

The Wind Blew by Pat Hutchins (New York: Macmillan, 1974). The wind whisks many things away, then dumps them down.

Follow-up activities for home or school:

Make a simple kite and run with it.

Make a paper pinwheel and blow it. Take a five-inch square of paper, punch holes in each corner, fold the four corners toward the center and thread their four holes onto a Q-tip stem. Stick the Q-tip stem into a straw—and blow.

13. Tools Work For Us!

Have a display of tools ready. Ask a parent to monitor if you allow exhibit handling. Or have a closed toolbox on display to excite curiosity.

Read: *The Toolbox* by Anne Rockwell and Harlow Rockwell (New York: Macmillan, 1971).

Show: Open toolbox and discover objects shown in the picture book. Pass them around (except for the saw).

Read: *Building a House* by Byron Barton (New York: Greenwillow, 1981). Steps in construction of a house.

Sing: "I Wish I were a Hammer" See Appendix for tune. Program 12.

> I wish I were a hammer
> A hammer, a hammer.
> If I were a hammer-
> I'd hammer just like this.

Let children suggest which tools to sing about—saw, drill, screwdriver, etc.

Talk about: Tools. How does a tool help us? What can a tool do that we can't do without it? Sometimes a tool is a simple machine.

Read: *Machines* by Anne Rockwell and Harlow Rockwell; illus. by Harlow Rockwell (New York: Macmillan, 1972). Simple pictures of cogs, levers, etc.

Play with simple machines:

Make a lever and fulcrum: Give each child two pieces of tagboard, one long and narrow, one square. Fold the square in half and set it upside down to form a fulcrum. The long piece is the lever. Try lifting a penny or other small object with your lever. You push down, the object goes up. Point out that you are changing the direction of your force with the assistance of the lever. Pull a nail with a hammer claw. You push down, the nail comes up.

Make a pulley: Give each child a piece of string tied to a weight. Golf pencils or crayons work well. Hang the string over your index finger. By pulling DOWN on the string you can make the object go UP. You are changing the direction of the force. Have the children take pulleys, levers and fulcrums home.

Closing songs. "Goodbye to the fulcrums," etc.

Film: With older groups you might show *Toolbox Ballet* (Xerox Films, 1972) 8 min. Object animation. A toolbox opens and drills, screwdrivers, pliers, etc. emerge to perform a ballet. A hammer attacks and is in turn routed by a fiery blowtorch. Tiny nail saves the day and all ends well. Scary sequences during the blowtorch battle may frighten smaller children. Fours and fives seem to handle it fine with a bit of warning beforehand that the scary blowtorch gets defeated in the end.

See also related programs: "Wheels and Gears," Program 14.

For your own information, see:

Simple Machines and How We Use Them by Tillie S. Pine and Joseph Levine; illus. Bernice Myers (New York: McGraw-Hill, 1965). Discusses levers, inclined planes, screws, pulleys, the wheel and axle (screwdrivers and wrenches); the wedge (knife).

More books to share:

Adventures With a String by Harry Milgrowm; illus. Tom Funk (New York: Dutton, 1965). More simple experiment ideas.

In Christina's Toolbox by Dianne Homan; illus. Mary Heine (Chapel Hill, NC: Lollipop Power, 1981). Christina fixes and constructs with her tools. Clear line drawings. This paperback could be added to the storytime for older children.

Tools by Ken Robbins (New York: Four Winds, 1983). Labeled photographs of twenty–three tools in picture book format.

Follow-up activities for home or school:

Examine some of the tools in your home. Learn where they are stored. Discuss safety points in handling tools.

Practice pounding. Younger children can use toy mallets and peg stools. If supervised, older children can try real hammers. Be sure that girls get a chance at this experience as well as boys. Cracking nuts can be fun hammering practice but needs close supervision.

Watch someone making something out of wood. What do you hear? Smell? With help, older preschoolers can participate in planning, sawing, sandpapering, hammering, or glueing together a small wooden toy.

Watch for simple machines around you. Can you spot fulcrums and levers? Pulleys?

14. Wheels and Gears

Opening songs.

Talk about: Bring in objects with wheels and talk about them, watch them roll.

Read: *Mr. Gumpy's Motor Car* by John Burningham (New York: Crowell, 1976). Mr. Gumpy and friends go for a ride.

Read:*Where Is My Friend?* by Betsy Maestro; illus. by Giulio Maestro (New York: Crown, 1976). Harriet looks up, down, and over for her friend. Watch for the wheels in the book.

Read:"Le Bicyclette" in *La Petite Famille* by Sesyle Joslin; illus. by John Alcorn (New York: Harcourt, 1964). A clown balances on a unicycle. Note that wheels are not very stable.

Sing:"Take me ridin' in your car car"

For music, see *Making Music Your Own* by Mary Tinnin Jaye (Morristown, NJ: Silver Burdett, 1971), p. 157.

Let kids suggest items for song—horn, brakes, etc. End song with "run out of gas."

Show: A set of gears. This could be an eggbeater, a toy cog board, etc. Talk about the way in which the motion of the cogs can change directions. Demonstrate.

Read: *Machines* by Anne F. Rockwell and Harlow Rockwell; illus. Harlow Rockwell (New York: Macmillan, 1972). Pictures of cogs, levers, etc.

Show: A tricycle. Notice how the wheels and gears work.

Film: *Remarkable Riderless Runaway Tricycle* (Phoenix, 1986) 11 min. A tricycle runs away and has adventures. Kids love it. If you have access to this film, show it at the end of your program, just for fun.

Closing songs: "Goodbye to the wheels, cogs, pulleys."

See also related programs: "Take Me Ridin' in Your Car!" Program 70.

More books to share:

Bears on Wheels by Stan and Jan Berenstain (New York: Random House, 1969). Disastrous riding.

Wheels by Byron Barton (New York: Crowell, 1979). Simple pictures of wheeled things.

Follow-up activities for home or school:

Look for wheels in your neighborhood; find wheels in your house; can you find cogs, pulleys in your house?

Young Scientists

15. Classifying Chairs

Opening songs.

Arrange in a circle as many different kinds of chairs as you can find. Ask the children "What can you do with a chair?" Sit on it, put something on it, etc.

Read: *Happy Birthday, Sam* by Pat Hutchins (New York: Greenwillow, 1978). Sam gets a chair on his birthday. Sam stands on his chair. Talk about the kinds of chairs you can safely stand on, the kind you should not stand on. Show a stool. Have the children tell you the difference between a stool and a chair.

Read: *Where is My Friend?* by Betsy Maestro; illus. Giulio Maestro. (New York: Crown, 1976). Harriet goes on, under, etc. looking for a friend. What does Harriet do with a chair? Do chairs move? Show a rocking chair and rolling or swiveling chair. What are chairs made of? Wood, plastic, fabric, rattan, metal, etc.

Read: *Peter's Chair* by Ezra Jack Keats (New York: Harper &

Row, 1967). Peter's father paints his chair for baby sister. What does Peter do with a chair? Paints it. Show a plain chair. What color could it be painted? Look at different colored chairs in the room. What happens when Peter tries to sit in his chair? It's too small. Look at sizes of chairs in the room. Line a few up in size order.

Game: Move to a circle of chairs. You may have to put some of those you discussed back into a circle. Sit on the chairs. Look at your chair carefully. Leader sings: "If You Have a Red Chair, Please Stand Up." For tune, see Appendix.

> If you have a red chair, please stand up.
> If you have a red chair, please stand up.
> If you have a red chair, please stand up.
> If you have a red chair, please stand up.
> Then sit back down.

Use colors, sizes, rolling chairs, stools, etc. After several rounds of this, play Musical Chairs. Put on music and have them march around until you stop the music. Have them look carefully at their new chairs. Have those with red chairs stand up, etc.

Read: *A Very Special House* by Ruth Krauss; illus. by Maurice Sendak (New York: Harper & Row, 1953). The lion thinks of one more thing to do with a chair.

Take a test: Go to work tables and give each child a crayon and worksheet. Ask them to wait for instruction and listen carefully. Read each direction several times. Have the parents help. There is no one right answer but the child should have a *reason* for his answer.

Questions: 1. Draw a line between two chairs which are similar (alike, the same).
2. Draw a circle around a chair which has arms.
3. Draw an *X* under a chair which is broken.
4. Find your favorite chair and color it.

To make a "Chair" worksheet I photocopied chairs from *Peter's Chair; Happy Birthday Sam; Where is My Friend?; A Very Special House;* and *Youngest One.* Cut out the chairs from the picture and paste all five chairs on one sheet of paper. Use this as your master and make enough copies for each child to have a sheet.

Closing songs.

See related program: "Foolish Furniture," Program 79.

More books to read:
  Ugbu by Ora Ayal; trans. by Naomi Löw Nakao (New York: Harper & Row, 1977). A chair becomes a horse, a giraffe, a dog in imagination.
  Youngest One by Taro Yashima (New York: Viking, 1962). A shy little boy is given a small chair as a gift.
Follow-up activities for home or school:
  See how many different kinds of chairs you can find. How do they differ? How are they the same? Compare and classify another kind of object—hats, perhaps, or buttons. Try to classify a group of leaves. How are they similar, different? With older children you can move on into a discussion of the characteristics scientists use to classify plants.

16. Take a Closer Look!

Opening songs.
Talk about: Looking carefully for things.
Read: *We Hide, You Seek* by Jose Aruego and Ariane Dewey (New York: Greenwillow, 1979). Animals camouflage themselves in the forest while rhinoceros tries to find them. Give the children time to look for the animals and point them out as they are discovered. Talk about looking closely at things.
Read: *Take Another Look* by Tana Hoban (New York: Greenwillow, 1981). Common objects are shown at very close range in photographs. Let the children try to guess what they are looking at, then turn the page and show the answer. Talk about magnifying things to take an even closer look.
Read: *The Microscope* by Maxine Kumin; illus. by Arnold Lobel (New York: Harper & Row, 1984). Anton Van Leeunhoek invents the microscope.
Activity: Use a magnifying glass. Pass it around and examine your skin, a leaf, or a flower.
Film: *Zea* by Andre LeDuc and Jean-Jacques LeDuc (National Film Board of Canada, 1981) 5 min. 17 sec. Close-up of a grain of popcorn popping. Let the children try to guess what they are watching. No one ever guesses the answer since it looks completely different in close-up shots.
Pop popcorn: If you cover the floor and walls well with newspaper, you can leave the lid off the popper and let the children watch the grains explode. Have plenty of adults to help you keep the children well back from the popping oil.

Closing songs.

See also related programs: "Down in the Grass," Program 6.

More books to share:

> *Greg's Microscope* by Millicent E. Selsam (New York: Harper & Row, 1963). Greg gets his own microscope and looks at lots of common objects.
>
> *The Trek* by Ann Jonas (New York: Greenwillow, 1985). Look for imaginary animals hidden in each picture.

Follow-up activities for home or school:

> Use a microscope to look closely at some common things—hair, salt, etc. Cut a hole in a sheet of cardboard and choose several photographs for your own "take another look" puzzle.
>
> Take your magnifying glass on a walk and look closely at things.

Geological Wonders

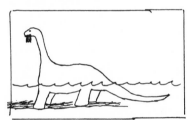

17. Dinosaurs

> Read: *Meg's Eggs* by Helen Nicoll and Jan Pienkowski; illus. by Jan Pienkowski (New York: Atheneum, 1972). Witch Meg hatches dinosaur eggs.
>
> Poems: Select from *Dinosaurs and Beasts of Yore* by William Cole; illus. by Susan Watt (New York: Philomel, 1979).
>
> Sing and act out: "Wooly Wooly Mammoth" from *Our Dinosaur Friends: For the Intermediate Years*, produced by Art Barduhn, Recording (Covina, CA: American Teacher's Aids, 1978).
>
> Read: *Patrick's Dinosaur* by Carol Carrick; illus. Donald Carrick (New York: Clarion, 1983). Patrick imagines dinosaurs everywhere where he looks.
>
> Read: *Dinosaurs* by Kathryn Jackson; illus. by Jay H. Matternes National Geographic Society, 1972). A look at several dinosaurs in action. Read pages 4–25, abbreviating slightly.
>
> Film: Older children will enjoy the Will Vinton claymation

film *Dinosaur* (Pyramid, 1981). It is long (14 min.) and could
be frightening; Tyrannosaurus Rex charges the screen with
his jaws open. Preview before showing.

Make a diorama. Put moss, rocks, small plants in a shoe box.
Use cut-out paper dinosaurs (photocopy from books, reduce,
mount on cardboard) or tiny plastic dinosaurs (usually
inexpensive at toy stores).

For a simpler project, pass out dinosaur cut-outs (photocopy
from books to make a montage, then reproduce) and green
crayons. Paste the dinosaurs on your picture then draw on
green foliage.

Closing songs.

More books to read:
Dinosaur Time by Peggy Parish; illus. by Arnold Lobel (New
York: Harper & Row, 1974). Simple descriptions of eleven
dinosaurs.

Fossils Tell of Long Ago by Aliki (New York: Crowell, 1972). A
Lets Read and Find Out Series book on fossil fish. Discuss
tracks, frozen mammoths, etc.

Follow-up activities for home or school:
Children love to learn the names of these dinosaurs. Your
job as an adult will probably be learning the names fast
enough to know what your children are talking about. Encourage this language play by providing them with pictures
and models to identify. If your nearest natural history mu-
seum includes a dinosaur exhibit, don't miss it.

Listen to the recording *Our Dinosaur Friends: The Early Years*
(Covina, CA: American Teaching Aids) and do the suggested
creative dramatic movements.

18. Your Own Special Rock

Read: *Too Many Stones* by David L. Krieger (New York: Young
Scott, 1970). A little girl collects stones until the house is
full.

Poem:"Rocks" by Florence Parry Heide from *A New Treasury of
Children's Literature* by Joanna Cole (Garden City, NY: Doubleday, 1984). Hold a handful of sand as you speak.

Read: *Everybody Needs a Rock* by Byrd Baylor; illus. Peter
Parnall (New York: Scribner's, 1974). How to choose a perfect stone.

Activity: Rock hunt. Go over Baylor's pointers for selecting a perfect stone. Then go outside and try to find one. Bring them back and test them against Baylor's criteria.

Read: *Sylvester and the Magic Pebble* by William Steig (New York: Simon & Schuster, 1969). A magic pebble turns Sylvester to stone.

Craft: Make a rock mosaic.

Closing songs.

See also related programs: "Volcanoes Erupt," Program 19.

Other books to share:

A First Look at Rocks by Millicent E. Selsam and Joyce Hunt; illus. by Harriet Springer (New York: Walker, 1984). Beginning identification.

On My Beach Are Many Pebbles by Leo Lionni (New York: Astor-Honor, 1961). A look at the varied pebbles on a beach in fine black and white illustrations by Leo Lionni.

Rock Collecting by Roma Gans; illus. by Holly Keller (New York: Crowell, 1984). Makes a good introduction to rock collecting as a hobby.

19. Volcanoes Erupt!

Opening songs.

Read: *Hill of Fire* by Thomas P. Lewis; illus. by Joan Sandin (New York: Harper & Row, 1971). A volcano erupts in a Mexican farmer's field.

Read: *How to Dig a Hole to the Other Side of the World* by Faith McNulty; illus. Marc Simont (New York: Harper & Row, 1979). Digging through the layers of the earth's crust. Condense this for younger groups.

Act out: A volcano. Form a circle and chant (fingerplay by author).

A mountain beautiful am I.
(hands extended pointing toward floor on either side)
I stand with my head against the sky (head held high)
But deep in my roots I feel lava flow (wiggle toes)
Look out! (stoop down)
I think I'm a VOLCANO!!!! (cheerleader leap into sky)

Sing: "The Volcano Song." See Appendix for tune (song by author)

"I'm a mountain oh so high
With my head up in the sky.

I look round the countryside.
Down my slopes the skiers slide.
Mountain Move.
Mountain Stop.
Mountain Mountain BLOW YOUR TOP!"

Read: *Earth Songs* by Myra Cohn Livingston, painting by Leonard Everett Fisher (New York: Holiday House, 1986). Use only a few of these double page spreads with poems for the younger children.

Paint a volcano: Pre-cut volcano shapes. Use red, orange, and yellow poster paint to drip lava down their sides. Suggest a paint dripping technique. Make your paint thick. Cover the table with plenty of protective newspaper before you start.

See also related programs: "Your Own Special Rock," Program 18.

More books to read:

Volcanoes by Franklyn M. Branley; illus. Marc Simont (New York: Crowell, 1985). Facts about volcanoes. Can be read aloud by older preschoolers. Appealing illustrations.

Volcano: The Eruption and Healing of Mount St. Helens by Patricia Lauber (New York: Bradbury, 1986). Text is for older readers but the excellent photos are fascinating for discussion with preschoolers.

The Village of Round and Square Houses by Ann Grifalconi Boston: Little, Brown, 1986). A Cameroon village's tale of a volcanic eruption which destroyed their village in the past.

Follow-up activities for home or school:

Watch movie *Colter's Hell*, Robin Lehman (Phoenix, 1973) 14 min. Erupting Yellowstone geyser. Encourage kids to talk about the images during screening.

Exploring Our Senses

20. Hear It!

Opening songs.
Read: A story about a loud sound. *Drummer Hoff* adapted by

Barbara Emberly; illus. by Ed Emberley (New York: Prentice-Hall, 1967). In this tongue-twisting chant soldiers construct a cannon, then Drummer Hoff fires it off. Let the children say the refrain with you, "Drummer Hoff—fired it OFF." Can they imagine how loud that cannon must have been?

Read: A story about quiet sounds.

The Quiet Evening by Thatcher Hurd (New York: Greenwillow, 1978). A mood book of evening's quiet.

Read: A noisy story. *Too Much Noise* by Ann McGovern (Boston: Houghton Mifflin, 1967). Peter's whistling teakettle annoys him. The wise man's remedy, get a cat. After Peter has added cat, dog, cow, horse, etc. to his household, the wise man advises him to let them all go. By contrast the teakettle now makes such a quiet sound. Let the children make all of the noises with you as you read. They can cover their ears and moan "too noisy" with Peter each time.

Act out: Let one child be Peter, another the Wise Man. The rest can be various animals, piling into the house and making their own rackets. Retell the story as the children walk through it.

Read: *All Sizes of Noises* by Karla Kuskin (New York: Harper & Row, 1962). Prepare a hidden performance stand for this story. Reach behind your screen and effect the sounds called for as a boy goes through his day. Splashing water, alarm clock, etc. Use a sound effects record for the difficult ones like traffic noises, or let the children invent them for you. With older groups you might retell the story letting *them* handle the sound effects.

Listen: Be very quiet and see what sounds you hear in the room. Clocks ticking? Cars passing outside? Breathing? Babies murmuring? If time allows, go for a brief "listening walk."

Activity: Make a rubber band "strumming box." First show a picture of the ear. Explain that sound is really waves in the air. Listen to a loud noise with ears covered and uncovered. Does keeping the air waves out keep the sound out too? Strum a rubber band stretched over an empty box. Let the children see the band "make waves," i.e. vibrate. Put rubber bands on empty boxes to make "strummers." Experiment with different sizes of rubber bands for different tones. Decorate the boxes with crayons if you like.

Closing songs.

More books to share:

Do You Hear What I Hear? by Helen Borton (New York: Abelard-Schuman, 1983).

Ears and Hearing, by Doug Kincaid and Peter Coles (New York: Rourke, 1983). A Read and Do Series Book. Simple experimentation, colorphotographs, vocabulary controlled, grade 2.

I Hear by Rachel Isadora (New York: Greenwillow, 1985). Simple text. Toddler book.

The Indoor Noisy Book by Margaret Wise Brown (New York: Harper & Row, 1942). One of a series of books about the sounds dog Muffin hears.

The Listening Walk by Paul Showers (New York: Crowell, 1961). Take a walk and see what you hear.

Night Noises by LaVerne Johnson; illus. by Martha Alexander (New York: Parents' Magazine Press, 1968). A small child hears and identifies noises in his house as he waits in his bed for sleep to come.

Peace At Last by Jill Murphy (New York: Dial, 1980). The night home is too noisy for father bear to sleep.

The Tiniest Sound by Mel Evans; illus. Ed Young (Garden City, NY: Doubleday, 1964). Poetic search for the world's tiniest sound—kitten on furry rug, fog against the windows.

Shhhhhh . . . Bang. A Whispering Book by Margaret Wise Brown (New York: Harper & Row, 1943). A saucy little boy wakes up a whispering town.

Sounds of a Summer Night by May Garelick; illus. by Beni Montresor (New York: Young Scott, n.d.).

Follow-up activities for home and school:

Play sound effects recordings and try to guess what each sound is.

Put objects in boxes. Shake and try to guess the contents by the sound.

Make two sets of boxes. Can you match boxes that have the same contents just by shaking them?

Collect noisy objects and "perform" them for the children. Can they guess the object with their eyes closed just by its sound?

To learn more yourself:

The Ears and Hearing by Brian W. Ward (New York: Watts, 1982).

21. Taste it!

Opening songs.

Talk about: Ask children to think of things they like to eat. Suggest strawberry jam, chocolate fudge, butterscotch syrup, etc. Have everyone pretend to dip a big spoon into a jar of their favorite gooey food. Take a lick. Imagine how it tastes. Put the spoon back in the jar. Take a napkin and wipe off your face if you got messy.

Announce a story about a caterpillar who likes LOTS of things to eat.

Read: *The Very Hungry Caterpillar* by Eric Carle (New York: Philomel, 1979). The caterpillar eats one apple on Monday, two pears on Tuesday, etc. Gets sick from overeating on Saturday, spins a cocoon and voila!—a butterfly!

Taste test: Serve the children a variety of things to taste. Find out how much their tongues can tell them about things. Try two kinds of cracker, salted and unsalted. Can they tell by tasting which is which? Try diced potato, diced apple. Parents can help execute the taste tests with smaller children. Older children can be served tastes on a paper plate or napkin.

Read: A story about a little girl who liked only one thing to eat. *Bread and Jam for Frances* by Russell Hoban; illus. Lillian Hoban (New York: Harper & Row, 1964). Frances likes just one thing, bread and jam. After eating this for breakfast, lunch, dinner, breakfast, lunch, snack, she begs for spaghetti at dinner.

This story must be cut for use with ages two and a half and threes. Keep the delightful songs and entire plot, but omit some of the dialogue. Families may share it later in its entirety. Fours and fives will enjoy the complete text.

Read: A poem Frances might have liked. "Spaghetti Spaghetti" from Jack Prelutsky's *Rainy Rainy Saturday*; illus. by Marylin Hafner (New York: Greenwillow, 1980).

Sing: Form a circle, standing to sing "The Peanut Butter Song." For tune, see Appendix.

Peanut—peanut butter—jelly.
Peanut—peanut butter—jelly.
First you take the peanut butter and you spread it—
You spread it—you spread it spread it spread it

Singing,
Peanut—peanut butter—jelly.
Peanut—peanut butter—jelly.
Then you take the jelly and you spread it—
You spread it—you spread it spread it spread it—

Other verses: "Then you take the bread and you squish it"; "Then you take the sandwich and you eat it";"Then you pat your tummy and you rub it."

Activity: Make peanut butter and jelly sandwiches and eat them. Have two crackers and knife on napkin at tables. Bowls of peanut butter and jelly for each table. Be sure adult helpers let the kids do the spreading and make the sandwiches. This takes quite a while. Let them wash up afterward and come back to the sitting circle for your goodbye songs.

Closing songs.

See also related programs: "Freaky Food," Program 78.

More books to share:

Eats by Arnold Adoff (New York: Lothrop, 1979). Exciting poetry about all sorts of food.

Taste and Smell by Doug Kincaid and Peter Cole (Windermere, FL: Rourke, 1983). A Read and Do Series book. Very simple experiments illustrate concepts. Color photographs and vocabulary controlled text.

To learn about the sense of taste yourself:

Touch, Taste and Smell by Brian R. Ward (New York: Watts, 1982). Has clear illustrations.

Follow-up activities for home or school:

Continue to experiment with tastes at home. Take small bites and think about how it tastes. Develop a vocabulary for talking about tastes.

Make a "favorite tastes" book by cutting pictures of favorite foods from magazines and pasting on pages. Staple pages together.

22. Touch It!

Opening songs.

Read: *I Touch* by Rachel Isadora (New York: Greenwillow, 1985). A very simple picture book about a toddler touching. "I touch the leaves, crunch, crunch."

Read: *Rosie's Walk* by Pat Hutchins (New York: Macmillan, 1968). Fox bumps his nose on a rake, falls into a pond, and a haystack, is covered with flour, and stung by bees. Let the children imagine how each of these events *felt* to the fox.

Experiment: Have the children touch various parts of their clothing. Which textures do they like best? Pass around swatches of fabric to feel.

Read: *My Bunny Feels Soft* by Charlotte Steiner (New York: Knopf, 1958). Simple illustrations and verse tell of hot, smooth, slippery, sticky, hard, wet, prickly, etc. Or read *Pat the Bunny* by Dorothy Kunhardt (Racine, WI: Western, 1942).

Experiment: Talk about what our hands can tell us. Pass around "feeling" sacks and let the children identify the contents by feel alone. Interesting "feels" could include a hardboiled egg, sand, crumpled paper, a spoon, rubber bands.

Read: *Don't Touch* by Suzy Kline; illus. by Dora Leder (Nile, IL: Albert Whitman, 1985). A child is told not to touch by father, brother, and others. He finally goes to the play area where he pounds, pokes, and pulls his play dough—something he *can* touch.

Activity: Pass out small handfuls of homemade clay. Let the children feel the clay. Squish it. Roll it. Make little balls of it. Make a flat pancake. How do these feel? Or, if you choose to do the alternate activity instead of using real clay, then let the children *imagine* playing with clay after reading *Don't Touch*. Lead them in imaginary play, punching, poking, rolling, etc.

Alternate Activity: Make a "touch" picture. Put a variety of textured objects on the table. Ask the children to paste "something smooth" on their paper, "something rough", and so forth. Shiny paper or tinfoil is "smooth and shiny", crumpled crepe paper is "crinkly", popcorn kernels are "smooth, hard, and round", yarn is "soft", etc.

Closing songs.

More books to share:

Is It Rough? Is It Smooth? Is It Shiny? by Tana Hoban (New York: Greenwillow, 1984). Color photos of textured objects.

Snow by Kathleen Todd (New York: Addison-Wesley, 1982). Sensory perceptions of a snowy day in brief text.

Touch and Feel. Doug Kincaid and Peter Cole (Windermere,

48

FL: Rourke, 1983). A Read and Do Series book. Simple experimentation, color photos and vocabulary controlled text, grade two.

Follow-up activities for home or school:

Experiment with "feely" foods. Give the children samples of peanut butter balls, honey, spaghetti, popcorn. Talk about the way these foods feel to the fingers, to the mouth.

Notice textures in the world around you. Encourage the children to touch and experience these.

Go for a "feeling" walk. Have the child close eyes and lead them. Can they tell they are walking on grass? Sand? Cement? Give the child a handful of coins. Can they be sorted with the eyes closed? Use size and texture for clues.

To learn more yourself:

Touch, Taste and Smell by Brian W. Ward (New York: Watts, 1982).

23. See It!

Opening songs.

Read: *The Look Book* by Jane Belk Moncure; illus. by Lois Axeman (Chicago: Children's, 1982). Eyes are for seeing colors, shapes, near, far, etc. Very simple concepts with watercolor illustrations.

Read: *Look at Your Eyes* by Paul Showers; illus. by Paul Galdone (New York: Crowell, 1962). A boy looks at his pupils, eyelashes, etc. May have to be cut slightly for two-and-a-half and threes, but reads aloud surprisingly well.

Activity: Pass out hand mirrors and let children look at their own eyebrows, eyelashes, pupils, etc.

Read: "Very Tall Mouse and Very Short Mouse" from *Mouse Tales* by Arnold Lobel (New York: Harper & Row, 1972). Different points of view.

Act out: Move into a standing circle. Walk around the inside of the circle showing the tiny pictures as you read/tell this story. The story is more important than the pictures for this activity so if everyone doesn't see every picture, it is probably o.k. Have the children repeat all of the mice lines— stretch tall to say "hello birds," "hello roof" with the very tall mouse. Stoop down to say "hello roots," "hello floor" with the very small mouse. Make a rainbow with your arms and all speak together on the final "hello rainbow." Don't forget to splash in the puddles.

Take a walk: Walk outside and look up. What do you see? Look down. Look around. Notice new things. Face one direction and have the children hold their heads still. Can they see some object or building to one side? Only out of the corner of one eye because eyes are in front of their heads. Let them turn their heads and look. Or do this walk inside the library visiting a room other than the storytime room. Most children *and* adults have never examined the library ceiling. Ours had lights, big beams, big bolts, wires, and a fire alarm with a gleaming red light!

Put out the lights: Go back into the story room and turn the lights down, then, if the group isn't panicking, turn them off for a moment. Tell them to get ready to look into a neighbor's eyes and watch to see if the pupils get smaller when the lights go on. They will. Fours and fives can choose their partners for this activity and will want to repeat it several times.

Read: *Bedtime for Frances* by Russell Hoban; illus. by Garth Williams (New York: Harper & Row, 1960). Sometimes things look different in the dark because we cannot see them as well as in the light. Frances thought she saw giants and tigers in her darkened bedroom.

Art project: Show bright colored cellophane sheets. Look through them at the children. Can they still see you? These sheets are "transparent." Let them say this word with you. "Trans" means through; "apparent" means visible.

Hold up a sheet of crepe paper or other translucent material. This is "translucent," permitting light to shine through. You can see light shining through this material but not clear images.

Make a transparent picture to put up in your window at home. Paste snippets of colored cellophane onto clear transparencies. Since transparencies cost a lot I bought paper protectors, the kind that are used for scrapbooks. I trimmed off the holes, removed the black papers and cut each in half. Clear plastic term paper covers would work as well. Some stores sell the covers without the plastic spine, the cheapest way to buy them. I cut my colored cellophane in quick-cut snippets but varied my snipping technique for each color to give variety. Greens were long and narrow, red rounded, blues triangular, yellows squared. I didn't take time to cut exact forms, just snipped rapidly with roundish or triangularish in mind, enough to give varied forms for the children to experiment with. Parents helped dab on the tiny spots of glue; kids pasted snippets on.

Closing songs.

See also related programs: "Color Me Red!" Program 26.

More books to share:

Do You See What I See by Helen Borton (New York: Abelard-Schuman, 1960).

Eyes and Looking by Doug Kincaid and Peter Cole (Windermere, FL: Rourke, 1983). Simple experiments.

For your information:

The Eye and Seeing by Brian R. Ward (New York: Watts, 1981). Clear illustrations. Good text.

Follow-up activities for home or school:

Continue the pupil examination using a flashlight and mirror in a darkened room.

Look at mirrors, reflections in water, windows, etc. Look through magnifying glasses, binoculars. Look at things up close, things far, far away. Look high, look low. Look closely.

24. Smell It!

Opening songs.

Read: *The Nose Book* by Al Perkins; illus. by Roy McKie. (New York: Random House, 1970). Lots of noses.

Talk about: What our nose does (smells, breathes).

Poem: "My Nose" from *The Random House Book of Poetry for Children* by Jack Prelutsky; illus. by Arnold Lobel (New York: Random House, 1983). "The only thing it does is blow."

Read: "Birthday Soup" from *Little Bear* by Else Holmelund Minarik; illus. by Maurice Sendak (New York: Harper & Row, 1957). Little Bear makes "birthday soup" when he thinks Mother Bear has forgotten to make a cake. Hen, Duck and Cat enter and ask what smells so good. They all stay for lunch, and SURPRISE—Mother Bear comes in with a birthday cake.

Singing Game: "Now the Chicken is A-Boiling." For tune, see Appendix.

Now the chicken is a-boiling
In the steamy pot he bubbles

Out he pops his head and asks us
DON'T YOU KNOW I NEED SOME ONIONS!

All form a circle with one or two "chickens" boiling in the middle. Circle them singing. On the last line, they pop up and call "Don't you know I need some onions!" (or carrots or potatoes, etc.) We all throw onions at them. Then another chicken gets a chance to go into the pot. With very small children I keep adding chickens until everyone who wants to play is in the pot, with only parents circling and singing. Older kids take turns being the "star" as a lone chicken while we all sing and circle.

Sing: "Put Your Finger on Your Nose." For tune, see Appendix.

> Put your finger on your nose on your nose.
> Put your finger on your nose on your nose.
> Put your finger on your nose.
> You smell with your nose.
> Put your finger on your nose on your nose.

Review all of the senses, singing of ear, eye, tongue, fingers.

Read: *This Can Lick a Lollipop: Body Riddles for Children; Esto Goza Chupando un Caramelo: Las Partes del Cuerpo en Adivinanaza Infantiles.* English by Joel Rothman, Spanish by Argentina Palacios; photographs by Patricia Ruben. (New York: Doubleday,1979). "This can wear a hat or bonnet. It has lots of hair upon it. It is your—." Read the riddles and have all point to the answer on their body. You can read only those riddles having to do with the senses, or use the entire book, depending on the age and attention span of your group.

Read: *Hamilton Duck's Springtime Story* by Arthur Getz (New York: Golden, 1974). Hamilton Duck smells the spring flowers, falls asleep under an apple tree and wakes up in a pink snowstorm that smells good; appleblossoms.

Smell test: Pass around paper cups containing a variety of strong-odored items. Cover the cups with wax paper. Punch a few holes to let the odor out, but not big enough to peek through. See how many scents the children can identify. Try things like peanut butter, orange peel, coffee grounds, chopped apple, soap.

Make a scent book: Give each child several small sheets of paper. Provide orange peels, perfumes, soap bars, etc. Let the children rub each scent onto a separate sheet of paper. Staple them together.

Closing songs.

See also related program: "Freaky Foods," Program 78.

More books to share:

Faces by Barbara Brenner; photographs by George Ancona (New York: Dutton, 1970). Eyes, ears, nose, mouth. A photographic close-up book of their senses.

A Tasting Party by Jane Belk Moncure (Chicago: Children's, 1982). Moncure has a series of books, one for each sense. Simple texts, water color illustrations.

Follow-up activities for home or school:

Make more "smell cups" for the child to experiment with.

Try smelling a variety of spices or perfumes.

Smell a variety of flowers.

Make a favorite smell book. Cut pictures from magazines of things that smell good and past onto papers. Staple into a book.

Basic Concepts

25. Number Rhumba

Opening songs.

Talk: Show large pictures of numbers. Ask if audience knows any numbers. They call out numbers.

Read: *Ten, Nine, Eight* by Molly Bang (New York: Greenwillow, 1987). Daddy counts in gentle bedtime book.

Read: *Harriet Goes to the Circus* by Betsy and Giulio Maestro; illus. by Giulio Maestro (New York: Crown, 1977). Animals line up for circus tent.

Fingerplay:

> Two little blackbirds; sitting on the hill
> (one finger on each hand)
> One named Jack; and the other named Jill
> (hold up by shoulders and wiggle)
> Fly away Jack; Fly away Jill
> (hide right, then left)
> Come back Jack; Come back Jill
> (bring back right, then left)

Read: *Jeanne-Marie Counts Her Sheep* by Françoise (New York: Scribner's, 1951). What if Patapon has 1, 2, 3, 4, 5 little lambs? We stop to count the sheep on each page.

Singing Game: Form a circle and sing "Five Little Buns." For tune, see Appendix.

> Five little buns in a baker's shop,
> Round and fat with sugar on the top.
> Along came a boy with a penny one day,
> Bought one bun and took it away.
> Four little buns, etc.

Put five children in middle. Take one out for each verse.

Do the number rhumba: Give every child a large number to hold. All dance to "Number Rhumba" from *Rise and Shine* by Raffi with Ken Whiteley (Willowdale, Ontario: Shoreline Records; 6043 Yonge St., Willowdale, Ontario M2M 3W3, SL-0023, 1982).

Read: *One Was Johnny* by Maurice Sendak (New York: Harper & Row, 1962). Johnny's house fills up till Johnny counts backwards and his intruders leave one by one.

Film: *One Was Johnny*. (Weston Woods, 1976) 3 min.

Fingerplay:

> Five little monkeys jumping on the bed
> One fell off and he bumped his head.
> Momma called the doctor and the doctor said
> "No more monkeys jumping on the bed!"

Repeat with one less monkey each time.

Read: *The Chicken Book: A Traditional Rhyme* by Garth Williams (New York: DeLacorte, 1970). "Said the first little chick with a queer little squirm—", etc.

Or show and sing: *Over in the Meadow* by John Langstaff; illus. by Feodor Rojankovsky (New York: Harcourt, 1957).

Make a Picture: Paste on your paper one circle, two squares, three triangles. Pre-cut shapes are handed out in varied colors.

Closing songs.

More books to share:

Anno's Counting House by Mitsumasa Anno (New York: Philomel, 1982). A counting book with possibilities for exploration of several mathematical concepts. See Anno's note at end.

Brian Wildsmith's 1, 2, 3's by Brian Wildsmith (New York: Watts, 1965). Multicolored geometric shapes to count.

How Much is a Million? by David M. Schwartz; illus. by Steven Kellogg (New York: Lothrop, 1985). Big, bright illustrations convey the concept "a million."

Over in the Meadow by Olive A. Wadsworth; illus. by Mary Maki Rae (New York: Viking Kestrel, 1985). Colorful illustrations.

Roll Over by Mordecai Gerstein (New York: Crown, 1954). Subtraction. One fell out and—.

Teddy Bears One to Ten by Susanna Gretz (Chicago: Follett, 1969). Count the teddies.

Follow-up activities for home or school:

Watch for numbers on signs and in print.

Make a set of cardboard numbers. Put a "3" on the table and let the child place three pennies (buttons, apples) beside the number three. When this becomes easy, build two sets of three. Push them together and re-count. Exchange the two threes for a six.

26. Color Me Red!

Opening songs.

Sing: "If You're Wearing Red Today." Can be sung to the tune of "Mary Had a Little Lamb."

> If you're wearing red today, red today, red today
> If you're wearing red today—please stand up!

Go on a hunt for colored shapes: Hide paper squares, triangles, circles around the room before storytime. Let the children hunt for them. Each should find a specific number and then stop hunting, no more than three each.

Sing: "If You Have a Red Square, Please Stand Up." See Appendix for tune. Program 15

Everyone who has a red square should stand and sit when song ends. Sing for green circles, blue squares, etc.

Form a circle and sing: "Bluebird, Bluebird, Fly Through My Window." See Appendix for tune.

> Bluebird, bluebird, fly through my window.
> Bluebird, bluebird, fly through my window.

Bluebird, bluebird, fly through my window.
Early in the morning.

Read: *Colors* by John Reiss (New York: Bradbury, 1969).

Read: *Little Blue and Little Yellow* by Leo Lionni (New York: Obolensky, 1959). Little blue and little yellow embrace and make green.

Fingerplay: Give each child a cellophane circle of blue and yellow and act this out. (Original fingerplay by Margaret MacDonald.)

Here's little yellow (hold yellow in right hand)
Here's little blue (hold blue in left)
Hello yellow! (bow blue)
Hello blue! (bow yellow)
Let's make GREEN! (put two together overlapping
    entirely)
Green, green, little green (holding green circle and asking
    audience)
Have you seen—little green?
Where's little yellow?
Where's little blue?
Here we are (separate the two colors)
Did we fool you?

I paperclip the two cellophane circles to a white three-by-five card with half overlapping so the children can see the three colors clearly before we begin the play. Paperclip them back on the card after the fingerplay is finished and let the children take them home.

Craft: Give the children snippets of colored cellophane in several colors. Let them paste them on white paper. Encourage overlapping to produce new colors. Be sure to set little blue-little yellow aside, clipped back to their card, or they will get glued down too.

Closing songs.

Selected books to display or substitute:

Freight Train by Donald Crews (New York: Greenwillow, 1978).

Green Says Go by Edward Emberley (New York: Little, Brown, 1968).

I Like Red by Robert Bright (New York: Doubleday, 1955).

Is It Red, Is It Yellow, Is It Blue by Tana Hoban (New York: Greenwillow, 1978).

El Libro de la Fresa de los Colores: Un libro de la Fresa. by
Richard Hefter; trans. by Enric Monforte (Barcelona: Editorial Juventud, S.A. Provenca, 101, 1975). Three bear pain-
ters mix colors through misadventures. Read it in Spanish
and let the kids give the meaning, or translate it.

A Rainbow of My Own by Don Freeman (New York: Viking,
1966).

Follow-up activities for home or school:

Paint with poster paints in red, blue and yellow. Experiment
with color mixing.

Experiment with glasses of water and drops of food coloring.
Stir to mix colors.

Put small amounts of vanilla pudding in ziplock bags. Dot
the pudding with two colors of food coloring. Let kids smush
the pudding in the bag to mix the colors by squeezing the
bag from the outside.

27. Is It Fast? Is It Slow?

Opening songs.

Read: *The Hare and the Tortoise* by Jean de La Fontaine; illus.
and rewritten by Brian Wildsmith (New York: Oxford University Press, 1966). Slow but steady tortoise wins the race.

Read: *Fast is Not a Ladybug* by Miriam Schlein; illus. by
Leonard Kessler (New York: W. Scott, 1953). A discussion of
fast and slow. Abridge this for the younger audiences.

Read: A book about something slow, *The Snail's Spell* by
Joanne Ryder; illus. by Lynne Cherry (New York: Warne,
1982). Imagine you are a snail. This book shows you how.

Act out: Curl up like a tiny snail, glide across the floor, put out
your feelers and see what you touch—you might try this
with your eyes closed—if you touch something pull your
feeler back quickly. Glide around playing at this for a while,
then curl back into your shell and go to sleep.

Read: A book about something fast, *Dance Away* by George
Shannon; illus. by Jose Aruego and Ariane Dewey (New York:
Greenwillow, 1982). Dancing Rabbit forces Fox to dance and
saves his rabbit friends from Fox's clutches. Encourage the
children to say Rabbit's chant with you as you read. They
can kick their feet slightly also, from a sitting position.

Act out: Form a circle and practice Rabbit's dance. Retell the
story briefly while acting out all of the dances. Choose one

mature child or an adult to be the fox, who gets dumped in the river in the middle of the circle at the story's end. Speed the dance up, faster and faster until the frenzied end.

Film: "The Wizard of Speed and Time" by Mike Jitlov (Pyramid, 1980) 3 min. Faster than the eye speeding green magician. Incredible pixilation film technique. This film is probably *too* fast for the younger children. Fours and fives love it.

An alternate activity for younger groups might be a round of "Motorboat, motorboat." Make a circle, begin to move around in a circle slowly chanting "Motorboat, motorboat go so slow." Go faster "Motorboat, motorboat go so fast. Motorboat, motorboat run out of gas!" All fall down. This can be repeated numerous times.

Make: Paper airplanes. See how fast you can make them fly, and how slow. With younger groups the parent will do most of the work on this, but try to get them to let the children press down the folds. This is a skill kids need to learn in order to do paperfolding themselves later.

Closing songs.

More books to read:

I like to use *Drummer Hoff* by Barbara Emberley; illus. by Ed Emberley (Englewood Cliffs, NJ: Prentice-Hall, 1967) with this unit as an example of *talking* rapidly or slowly. Read the list of soldiers very rapidly; let the children join you on a slow recitation of the refrain "Drummer Hoff— fired it off."

Follow-up activities for home or school:

Put on a record with movements of various speeds. Dance slowly. Dance fast.

Set up a race course and see how fast you can run.

Play a slow motion game. At one clap everyone begins making a motion—rolling bread dough, dancing, sawing— at two claps or a vocal command all do the motion in slow motion. Three claps and all do a speeded up motion.

28. What Then? A Sequencing Storytime

Opening songs.

Read: *The Runaway Bunny* by Margaret Wise Brown; illus. Clement Hurd (New York: Harper & Row, 1942). Mother Bunny follows her little bunny through many changes.

Read: *Fish for Supper* by M.B. Goffstein (New York: Dial, 1976).
The illustrations are very tiny. I hold the book close to the
audience and move it from person to person as I tell the
story. It's not important for everyone to see every picture
but all must see some of them clearly. (At the end of the
program they'll be given several of these pictures to take
home and can look at them more closely.)

Read: *If You Give a Mouse a Cookie* by Laura Joffe Numeroff;
illus. by Felicia Bond (New York: Harper & Row, 1985). A
sequence of events occurs when you give a mouse a cookie,
then he wants . . .

Do a magic cookie trick: Open a magazine and read a recipe
for cookies. Pretend to put each ingredient in a big pot as
you read. Stir it all up. Say a magic word and shake the
magazine upside down—a cookie falls out! The trick: paste
bottom and side of two pages together. Slip a cookie in
between the pages. The magazine will look normal when
shown casually as you read from it. Now wave the magazine
over a covered basket, say your magic word and remove the
covering to reveal COOKIES FOR EVERYBODY! Relax and
chat while you eat your snack.

Read: *Fortunately* by Remy Charlip (New York: Four Winds,
1964). What happens next is not always predictable. This is
the old "Good news—bad news—" tale.

Film: "Charlie Needs a Cloak." (Weston Woods, 1977) 7 min.
From the book *Charlie Needs a Cloak* by Tomie de Paola (New
York: Prentice-Hall, 1973). Shows the steps in making a new
cloak, from sheep to stitch. Talk about the sequence of events
Charlie went through to get his new cloak.

Solve a picture sequence puzzle: Any cartoon could be cut up
for this exercise. I make a story sequence by photocopying
selected scenes from *Fish for Supper*. I photocopied grand-
mother rowing out, fishing, catching a fish, frying it, and
eating it. These five pictures just fit across a legal size paper.
You can fit two sequences on a legal page. Make a master,
then run enough copies for your class. Cut them up and give
each child a set. The children put them in correct sequence,
then color them. This has the added benefit of allowing each
child to study Goffstein's tiny drawings at leisure.

Closing songs.

More books to read:

The Camel Who Took a Walk by Jack Tworkov; illus. by Roger

Duvoisin (New York: Dutton, 1951). A sequence that *doesn't* happen.

Paddy's New Hat by John S. Goodall (New York: Atheneum, 1980). Books in the Paddy Pork series are wordless. Most have half pages which turn to reveal a new bit of action in the same scene. It could be fun to read the whole book again *backwards*, like a reversed movie.

Follow-up activities for home or school:

Cut up cartoons and let the children put them back in correct order.

Make a batch of real cookies. Plan the sequence in which you will put ingredients into your bowl.

Through The Year:
Seasons

Fall

29. All Falling Down

Opening songs

Talk about: Seasons.

Read: *Green Eyes* by A. Birnbaum (New York: Golden, 1953). The four seasons of a cat's life.

Talk about: Leaves falling.

For younger children read: *Yellow Leaf* by Cindy Wheeler (New York: Knopf, 1982). A cat chases a leaf. Few words.

For older children read: *Mr. Tamarin's Trees* by Kathryn Ernst; illus. by Diane de Groat (New York: Crown, 1976). Mr. Tamarin hates raking leaves so he cuts down his trees. He regrets this and replants.

Read: *All Falling Down* by Gene Zion and Margaret Bloy Graham (New York: Harper & Row, 1951). Leaves, rain, many things fall down.

Sing and act out: "I Wish I Were a Leaf" See Appendix for tune. Program 12.

> I wish I were a leaf,
> a leaf, a leaf.
> If I were a leaf,
> I'd float in the wind like this.

Float, twirl, let the wind blow you very hard, on succeeding verses.

Sing:"Autumn Leaves are Falling Down" to the tune of "London Bridge" or for descending tune that I use, see Appendix.

> Autumn leaves are falling down,
> falling down,
> falling down.
> Autumn leaves are falling down
> All over town.

Let some children go into the middle of the circle and float around as you sing, fall down on last line. Make up other verses. "The wind can blow them round and round"; "They're drifting gently to the ground"; "Take a rake and rake them up."

Go for a walk and pick up leaves.

Experiment: Let your leaves fall to the floor. Drop some one at a time for the children to observe. Some will twirl, some fall straight down, some glide, depending on their shape and the way the air supports them (aerodynamics). Let the children drop their leaves and watch them fall. Sing "Autumn Leaves are Falling Down" again and drop your leaves as you sing.

Make a leaf rubbing: Tape leaves to the table top. Tape a piece of paper over the leaves. Use a crayon with no wrapper. Lay it on its side and scrub over the top of the paper. Marvelous leaf pictures will appear.

Closing songs: "Goodbye to the Leaves."

See also related programs: "Habitat: The Tree," Program 2.

More books to share:

Johnny Maple Leaf by Alvin Tresselt; illus. by Roger Duvoisin (New York: Lothrop, 1948). The seasons of a leaf.

The Life Cycle of the Oak Tree by Paula Z. Hogan; illus. by Kinuko Craft (Milwaukee: Raintree, 1979). Simple enough to read aloud to preschoolers.

Follow-up activities for home or school:

Notice the way various leaves drift to the ground as they fall. Continue to play at dropping leaves to observe this fall. Collect leaves, press them, learn to identify them.

Arrange leaves on a sheet of clear contact paper. Cover with another sheet of clear contact paper. Seal by pressing the two together. Trim the edges. You now have a place mat or window hanging. Leaves which will lie flat and do not have bulky stems work best for this.

Smell dry leaves, compare their scents. Stroke their surfaces, crunch them, stomp in them. It may be messy, but there is great sensory pleasure in jumping into a pile of fallen leaves.

30. Apple Day

Opening songs.

Read: *The Apple and the Moth* by Ielo and Enzo Mari (New

York: Pantheon, 1969). Apple tree and moth around the seasons.

Read: *The Seasons of Arnold's Apple Tree* by Gail Gibbons (San Diego: Harcourt, 1984). Seasons of the year with Arnold and his tree.

Fingerplay:

> Way Up High in the Apple Tree (arms high)
> Two little apples looked at me (hands form apples)
> I shook the tree as hard as I could (act out)
> And down fell the apples (hands fall)
> MMMM were they good! (rub tummy)

Circle song: "I Wish I were an Apple Tree" For tune, see Appendix. Program 12. Invent motions to go with each verse.

> I wish I were an apple tree
> an apple tree
> an apple tree
> If I were an apple tree
> I'd blossom in the spring like this . . .
> Add verses:
> "I'd have little green apples like this . . ."
> "I'd grow ripe red apples like this . . ."
> Last verse:
> "I wish I were a kid under an apple tree.
> If I were a kid, I'd eat ripe apples like this . . . !"

Read: *Apple Pigs* by Ruth Orbach (New York: Collins-World, 1977). Lots of uses for apples, including making apple pigs. Use this book if you plan to do an apple pig craft with the program.

Film: *Legend of Johnny Appleseed* (Disney, 1948). 20 min. This old Disney classic still presents an imaginative look at Johnny's trek through the wilderness.

Read: *Rain Makes Applesauce* by Julian Scheer and Marvin Bileck; illus. by Marvin Bileck (New York: Holiday House, 1964). Let children chant the refrain: "Oh you're just talking silly talk." Point out the tiny inset pictures on each page which show applesauce being made. I usually go back through the book quickly at the end just pointing out these tiny vignettes.

Make: Apple pigs. Directions are in *Apple Pigs*. This makes a rather long program and requires a bit of adult help in the apple pig making. You may want to omit the craft and simply end the program with an apple tasting session.

Closing songs.

See also related programs: "Habitat: The Tree," Program 2.

More books to read:

Apple Tree Christmas by Trinka Hakes Noble (New York: Dial, 1984). A beloved apple tree breaks in the storm but provides wood for winter and a drawing board for Katrina.

Apples by Nonny Hogrogian (New York: Macmillan, 1972). Wordless, apple seed to orchard.

The Story of Johnny Appleseed by Aliki (Brandenberg) (Englewood Cliffs, NJ: Prentice-Hall, 1963). Legend of John Chapman.

Follow-up activities for home or school:

Eat apples in various forms—pies, applesauce, juice, cider. Notice the different varieties of apples at a grocery or fruit market. Buy one each of several and compare their flavor, texture, color, shape.

Cut open an apple and examine its seed structure.

Visit an apple tree at different times of the year to see it bud, blossom, bear fruit.

31. The Harvest Moon

Opening songs.

Read: *Goodnight Moon* by Margaret Wise Brown; illus. by Clement Hurd (New York: Harper & Row, 1947). Let the children repeat the "goodnight bears, goodnight chairs" as you read. You read the "goodnight" first. Let them echo. It becomes a gentle litany and very soporific.

Read: *Cabbage Moon* by Jan Wahl; illus. by Adrienne Adams (New York: Holt, 1965). Squink steals the "cabbage moon" but Princess Adelgiltha and dog Jenny save it. A magical action story, evocative.

Sing:"Mr. Moon, Mr. Moon You're Out Too Soon." For tune, see Appendix.

> Mr. Moon, Mr. Moon, you're out too soon
> The sun is still in the sky.
> Go back to your bed and cover up your head
> and wait till the day goes by.

Fingerplay:

> Reach for the stars
> Reach for the moon
> Fly through the sky like a witch on her broom!

Reach with one hand, then the other, then gallop around the room. Original fingerplay by Margaret MacDonald.

Read or sing: *A Fox Went Out on a Chilly Night* illus. by Peter Spier (New York: Doubleday, 1961). Autumn backdrops for a rollicking song. All can sing along on choruses.

Listen and look: *Moon Cycle* A Little Nature Book by Bill Martin, Jr.; illus. by Colette Portal. Read by Bill Martin, Jr; guitar by Al Caiola (Chicago: Encyclopaedia Britannica Educational Corp., 1975).

Make: A picture of the phases of the moon. Pass out pre-cut moons in various phases. Help the children arrange them in order on their papers, and paste.

Closing songs: (Hold up phases) "Goodbye gibbous moon," etc.

See also related programs: "The Don't Be Scared Storytime," Program 60; "Sleepy Storytime," Program 65.

More books to share:

The Moon Seems to Change by Franklyn M. Branley; illus. by Helen Borten (New York: Crowell, 1960). Phases of the moon. *Wynken, Blynken and Nod* by Eugene Field; illus. by Barbara Cooney (New York: Hastings House, 1964). A moonlit dream poem.

Follow-up activities for home and school:

Look at a calendar which shows the phases of the moon. Watch the moon for several nights to see how it changes. If this is fall try to see it when it first rises in the "Harvest Moon" role.

32. Owls in the Night

Opening songs.

Read: *Georgie* by Robert Bright (New York: Doubleday, 1958). Miss Oliver the owl is friend to Georgie the ghost.

Fingerplay:

> The owl's eyes open wide at night. (Make round owl eyes hands and act out.)

He looks to the left.
He looks to the right.
He turns his head around and around
And then he makes the *scariest* sound (call—Hoooooo)

(Fingerplay by author)

Read: *Good-night Owl!* by Pat Hutchins (New York: Macmillan, 1972). Owl tries to sleep. Group participation on the bird calls.

Read: *Bears in the Night* by Stan and Jan Berenstain (New York: Random House, 1971). Set up an obstacle course before you begin. Flagpoles make good trees, table can be bridge, etc. I put up an owl cutout at the end of the course. Take the kids on a hike over and around your obstacles to act out the story. Retrace your steps after you see the scary owl. Keep the excitement down so you don't actually terrorize anyone.

Read: *The Happy Owls* by Celestino Piatti (New York: Atheneum, 1964). Two happy owls in all seasons.

Poem: "Who" from *The Birthday Cow*, poems by Eve Merriam; illus. by Guy Mitchell (New York: Alfred Knopf, 1978).

Play and sing: "We Are Mice." Mice form circle around owl. Mice sing and dance around. For tune, see Appendix. (Original song by Margaret MacDonald)

Mice:	We are mice!
	We are mice!
	We think mice are very nice!
The owl calls:	"Whoooo" and the mice all FREEZE.
Mice sing:	Owlll, Owlll,
	Up in the tree.
	Owlll, Owlll,
	Don't look at me.

Owl chooses a mouse to become an owl with him in the circle center. Repeat with each owl choosing another after each chorus until all are owls. "Whooo" a few times and quit.

Craft: Make a simple paper fold owl using stick-on round labels for eyes and cut paper for ears. The fold forms the beak.

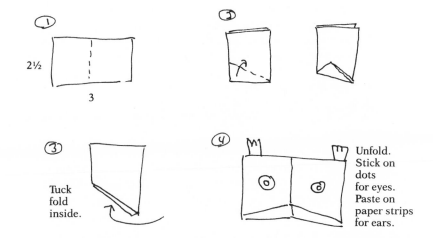

Closing songs.

More books to share:

> *The Owl and the Mouse.* A Little Woodland Book by Bill Martin, Jr.; illus. by Ted Rand. Read by Bill Martin, Jr; guitar by Al Caiola (Chicago: Encyclopaedia Britannica Educational Corp., 1979). Owl catches a mouse for the babies. Realistic, could be frightening.

Follow-up activities for home or school:

> Go near a forest at night. Close your eyes and listen. You probably won't hear an owl but what interesting night sounds *do* you hear?

> Visit a zoo to watch an owl. Be patient.

33. Black Cats

Opening songs.

Read: *John Brown, Rose, and the Midnight Cat* by Jenny Wagner; illus. by Ron Brooks (New York: Bradbury, 1977). A black cat intrudes on dog John Brown's home life.

Act out poem: "Cat" by Mary Britton Miller in *The Random House Book of Poetry* by Jack Prelutsky (New York: Random House, 1983). "The black cat yawns . . ." Assume cat posture on the floor and act this poem out.

Read: *Cat* by Sara Bonnett Stein; illus. by Manual Garcia (New York: Harcourt, 1985). A look at the life of a real cat.

Fingerplay:

Five little mice on the pantry floor (five fingers)
Looking for bread crumbs and something more.
Five little mice on a shelf up high (up high)
Nibbling so daintily on a pie. (nibble)
But the great round eyes of the wise old cat (circles eyes
with fingers)
Sees what the five little mice are at.
Quickly she JUMPS (pounces)
And the mice run away (hands behind back)
And hide in their snug little holes all day.
Feasting in pantries may be nice (clasp hands smugly)
But home is the best, say the five little mice.

Sing and play: "The Old Grey Cat is Sleeping." See Appendix
for tune.
Make a circle with a "cat" sleeping in the middle. All of the
mice circle her making the song's motions. On the last verse
the cat rises and chases the mice, who scurry for cover. You
can use several cats if you like. Keep the "chase" part down
to a simple feint and scurry bit. Stop the action right away
so it doesn't develop into an actual chase scene which might
frighten the younger set.

The old grey cat is sleeping,
sleeping,
sleeping.
The old grey cat is sleeping
in the house.

Other verses: "The little mice are nibbling." (nibbling your
cheese) "The little mice come creeping." (on tiptoe) "The
old grey cat is waking." (yawns and stretches) "The little
mice all scamper." (quickly)
Read: *Angus and the Cat* by Marjorie Flack (Garden City, New
York: Doubleday, 1971). A black cat and a calico cat. Angus
scares off the new cat, then misses her.
Fingerplay: "Five Little Kittens."

Five little kittens (five fingers of right hand)
Standing in a row,
See them bow to the children so.
They run to the left.
They run to the right.

They stand up and st-r-e-tch
in the bright sunlight.
Along comes a dog (left fist comes from behind back)
Looking for some fun.
MEOW! See those kittens run (hands behind back).

Film: *House Cats*. (Phoenix, 1986) 5 min. Two cats, one easy-going, one a grouch.

Draw: *The Tale of a Black Cat* by Carl Withers; illus. by Alan Cober (New York: Holt, 1969). A drawing story culminating in the drawing of a cat. Draw and tell this without showing the picture book. Use a wide black felt tip pen to draw the black cat. The story is also found in *When the Lights Go Out* by Margaret Read MacDonald (New York: H.W. Wilson, 1988).

Draw: Give each child-parent team a piece of paper and a marker and let them retell and redraw the story with you. White chalk on black construction paper makes a handsome picture. For younger children, the parent should do the drawing while the child tells what to draw next.

Closing songs.

See also related programs: "Spring Kittens," Program 38; "Mice Are Nice," Program 75.

More books to share:
King of the Cats by Paul Galdone, adaptor and illustrator; written by Joseph Jacobs (New York: Houghton, Mifflin, 1980). Scary, Halloween black cat tale.

Meg and Mog by Helen Nicoll and Jan Pienkowski (New York: Atheneum, 1972). A witch and her cat in a series of cheerful adventures. See also *Meg on the Moon, Meg's Eggs, Meg at Sea*, and others.

Pitschi by Hans Fischer (New York: Harcourt, 1953). Antics of a black kitten.

Rotten Ralph by Jack Gantos; illus. by Nicole Rubel (New York: Houghton, Mifflin, 1976). Ralph is not a *black* cat, but *is* a troublemaker.

Follow-up activities for home or school:
Visit a cat or have a cat visit you. Learn how the cat likes to be handled and how it must be cared for. Watch its movements. Stroke its fur.

Watch for cats in your neighborhood. How many different kinds of cats can you see?

Winter

(See also Thanksgiving Turkeys, Program 52; Happy Hanukkah, Program 53; Christmas, Programs 54, 55, 56)

34. The Snowy Day

Opening songs.

Read: *The Snowy Day* by Ezra Jack Keats (New York: Viking, 1962). Peter plays on a snowy day.

Poem: "First Snow" by Marie Louise Allen in *Surprises* by Lee Bennett Hopkins; illus. by Megan Lloyd (New York: Harper & Row, 1984).

Read: *The Winter Picnic* by Robert Welber; illus. by Deborah Ray (New York: Pantheon, 1970). A picnic in the snow.

Read: *The Runaway Giant* by Adelaide Holl; illus. by Mamoru Funai (New York: Lothrop, 1968).

Sing: "I'm a Little Snowman" to tune of "I'm a Little Teapot." On "Down, down . . ." begin descending notes and end in spoken exclamation "Whoops! I'm a puddle!"

> I'm a little snowman,
> Short and fat.
> Here is my broomstick.
> Here is my hat.
> When the sun comes out I'll melt away
> Down, down, down, down—
> Whoops! I'm a puddle!

Let the kids suggest things to sing about. "We'll build with blocks on a winter day"; "We'll drink hot chocolate on a winter day," etc. See Appendix for tune.

Read: *The Tomten and the Fox* by Astrid Lindgren; illus. by Harold Wiberg (New York: Coward, 1956). Tomten feeds a hungry fox.

Read: *Stopping by Woods on a Snowy Evening* by Robert Frost; illus. by Susan Jeffers (New York: Dutton, 1978). A snowy woods, a horse and driver.

Paint snowman: Paint snowmen on black or navy paper, using thick soap suds or paint. Use your fingers to paint. Ivory flakes works when whipped to consistency of whipped cream.

Closing songs.

See also related programs: "Snow Bears," Program 35.

More books to share:

Katy and the Big Snow by Virginia Lee Burton (Boston: Houghton Mifflin, 1943). Katy the snowplow clears the way.

Marmalade's Snowy Day by Cindy Wheeler (New York: Knopf, 1982).

The Mitten: An Old Ukranian Folktale by Alvin Tresselt; illus. by Yaroslava (New York: Lothrop, 1964).

Snow by Kathleen Todd (New York: Addison-Wesley, 1982). Sensory perception of a snowy day in brief text.

Snow by Isao Sasaki (New York: Viking, 1980). No words. A day passes at a train station.

The Snowstorm by Selina Chönz; illus. by Alois Carigiet (New York: Walck, 1958). Selina is caught in a snow drift. Somewhat lengthy rhyme, text for older listeners. Set in the Alps. Originally published in German.

Follow-up activities for home or school:

Catch snowflakes on a black slate and look at them. Use a magnifying glass.

Make snow ice cream. Add sugar and vanilla to clean, fresh snow and stir. Eat right away.

Snow play! Make snowmen; throw snow balls; make snow angels.

Play fox and geese in the snow. Tromp out a circle with spokes. The fox is in the center, the geese run around the edges. Fox and geese must all use only the plowed out path.

Watch movie *The Snowy Day*. (Weston Woods, 1964) 6 min. Based on Ezra Jack Keats's book.

35. Snow Bears

Opening songs.

Read: *Bears Are Sleeping* by Yulya; illus. by Nonny Hogrogian (New York: Scribner's, 1967). Bears, deer, etc. sleep in a Russian winter.

Read: "What Will Little Bear Wear?" in *Little Bear* by Else Holmelund Minarik (New York: Harper & Row, 1957). Mother Bear makes Little Bear pants, shirt, and coat to keep warm.

Act out: Act out the story "What Will Little Bear Wear?" Let each parent be Little Bear's mother. With parentless groups, you can be the mother.

Read: *Fergus and the Snow Deer* by Yasuko Kimura (New York: McGraw-Hill, 1978). Hibernating Fergus wakes and frolics with the snow deer. Fergus is an indeterminate creature— not really a bear but I like the book in this program.

Sing and act out: "The Sky Bears." "Oh it snowed last night, . . . The sky bears had a pillow fight. They tore up every cloud in sight and threw down all the feathers white. For source, see *Making Music Your Own* by Mary Tinnan Jaye (Morristown, NJ: Silver Burdett, 1971), p. 106. Make lots of paper snowflakes beforehand, or use confetti. Put a few children up on a table as "snow bears." Let them toss down flakes on the rest of us as we bundle coldly around the table singing "They tore up every cloud in sight and threw down all the feathers white." Might let the walkers in the snow put on stocking caps or scarves. This makes their part more exciting.

Say and stomp a Pooh Bear Poem:
"The more it snows, tiddely pom," from *The House at Pooh Corner* by A.A. Milne (New York: Dutton, 1928), p. 4.

Cut tissue paper snowflakes: Use very thin paper. Hand out pre-folded or have parents help fold. Parents will have to help youngest children with cuts.

Closing songs.

See also related programs: "The Snowy Day," Program 34.

More books to read:
Paddy's Christmas by Helen A. Monsell; illus. by Kurt Wiese (New York: Knopf, 1942). Paddy Bear wakes and discovers Christmas.

Osito Pardo Va de Vacaciones by Daniele Bour (Madrid: Editiones Altea, 1985). Little Bear plays in the snow. Bright illustrations, simple Spanish text. Available in the United States through distributors.

Otto the Bear by Ivan Gantschev; trans. from the German by Karen M. Klockner (Boston: Little, Brown, 1985). A young woodsman fences his orchard to keep the animals out, but after Otto saves his life he decides to share his fruit.

Shadow Bear by Joan Hiatt Harlow; illus. by Jim Arnosky (New York: Doubleday, 1981). A small boy and a small bear scare each other. Condense text slightly for under threes.

Sleepy Bear by Lydia Dabcovich (New York: Dutton, 1980).
Hibernating bear.

Snow on Bear's Nose: A Story of a Japanese Moon Bear Cub by
Jennifer Bartoli; illus. by Takeo Ishida (Chicago: Albert
Whitman, 1972). A Japanese bear cub's first winter.

The Winter Bear by Ruth Craft and Erik Blegvad (New York:
Atheneum, 1975). An abandoned teddy bear stuck in a tree
is rescued from a wintery day.

Follow-up activities for home or school:

Make a snow "bear" instead of a snowman.

Make a cave of branches and leaves or other materials and
hide a hibernating bear in it.

Visit a zoo in winter. Some zoos have cutaway displays so
you can watch animals in their dens.

Spring

(See also Easter Rabbit, Program 47; May Day, Program
101; Wind Power, Program 12.)

36. It's Spring

Opening songs.

Read: *The Happy Day* by Ruth Krauss; illus. by Marc Simont
(New York: Harper & Row, 1949). First flower of spring.

Read: *Hamilton Duck's Springtime Story* by Arthur Getz (Racine, WI: Golden, 1974). A pink snowflower or apple blossoms?

Form a circle and act out: "Spring" by Karla Kuskin in *Piping
Down the Valleys Wild* by Nancy Larrick (New York: Dela-
court, 1968). Go outside to do this if possible.

Read: *Springtime for Jeanne-Marie* by Françoise (New York:
Scribner, 1955).

Read: *In a Spring Garden* edited by Richard Lewis; illus. by
Ezra Jack Keats (New York: Dial, 1965). Haiku arranged and
illustrated to work well as a picture book.

Make: Make a spring blossom picture: Draw three lines for
branches on a piece of paper. Litter the table with small
pieces of crepe paper. Kids wad them up, touch to a plate of
glue and stick onto branch.

Closing songs.

See also related programs: "Habitats: The Garden," Program 3; "Feathered Babies," Program 37; "Spring Kittens," Program 38; "Spring Hats," Program 39; "May Day," Program 101.

More books to share:

The Boy Who Didn't Believe in Spring by Lucille Clifton; illus. by Brinton Turkle (New York: Dutton, 1973). Two inner city boys discover spring in an abandoned lot.

First Comes Spring by Anne Rockwell (New York: Crowell, 1985). The four seasons in simple illustrations, with lots of tiny illustrations showing the things we do each season.

Really Spring by Gene Zion; illus. by Margaret Bloy Graham (New York: Harper & Row, 1956). Spring in the city.

When the Root Children Wake Up by Helen Dean Fish; illus. by Sibylle Von Olfers (New York: Lippincott, 1930). Fanciful story of the flower children who live among the roots underground.

37. Feathered Babies

Opening songs.

Read: *The Chick and the Duckling* by Mirra Ginsburg; illus. by Jose Aruego and Ariane Dewey (New York: Macmillan, 1972). Copycat chick.

Act out: Walk around in circle saying "Mother Duck says quack, quack, quack! Follow me to the pond and back!"

Circle chant: Form a circle. Children act this out while parents play mother ducks and "quack" for them to come back. Leader recites:

> Ten little ducklings,
> Dash! Dash! Dash!
> Jumped in the duck pond,
> Splash! Splash! Splash!
> Then the mother duck called them,
> Quack! Quack! Quack!
> And ten little ducklings
> swam right back.

Act out poem: "Duck's Ditty" by Kenneth Grahame from *The Random House Book of Poetry for Children* by Jack Prelutsky (New York: Random House, 1983), p. 83.

Circle song: "All the Ducks are Swimming in the Water" For tune, see Appendix, Program 4.

> All the ducks are swimming in the water,
> swimming in the water,
> swimming in the water.
> All the ducks are swimming in the water
> All this sunny, sunny day.

Sing additional verses: "Diving in the water"; "Calling to their mothers"; "Sleeping on the bank."

Read: *The Golden Egg Book* by Margaret Wise Brown; illus. by Leonard Weisgard (New York: Simon & Schuster, 1947). Bunny wonders what is inside an egg.

Action poem: "Baby Chick" by Aileen Fisher. For text, see *I Went to the Animal Fair* by William Cole (Cleveland: World, 1958), or *Making Music Your Own* by Mary Tinnan Jaye (Morristown, NJ: Silver Burdett, 1971) p. 149. Curl up in egg shape and act out "peck peck peck on the warm brown egg and out comes a wing and out comes a leg!" The fun part of this is the ending in which you all leap up crying, "How does a chick who's not been about, discover the trick of how to get OUT!"

Action Record: "Birds in the Nest" from *Cloud Journeys* by Anne Lief Barlin and Marcia Berman. Van Nuys, CA: Learning through Movement, n.d. Every "mother" should have her birds in her nest. Teacher can hold a few birds or all birds if this is a class without parents. Instructions on the record are clear.

Read: *The Happy Egg* by Ruth Krauss; illus. Crockett Johnson (New York: O'Hara, 1967). A chick hatches.

Craft: Yellow cottonball chicks. Needs quite a bit of supervision to avoid too much glue. Pass out two cotton balls to each child. Pass around plate of glue and let each dip one ball *gently* in glue. Pass out two blue hole-punches per child for eyes. I punch them out into their hands. Pass glue again (this gets tricky). Pass out small yellow triangles, one to each. Fold triangles in half and *dip* edge in glue. Stick on bird. Talk about soft bodies, sharp beaks.

Sing: "All the Ducks" again using our ducks as puppets.

Closing songs: "Goodbye to the Ducks."
More books to read:

> *Seven Diving Ducks* by Margaret Friskey; illus. by Jean
> Morey (Chicago: Children's, 1965). Pleasing rhyme of seven
> diving ducks.
>
> *Three Ducks Went Wandering* by Ronald Roy; illus. by Paul
> Galdone (New York: Seabury, 1974). Simple rhyme as ducks
> escape dangers.

Follow-up activities for home or school:

> Visit a lake and feed the ducks. Observe how they walk,
> swim, dive. Notice their different colorings. Listen to the
> sounds they make. How do they relate to each other?
>
> Find a nest with eggs or baby birds. Visit them repeatedly
> and watch their changes. Don't touch the nest.
>
> Eat hard-boiled eggs. Hold one in your hand and feel the
> shape. Crack it and examine the shell. Slice it and look at
> its yolk.
>
> Most children's zoos have incubators where you can watch
> eggs in stages of hatching.

38. Spring Kittens

Display pussywillow branches.
Opening songs.
Read: *Green Eyes* by Abe Birnbaum (Racine, WI: Western,
1953). A kitten grows through the seasons.
Read: *Millions of Cats* by Wanda Gag (New York: Coward,
1928). The little old man brings home hundreds of cats,
thousands of cats. . . .
Fingerplay: "Five Little Kittens." See Program 33 for text.
Read: *Three Kittens* by Mirra Ginsburg; trans. by V. Suteyev;
illus. Giulio Maestro (New York: Crown, 1973). Three kittens
turn black from a stovepipe, white from flour.
Read: *Three Little Kittens*; illus. by Masha (Racine, WI: Golden,
1943). Bright, sentimental illustrations for the traditional
rhyme.
Show: Pussywillows. If possible give each child one pussywillow to hold.
Poem:

> Tiny little pusswillow,
> You're soft as a baby's pillow.

When I stroke your silky fur
I can almost hear you purr. (stroke pussywillow)

Sing: "I Know a Little Pussy" For tune, see Appendix.
(Start crouched in cat on floor position. Rise gradually as
you sing lines.)

I know a little pussy,
Her coat is silvery grey.
She lives down in the meadow
Not very far away.
She'll always be a pussy.
She'll never be a cat.
'Cause she's a pussywillow.
Now what do you think of that!
(Arms in air, you are now standing!)
MEOW MEOW MEOW MEOW (crouch down gradually as
you sing these lines rapidly)
MEOW MEOW MEOW MEOW
MEOW MEOW MEOW MEOW
MEOW—SCAT! (SPRING UP!)

Make a pussywillow picture: Start with plain navy construction paper, draw three brown twigs on each paper. Children
dip index finger in white paint and "print" pussywillows
along stem. Or, if you have plenty of pussywillows, give one
to each child. Glue to paper and draw ears and tail on paper
to make a pussywillow cat.

Film: *One Little Kitten* (Texture, 1981) 2 min. could be used
with this program also.

See also related programs: "Black Cats," Program 33.

More books to read:

Annie and the Wild Animals by Jan Brett (Boston: Houghton
Mifflin, 1985). Annie's cat runs off but comes back with
spring kittens.

Momo's Kittens by Mitsu Yashima; illus. by Taro Yashima
(New York: Viking, 1961). New kittens for Momo.

Oh No Cat! by Janice May Udry; illus. by Mary Chalmers
(New York: Coward, 1976). A pet cat creates havoc.

Where Does My Cat Sleep by Norma Simon; illus. by Dora
Leder (Niles, IL: Albert Whitman, 1982). Cat looks for a
sleeping spot.

Follow-up activities for home or school:

Watch some kittens at play.

Observe other baby animals.

Children's farms and zoos may have baby animals at this time of year.

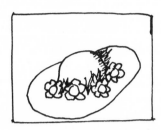

39. Spring Hats

Opening songs.

Read: *Old Hat, New Hat* by Stan and Jan Berenstain (New York: Random, House, 1970). Bear tries many hats. All are wrong: "Too red . . . too fancy." Finally settles on old hat.

Read: *Caps for Sale* by Esphyr Slobodkina (New York: Addison-Wesley, 1940). Monkeys steal a peddler's caps.

Act out: *Caps for Sale*. With younger groups choose a lively parent to be the peddler and the rest of you can all be monkeys.

Sing and play: "I'm Putting on My Spring Hat." See Appendix for tune. Program 12.

Form a circle. Let children suggest different kinds of hats to try on.

> I'm putting on my baseball hat,
> my baseball hat, my baseball hat.
> I'm putting on my baseball hat
> and playing baseball.

Verses could include: "Putting on my cowboy hat and riding on my horse"; "Putting on my beach hat and lying in the sun"; "Putting on my rain hat and walking in the rain."

Read: *Jennie's Hat* by Ezra Jack Keats (New York: Harper & Row, 1966). The birds help Jennie decorate her hat.

Make: Paper plate hats. Punch holes in sides and run ribbon through to tie hat on. Paste on curled paper ribbons, feathers, paper flowers. Pile the table high with colorful, interesting things to affix to the hats.

Model your hats: Put on some music and let each child walk slowly past showing off the marvelous hat.

Closing songs: "Goodbye to the Hats."

More books to read:

The Hat by Tomi Ungerer (New York: Parents' Magazine Press, 1970). A magic hat.

The Horse With the Easter Bonnet by Catharine Woolley; illus. by Jay Hyde Barnum (New York: Morrow, 1952). Useful for Easter adaptations of this program.

Tan Tan's Hat by Kazuo Iwamure (New York: Bradbury, 1983). For the very young. A little monkey and his hat.

Follow-up activities for home or school:

Have a hat modeling show with hats from your own closets. Talk about the functions of various hats. Does their form reflect the use for which they are designed? For example, why does a cowboy's hat have a wide brim?

Collect pictures of hats from magazines and make a "funny hat" bulletin board or picture.

Get silly and try on various objects as possible hats. Do they perform any of a hat's functions? Keep off the sun, rain, wind? Keep your head warm? Look interesting?

40. The Rainy Day

Opening songs.

Read: *Umbrella* by Taro Yashima (New York: Viking, 1958). A little girl waits for rain so she can use her new umbrella.

Act out poem: "Happiness" from *When We Were Very Young* by A.A. Milne (New York: Dutton, 1927). Put on your boots and mackintosh as you chant "John had great big waterproof boots on . . ."

Act another poem: "It Rained on Ann." from *Resource Handbook for Early Learning* by Gloria Polis (Bellevue, WA: Bellevue Community College, 1978).

> It rained on Ann,
> It rained on Dan,
> It rained on Arabella.
> It did not rain on Mary Jane.
> She had a big umbrella.

Read: *Rain Rain Rivers* by Uri Shulevitz (New York: Farrar, 1969). Drops to puddles to rivers to sea.

Poem: "The Elf and the Dormouse." See program 9.

Read: *Mushroom in the Rain* by Mirra Ginsburg; illus. by Jose

Aruego and Ariane Dewey (New York: Macmillan, 1974). A mushroom grows in the rain as animals shelter under it.

Act out: *Mushroom in the Rain.*

Read: *Rain Makes Applesauce* by Julian Scheer; illus. by Marvin Bileck (New York: Holiday House, 1964). Delightful nonsense rhyme. Encourage the children to chime in with you on the refrain, "Oh you're just talking silly talk." Note the applesauce being made in inset illustrations on each page.

Action Record: Sequence from *Rainy Day Dances, Rainy Day Songs* by Patty Zeitlin and Marcia Berman, with Anne Lief Barlin. Freeport, NJ: Educational Activities AR 570, 1975. Begin at "Picture of Me in the Puddle" on side B and act this out with the children to the end of the track.

Make: Raindrop pictures. Dip index finger in water. Hold finger over sheet of construction paper pointed down at paper and let drop of water fall onto paper. Repeat to form a picture.

Closing songs.

More books to share:

The Big Rain by Françoise (New York: Scribner's, 1961). Too much rain floods Jeanne-Marie's world.

Let's-Try-It-Out Wet & Dry by Seymour Simon; illus. by Angie Culfogienis (New York: McGraw-Hill, 1964). Some effects of wetting and evaporating are noted.

Rain Drop Splash by Alvin Tresselt; illus. by Leonard Weisgard (New York: Lothrop, 1946). Mood book. Raindrops become lake, flood, river to the sea.

The Storm Book by Charlotte Zolotow; illus. by Margaret Bloye Graham (New York: Harper & Row, 1952). Moods of the weather.

A Walk in the Rain by Unsel Scheffter; trans. by Andrea Mernan; illus. by Ulises Wensell (New York: Putnam's, 1984, 1986). Bright colored rainy day walk.

Follow-up activities for home or school:

Put on boots and raincoat and go out and *enjoy* the rain. Splash in puddles. Catch the rain on your face. Listen to the rain on your umbrella. Watch the rain make rivulets, follow them. Dam one up and see what happens. Can you find insects, birds, animals sheltering from the rain?

Take a walk right after a rain and see the rain's effects— water running away in rivulets, drops hanging from the branches, worms out of their flooded holes.

Dance with scarves to "Hello Rain" on side A of *Rainy Day Dances, Rainy Day Songs* above. Anne Lief Barlin describes this activity in her *Teaching Your Wings to Fly* (Santa Monica, CA: Goodyear 1979).

Summer

(For related programs, see also Fourth of July Parade, Program 48; Habitat: The Sea, Program 4; Mold It!, Program 94.)

41. Sun!

Opening songs.

Read: *The Strongest One of All* by Mirra Ginsburg; illus. by Jose Aruego and Ariane Dewey (New York: Greenwillow, 1977). Cloud stronger than sun, etc. Folktale.

Read: *Where Does the Sun Go at Night?* by Mirra Ginsburg; illus. by Jose Aruego and Ariane Dewey (New York: Greenwillow, 1977). Simple tale.

Read: *The North Wind and the Sun* by Jean de la Fontaine; illus. by Brian Wildsmith (New York: Watts, 1964). Sun and wind compete.

Act out: *The North Wind and the Sun.* Let half the children be the North Wind, half the sun. Blow and beam on one lone rider.

Sing: "What Can We Do On a Sunny Day?" For tune, see Appendix, Program 34.

> What can we do on a sunny day?
> A sunny day, a sunny day.
> What can we do on a sunny day
> When we all go out to play?

Sing: "The Eensy, Weensy Spider." For music, see *Music for Ones and Twos by Tom Glazer (Garden City, NY: Doubleday, 1983).*

Read: Why the Sun and Moon Live in the Sky by Elphingstone Dayrell; illus. by Blair Lent (New York: Houghton Mifflin, 1968). How water drove the sun and moon into the sky.

Act it out: You'll need a table or chair for the sun and moon to escape. You can lift them away to the heavens at the end.

Make a collage and crayon sun: Hand out yellow circles and crayons. Show several different sun illustrations. With older children, talk about the artists' styles. Suggest ways to make rays and design suns.

Closing songs.

See also related programs: "Shadow Play," Program 42.

More books to share:

> *The Day We Saw the Sun Come Up* by Alice E. Goudey; illus. by Adrienne Adams (New York: Scribner's, 1961). Greeting the sunrise.
>
> *How the Sun Was Brought Back to the Sky* by Mirra Ginsburg; illus. by Jose Aruego and Ariane Dewey (New York: Macmillan, 1975). Slovenian folktale.
>
> *The Way to Start a Day* by Byrd Baylor; illus. by Peter Parnall (New York: Scribner's, 1978).

Follow-up activities for home or school:

> Learn never to look directly at the sun, but follow its path across the sky during one day. Notice where it shines in your yard. Notice how the sunshine feels on your hands. Examine your skin for tan lines.
>
> Leave some foods in the sun for a while—a square of chocolate, a slice of fruit. What affect did the sun have on them?

42. Shadow Play

Opening songs.

Read: *Nothing Sticks Like a Shadow* by Ann Tompert; illus. by Lynn Munsinger (Boston: Houghton Mifflin, 1984). Rabbit tries to get rid of his shadow.

Show: How a shadow is made. Use a light source to cast a shadow. Show how it can be lengthened or shortened by the object's relationship to the light.

Read: *Dreams* by Ezra Jack Keats (New York: Collier, 1974). A paper mouse's shadow becomes a giant.

Read: *The Moon Jumpers* by Janice May Udry; illus. by Maurice

Sendak (New York: Harper & Row, 1959). Even the moon casts shadows. Watch for them in these illustrations.

Activity: Play with your own shadow.

Do this program on a sunny day if possible, so you can go outside and play shadow tag, make your shadows dance together.

Alternate activity: Play with your shadow on the wall. Use a bright light source in a semi-darkened room (a movie or slide projector will do) to cast shadows. Make your body shadows *bigger* and then smaller. Learn how to cast a simple hand shadow.

Closing songs.

See also related programs: "Sun!" Program 41.

More books to read:

Shadow by Blaise Cendrars; trans. and illus. by Marcia Brown (New York: Scribner's, 1982). Caldecott award-winning illustrations evoke the dark and magical side of shadow in a primitive African setting.

Shadow Bear by Joan Hiatt Harlow; illus. Jim Arnovsky (New York: Doubleday, 1981). An Eskimo boy and a baby bear see each other's elongated shadows and flee.

The Shadow Book by Beatrice Schenk de Regniers, photographs by Isobel Gordon (New York: Harcourt, 1960). Suggests things to do with a shadow as a boy goes through a day with his.

Follow-up activities for home or school:

Use *Shadows* by Larry Kettlekamp (New York: Morrow, 1957) or *Hand Shadows to be Thrown Upon the Wall* by Henry Bursill (New York: Dover, 1967) to learn how to create shadow effects.

Use a sheet with a light source behind it and paper cut-outs or real objects to put on a simple shadow play.

Celebrations

Valentine's Day

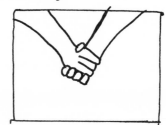

43. Be My Friend

Opening songs.

Read: *Where is My Friend* by Betsy Maestro; illus. by Giulio Maestro (New York: Crown, 1977). Harriet looks over, under, everywhere for her friend.

Read: *Youngest One* by Taro Yashima (New York: Viking, 1972). Youngest one is too shy to be friends.

Stand and sing: "Shake My Hand and You'll Be My Friend." See Appendix for tune.

> Shake my hand and you'll be my friend,
> Be my friend,
> Be my friend.
> Shake my hand and you'll be my friend.
> We'll all be friends.

Change hand shaking partners and repeat several times.

Read: *The Wedding Procession of the Rag Doll and the Broom Handle and Who Was in It* by Carl Sandburg; illus. by Harriet Pincus (New York: Harcourt, 1922). Wonderfully evocative poetry as the spoon lickers, soup slurpers, and others join in the parade. Have everyone act it all out as you go along, dipping their big spoons into something slickery sweet and good to eat and licking them, eating chocolate (pretend) and getting it all over their chins, wiping it off on their dirty bibs, etc.

Act out: After the story has been read, form a circle. Put on some walking music and act it all out again!

Read: *Hilary Knight's The Owl and the Pussycat*. Based on a poem by Edward Lear; illus. by Hilary Knight (New York: Macmillan, 1983). Fanciful illustrations and a boy and girl as observers to the poem.

Make: Valentine collages. Provide cut-out hearts; paper lace pieces cut from doilies; pink, red, and white paper; paste and scissors, and let them create.

Closing songs.

See also related programs: "The Caring Day," Program 61.

More books to share:

Best Friends. Poems selected by Lee Bennett Hopkins; illus. by James Watts (New York: Harper & Row, 1986). Especially nice selections on missing the friend who's moved away.

The Friend by John Burningham (New York: Crowell, 1975). Brief text. Friends play together, fight and are still best friends.

One is Good But Two are Better by Louis Slobodkin (New York: Vanguard, 1956). Litany of all the things it takes *two* to enjoy.

Follow-up activities for home or school:

Invite a friend to visit. Think of ways to be a good host.

Plan activities a friend will enjoy. Serve a tasty snack. Try to help them have a pleasant visit.

Talk about being friends. Who are some of your friends? What responsibilities does friendship entail?

44. Mailman, Mailman, Bring Me a Letter!

Opening songs

Read: *May I Bring a Friend?* by Beatrice Schenk de Regniers; illus. by Beni Montresor (New York:Atheneum, 1967). A boy is invited to visit the king and queen. He brings his animal friends. Shows the invitation, card, letter that the king and queen sent him. After the story talk about why we send letters. How else did the king and queen communicate? Sent a man with a horn! Told him in person.

Read: *Jen the Hen* by Colin and Jaqui Hawkins (New York: Putnam's, 1985). "*Jen* the *hen* sets in her *pen*, writes a letter to the *men* inviting them to come at *ten*." Point out the bold type "en" words as you read and let the audience repeat them with you.

Sing: "Mailman, Mailman Bring Me a Letter." See Appendix for tune.

> Mailman, mailman bring me a letter.
> Mailman, mailman bring me a letter.
> I can hardly wait to see
> What is in your bag for me!!

One child is the mailman. The mailman carries a shoulder bag full of valentines around the outside of the circle and chooses someone to present with a 'letter.' Choose another mailman and repeat until all have received a valentine.

Another singing game which could be used with older children: "I Wrote a Letter to My Love" sung to the tune of "Yankee Doodle."

> I wrote a letter to my love
> And on the way I dropped it.
> A little doggie picked it up
> And put it in his pocket.

Child goes around outside of circle and drops letter behind someone. That child picks it up and chases first child around circle. That child must reach second child's empty space to be "safe." Fours and fives and older enjoy this.

Read: *A Letter to Amy* by Ezra Jack Keats (New York: Harper & Row, 1968). Peter writes inviting Amy to his birthday party.

Film: "Pedro" (Walt Disney, 1943) 8 min. Disney classic. Chilean-Argentine setting is well done. A little airplane must carry the mail over the Andes. Has some scary scenes. Warn children beforehand that the mountain scares Pedro but doesn't hurt him.

Send a letter: Give each child a piece of paper, an envelope and a play stamp (seals, stickers). Let the children draw pictures and dictate a few words about the picture for an adult to write on the paper. Provide paper which will fit into the envelope when folded in half. Show the children how to line up the edges and fold the paper. Stuff the envelopes and have helping adults address to dad, grandma, or whomever.

Closing songs.

More books to share:

The Post Office Book: Mail and How It Moves by Gail Gibbons (New York: Crowell, 1982). Clear illustrations. Basic information on postal system.

Richard Scarry's What Do People Do All Day? by Richard Scarry (New York: Random House, 1968). Informative section on the postal system, p. 15–18.

Follow-up activities for home and school:

Make valentines for your neighbors. Stick pretend stamps (seals, stickers) on the envelopes and deliver them.

Go to the post office and ask to see their commemorative stamps. Buy a few.

Cut stamps off of envelopes you receive and paste them in a scrapbook. (Affixing stamps properly to a stamp collecting album requires more dexterity than most preschool children can muster.)

Make a collage picture of used stamps.

St. Patrick's Day

45. A St. Patrick's Day Parade

Opening songs.

Read: *Fin M'Coul: The Giant of Knockmany Hill* by Tomie de Paola (New York: Holiday House, 1981). Finn's wife Oona outwits the Giant Cuculain. This story is so lively that with a little cutting it will hold even the smallest listeners. Once I tied bright colored yarn strands around everyone's wrist for good luck as Oona does in the story. The kids loved it, but one fell off the bed and broke her tooth that night and blamed the "charm."

Read: *Little Bear Marches in the St. Patrick's Day Parade* by Janice; illus. by Mariana (New York: Lothrop, 1967). When Little Bear raises his umbrella it *stops* raining; when he puts it down it *starts*. The text is too long for younger listeners. I abbreviate, concentrating on the parade plot.

Act out: *Little Bear Marches in the St. Patrick's Day Parade.* Form a circle. Let one child be Little Bear and hold an umbrella (a child's umbrella decorated with green crepe paper works well). When this child raises the umbrella it rains! We all cover our heads and duck down. When the child lowers the umbrella the sun shines! We all raise our heads to the sun and march happily around in our circle again. Play lively music for marching.

Poem: "The Elf and the Dormouse" by Oliver Hereford. See Program 9.

Shamrock hunt: Hide green paper shamrocks around the room before you start the class. Have a shamrock hunt. I tell each child to find *one* shamrock, then come back and sit down.

Sing: "If you have a green shamrock, please stand up." For tune, see Appendix, Program 15.

> If you have a green shamrock, please stand up.
> If you have a green shamrock, please stand up.
> Then sit right down!

Say: "An Irish Benediction"

> May the road rise up to meet you; (rising motions with hands)
> May the wind be always at your back; (hands over shoulders)
> May the sun shine warm upon your face; (hands on face)
> May the rain fall soft upon your fields; (rain motion)
> And until we meet again, (point to audience, then self)
> May your God hold you (hands extended palm up to audience)
> in the palm of His hand. (fingers of right hand in palm of left hand)

Closing songs: "Goodbye to the Shamrock."
More books to share:
> *Field of Buttercups: An Irish Story* by Alice Boden (New York: Walck, 1974). A leprechaun's pot of gold is found.
> *The Hungry Leprechaun* by Mary Caloun; illus. by Roger Duvoisin (New York: Harper & Row, 1962).
> *St. Patrick's Day in the Morning* by Eve Bunting; illus. by Jan Brett (Boston: Houghton Mifflin, 1980).

Follow-up activities for home and school:
> Listen to an Irish jig and dance to it.
> Make a pipe cleaner leprechaun. You need two pipe cleaners. (1) Cut one in half; (2) wind a half pipe cleaner around the bottom half of the whole pipe cleaner; (3) wrap second half around middle of whole pipe cleaner; (4) bend top of whole cleaner in circle to form head. All this can be done by an adult for most preschoolers. The children can now paste on green construction paper pants, caps and shoes.

April Fool's Day

46. Feeling Foolish

Opening songs
Read: *Hamilton Duck's Springtime Story* by Arthur Getz (Ra-

cine, WI: Golden, 1974). Hamilton Duck mistakes falling apple blossoms for a snowstorm.

Read: *George and Martha One Fine Day* by James Marshall (Boston: Houghton Mifflin, 1978). George tries to get the best of Martha but he is the one who ends up feeling foolish.

Read and sing: *This Old Man* illus. by Pam Adams (Restrop Manor, Purton Wilts, England: Child's Play, 1974). The book ends with the number six. Let the group suggest rhyming words to continue the song through ten. Traditional solutions include "seven . . . up to heaven", "eight . . . on my gate", "nine . . . on my spine", "ten . . . on my shin" or "then we start again." Use motions as you sing—one finger for one, tap pretend drum, then make rolling motion with hands as the old man "comes rolling home."

Stand and sing: "The Grand Old Duke of York" For tune see *Wee Sing and Play* by Pamela Conn Beall and Susan Hagan Nipp (Los Angeles: Price/Stern/Sloan, 1981).

The grand old Duke of York (bend with hands on knees)
He had 10,000 men.
He marched them up to the top of the hill (straighten up)
And he marched them down again. (squat to floor)
And when you're up, you're up. (stand up)
And when you're down, you're down. (squat)
And when you're only half way up, (hands on knees)
You're neither up (stand straight)
Nor down! (squat)

Do it over several times, faster and faster.

Read: *Circus Baby* by Maud and Mishka Petersham (New York: Macmillan, 1950). The elephant mother tries to train her baby elephant to eat like the clown family and ends up feeling foolish.

Make an April Fool's Day hat:
Fasten a two-and-a-half inch wide band around each child's head. Litter the table with brightly colored paper strips, colored pipe cleaners, feathers, etc. to be fastened to the band. A strip of paper becomes an attractive curl when rolled around a fat magic marker. Pipe cleaners can be curled in the same way. With a little help most children catch on to this technique.

Have an April Fool's Day parade: Show off your hats by parading through the library. Or put on a record and parade for each other.

More books to read:
    Foolish Rabbit's Big Mistake by Rafe Martin and Ed Young (New York: Putnam's, 1985). An apple falls and rabbit thinks the earth is breaking apart.
    Harriet and the Roller Coaster by Nancy Carlson (Minneapolis: Carolrhoda, 1982). George brags about the roller coaster, then "turns to jelly" with fright once aboard.
Follow-up activities for home or school:
    Talk about things you have done that made you feel foolish. Put on a silly hat and sing a silly song. Feeling foolish can be okay if you learn to laugh at yourself.

Easter

47. Easter Rabbits

Opening songs
Read: *Home for a Bunny* by Margaret Wise Brown; illus. by Garth Williams (Racine, WI: Western, 1983). Where can a bunny find a home?
Read: *The Runaway Bunny* by Margaret Wise Brown; illus. by Clement Hurd (New York: Harper & Row, 1942). Mother bunny follows him everywhere.
Act out: *The Runaway Bunny*. Children are little bunnies; parents and you are mother bunny.
Form a circle, sing and dance: "Easter Bunny Hop Hop Hop." For tune, see Appendix. (Original song by author.)

Easter bunny hop hop hop, (hop in a circle)
Wiggles his nose when he stops stops stops. (stop and
    wiggle nose)
Easter bunny hop hop hop,
Wiggles his ears with a flip flip flop. (arms overhead for
    ears flopping)
Easter bunny hop hop hop,
Wiggles his tail with a bip bip bop. (stick out tail and
    wiggle)
Easter bunny hop hop hop,

Bringing us baskets for Easter Day. (stop and pick up
imaginary baskets and offer to friend)

Sing and dance: "Happy Peter Pink Ears." For tune, see Appendix. (Song by Martha Nishitani)

Happy Peter Pink Ears (arms over head inside out, flapping
forward as "pink ears" in time to tune)
Happy Peter Pink Ears
Happy Peter Pink Ears
Happy Peter Pink Ears
Run run run run hop hop (run and hop as directed)
Run run run run hop hop
Run run run run hop hop
Run run run run jump jump!

This song was designed by creative dance artist Martha
Nishitani as a movement activity for very young dancers.
Her choreography is more elaborate than that which I suggest and is designed to teach certain points of coordination.

Read: *The Whiskers of Ho Ho* by William Littlefield; illus. by
Vladimir Bobri (New York: Lothrop, 1958). Ho Ho the Rabbit
lives in a mystical China where he paints eggs with great
finesse. An elegant, magical tale.

Craft: Pass out paper egg shapes and let the children decorate
them with crayon markers. On the bulletin board prepare a
field of grass with green paper strips. Let the children hide
their eggs in the bulletin board grass.

NOTE: If you are not using the "Feathered Babies," Program
37 in your spring series, add *The Golden Egg Book* by Margaret Wise Brown; illus. by Leonard Weisgard (New York:
Simon & Schuster, 1947) to this program.

Closing songs.

See also related programs: "It's Spring," Program 36; "Feathered Babies," Program 37; "Spring Hats," Program 39.

More books to read:

The Country Bunny and the Little Gold Shoes by Du Bose
Heyward; illus. by Marjorie Flack (New York: Houghton
Mifflin, 1939).

Mr. Rabbit and the Lovely Present by Charlotte Zolotow; illus.
by Maurice Sendak (New York: Harper & Row, 1962). Mr.
Rabbit helps little girl make a basket of fruit for her mother.

A Rabbit for Easter by Carol Carrick; illus. by Donald Carrick
(New York: Greenwillow, 1979).

Follow-up activities for home or school:
> Dye eggs. Paint some using a brush as Ho Ho did.
> Eat hard boiled eggs. Watch them boiling as Shen Shu did.
> Find a bunny to watch and pet.
> Have an egg hunt.
> Read *Home for a Bunny* and *The Golden Egg Book* by Margaret Wise Brown again and look for the wildflowers. See if you can locate some wildflowers in bloom.

Arbor Day

(See "Habitat: The Tree," Program 2; "All Falling Down," Program 29; Apple Day," Program 30.)

May Day

(See "May Day," Program 101.)

Fourth of July

48. Fourth of July Parade

Parade music should play as the children enter the room.
Opening songs.
Read: *Parade* by Donald Crews (New York: Greenwillow, 1983). Bright pictures of patriotic parade, almost wordless.
Read: *Fourth of July* by Barbara M. Loasse; illus. by Emily Arnold McCully (New York: Knopf, 1985). An "almost six" year-old marches in the Fourth of July parade, gets hot and tired, and is rewarded with sparklers that night.
Read: *Harbor* by Donald Crews (New York: Greenwillow, 1982). Clear illustrations of a variety of boats in the harbor. Ends with fire boat spraying water in celebration.
Have a parade: Put on a Sousa march and parade around the room. Play rhythm instruments if possible. If not, a book to beat on will do. Do some intricate moves—like lifting your knees really high, marching out a door and back in again, or marching under a bridge made by two parents' uplifted arms.

Read: *The Story of the Statue of Liberty* by Betsy and Giulio Maestro (New York: Lothrop, Lee & Shepard, 1986). Brief text. Large, colorful pictures. Tells of construction of the Statue of Liberty.

Read and sing: *The Star Spangled Banner* by Francis Scott Key; illus. by Peter Spier. (New York: Doubleday, 1963). Large page, intricate illustrations.

Poem: "Fourth of July" from *Celebrations* by Myra Cohn Livingston; illus. by Leonard Everett Fisher (New York: Holiday House, 1985). Show the painting as you recite the poem.

Make a skyrocket picture: Give each child a large sheet of white paper, a straw, and diluted paints in red, pink, and blue. Show them how to pick up a drop of paint water by dipping the straw in the paint water, then putting a finger over the straw's top opening. Hold the straw high above the white paper and lift the finger—a drop of colored paint water drops onto the paper and splatters. Cover the paper with these "skyrockets."

Closing songs.

More books to read:

And To Think That I Saw It On Mulberry Street by Dr. Seuss (New York: Vanguard, 1937). The weirdest parade possible.

Another Day by Marie Hall Ets (New York: Viking, 1953). A small boy and forest animals have a parade.

Crash! Bang! Boom! by Peter Spier (New York: Doubleday, 1972). A noisy parade.

In the Forest by Marie Hall Ets (New York: Viking, 1944). A small boy goes walking alone in the forest and meets several animals. His father finds him and they parade home.

Lentil by Robert McCloskey (New York: Viking, 1940). A sourpuss sucking a lemon is enough to stop a whole parade.

Nini at Carnival by Errol Lloyd (New York: Crowell, 1978). Small Nini has no costume for the carnival parade, until a fairy godmother friend helps her out.

The Parade Book by Ed Emberley (Boston: Little, Brown, 1962). A look at a parade.

Follow-up activities for home or school:

Plan a play parade with costumes and music. Practice it and perform it for some friends or relatives.

Go to watch a real parade. Even the smallest live parade is exciting.

Halloween

49. Pumpkin Magic

Opening songs.

Say poem: "A Riddle: What Am I?" by Dorothy Aldis from *Hey-How for Halloween!* by Lee Bennett Hopkins; illus. by Janet McCaffery, (New York: Harcourt, 1974) p. 19.

Read: *Pumpkin Pumpkin* by Jeanne Titherington (New York: Greenwillow, 1986). A pumpkin grows. Very brief text.

Fingerplay:

Five little Jack-o-Lanterns
Sitting on a gate. (five fingers upright)
First one said,
"It's getting late." (first wiggles)
Second one said,
"There're witches in the air." (second)
Third one said,
"I don't care."(third)
Fourth one said,
"Let's have some fun."(fourth)
Fifth one said,
"Let's run and run and run." (fingers run back and forth)
"Ooooh" went the wind.
"Out" went the light. (clap hands on "out")
And five little jack-o-lanterns
Rolled out of sight. (hand runs behind back)

Read: *Mousekin's Golden House* by Edna Miller (Englewood Cliffs, NJ: Prentice-Hall, 1969). A discarded jack-o-lantern makes a perfect house for mousekin.

Fingerplay:

This is pumpkin happy.
This is pumpkin sad.
This is pumpkin sleepy.
This is pumpkin mad.
Cut them up in pieces small
In pumpkin pie they're best of all!

Sing and act out: "The Pumpkin Tells" from *Halloween*. Golden LP242 (Port Washington, NY: Den-Lan Music, 1969. Chil-

dren act like monsters as pumpkin tells them what to be
and do.

Read: *The Magic Pumpkin* by Gloria Skurzynski; illus. by
Rocco Negri (New York: Four Winds, 1971).

Make a pumpkin face: Pass out orange pumpkin shapes. Paste
on eyes, nose, mouth. Selected from assorted shapes.

Closing songs.

More books to share:

From Seed to Jack-o-Lantern by Hannah Lyons Johnston;
photos by Daniel Dorn (New York: Lothrop, 1974). Pumpkin
facts and activities.

The Old Woman and the Red Pumpkin: A Bengali Folktale by
Betsy Bang; illus. by Molly Garrett Bang (New York: Macmillan, 1975). Old woman in a rolling pumpkin outsmarts
the animals.

Pumpkin Moonshine by Tasha Tudor (New York: Oxford University Press, 1938). Nostalgic. Pumpkin in an old-fashioned
community.

Follow-up activities for home and school:

Carve a pumpkin. Toast the seeds.

Visit a pumpkin farm.

Eat a pumpkin pie.

50. Ghosts and Witches

Opening songs.

Read: *A Woggle of Witches* by Adrienne Adams (New York:
Scribner's, 1971). Witches ride but are frightened off by
trick or treaters.

Read: *Humbug Witch* by Lorna Balian (Nashville: Abingdon,
1965). When humbug witch undresses, she's just a little girl.

Say and act out: "Reach for the Stars." (Fingerplay by author)

Reach for the stars. (reach with right hand)
Reach for the moon. (reach with left hand)
Fly through the sky
Like a witch on her broom. (Climb on broom and gallop
around room)

Sing: Form circle and all pretend to stir cauldron in middle.
For tune, see Appendix. (Song by author)

> Halloween,
> Halloween,
> Witches stir their big black pot.
> Halloween,
> Halloween,
> Witches stir their brew so hot.
> oooooooooooo
> oooooooooooo

> *Boo*!

Sing and dance to: "Pass the Witches' Broomstick" from *Halloween* Golden LP242 (Port Washington, NY: Den-Lan Music, 1964).
A toy broomstick works best. Pass it around as directed by the record. The game suggests that any child caught holding the broom when the music stops is "out." Being "out" is no fun so we all stay in the game.

Listen and dance to: "She's Stuck on Her Broomstick" from *Halloween*. See above citation. Plop on floor and listen to verse. Jump up and dance pretending to be stuck to your broomstick on chorus.

Read: *Georgie* by Robert Bright (New York: Doubleday, 1944).
Georgie the little ghost is frightened of everything.

Make a "Georgie" puppet: Wad a paper towel into a ball. Set the ball in the middle of another paper towel (white, soft) and pull up the sides. Tie with orange yarn making a neck. Tie loosely enough for a child's finger to fit up into the head. You have a ghost puppet. You'll need adult help to tie the puppet necks.

Say a chant with puppet:

> I'm a little ghost,
> Whoo whoo whoo. (making sweeping motions)
> I've come to haunt
> You you you. (swoop at friends)

Closing songs: "Goodbye to Georgie"
More books to read:

> *Halloween* by Gail Gibbons (New York: Holiday House, 1984).
> Simple picture book descriptions of Halloween traditions.

The Halloween Party by Lonzo Anderson; illus. by Adrienne Adams (New York: Scribner's, 1979). Boy out to trick-or-treat visits witches' party.

Follow-up activities for home or school:

On a shopping trip in October, count the ghosts you see in displays, or packaging, or anywhere else.

Make a ghost mobile. Cut body from white paper, paste on circles for eyes and mouth. Paste white crepe paper streamers to bottom. Hang it by string from the top.

51. Trick or Treat

Opening songs.

Read: *Hester* by Byron Barton (New York: Greenwillow, 1975). Crocodile Hester trick or treats a real witch.

Read: *The Trip* by Ezra Jack Keats (New York: Greenwillow, 1978). Halloween brings new friends after a move.

Dance: To "Guess What I Am?" from *Halloween*. Golden LP242 (Port Washington, NY: Den-Lan Music, 1969). Sing and dance to chorus. Act out character after you guess the riddle.

Dance: "Halloween Dance" from *Halloween*. See above citation.

Read: *Harriet's Halloween Candy* by Nancy Carlson (Minneapolis: Carolrhoda, 1982). Harriet tries to hog her candy, until she gets sick.

Read: *One Dark Night* by Edna Mitchell Preston; illus. by Kurt Werth (New York: Viking, 1969). A mouse scares trick or treating children.

Act out: *One Dark Night* as a finger play. Use five characters only and let right hand fingers be trick or treat kids. Left thumb should be the mouse.

Make *One Dark Night* puppets: Pass out pre-printed sheet to color. They can be cut into finger puppets at home.

Closing songs.

See also related programs: "Black Cats," Program 33; "Owls in the Night," Program 32.

More books to share:

The Ghost with the Halloween Hiccups by Stephen Mooser; illus. by Tomie de Paola (New York: Watts, 1977).

A Tiger Called Thomas by Charlotte Zolotow; illus. by Kurt Werth (New York: Lothrop, 1963). Shy Thomas finds security in a tiger costume.

Follow-up activities for home or school:
  Play at trick-or-treat visits. Divide the children into groups
  and give each group a bowl of peanuts or small candies. Let
  some groups go into an adjoining room. The trick-or-
  treaters knock and call out. The hosts open the door and
  give out treats.
  Decorate a bag to use for Halloween night.

Thanksgiving

52. Thanksgiving Turkeys

Opening songs.
Read: *The Four Riders* by Charlotte Krum; illus. by Katharine
  Evans (Chicago: Follett, 1953). A turkey and friends hop a
  ride on a donkey.
Read: *Sometimes It's Turkey, Sometimes It's Feathers* by Lorna
  Balian (Nashville, TN: Abingdon, 1980). A turkey comes to
  dinner.
Form a circle and sing: "The Turkey is a Funny Bird." See
  Appendix for tune.

> The turkey is a funny bird,
> His head goes bobble bobble.
> And all he says is just one word,
> Gobble gobble gobble
> Gobble gobble gobble.

Act this out while walking turkey-like in a circle bobbing
your necks and gobbling.
Sing: "Five Fat Turkeys Are We." See Appendix for tune. For
  complete tune, see *Dancing Games for Children of All Ages* by
  Esther L. Nelson (New York: Sterling, 1974).

> Five fat turkeys are we.
> We slept all night in a tree.
> When the cook came around
> We couldn't be found,
> And that's why we're here, don't you see!
> Gobble Gobble Gobble Gobble Gobble.

All may strut around as turkeys during song, or five may
strut in center. Break into gobbling at song's end.

Listen and look: *The Wild Turkey and Her Poults*, A Little Woodland Book by Bill Martin, Jr.; illus. by Laura Cornell; read by Bill Martin, Jr; guitar by Al Caiola (Chicago: Encyclopedia Britannica Educational Corp., 1979). A wild mother turkey with her young. Show the pictures while Bill Martin reads on cassette tape.

Show and sing: *Over the River and Through the Woods* by Lydia Maria Child; illus. by Brinton Turkle (New York: Coward, 1974). I tape the words to the back of the book and show only the colored page spreads as we sing. All can join in on the "over the river and through the woods" lines.

Fingerplay:

Everyday when we eat our dinner
Our table is just this small. (small circle with both hands)
There is room for father and mother and brother (point to fingers)
And sister and me. That's all.
But Thanksgiving Day, when company comes,
You'd scarcely believe your eyes. (point to eyes)
Our little table grows bigger and bigger,
Until it is just this size. (make circle grow larger and larger with hands and arms)

Crafts: Make an apple turkey. You will need one pre-cut turkey head of stiff posterboard. Make small slit in front of each apple to slide neck into. You'll need lots of toothpicks. Children can poke toothpicks into rear of apple forming tails.

Draw a turkey. Trace around the child's spread-fingered hand. Let the child color a turkey's tail feathers and draw an eye on the thumb.

Let the child assemble a pre-cut turkey. You'll need one large brown circle (body); two small yellow strips (feet); one pre-cut head; many pre-cut feathers of various colors. Glue.

Closing songs.

See also related programs: "Feeling Glad," Program 58; "Chicken Soup," Program 98

More books to share:

Autumn Harvest by Alvin Tresselt; illus. by Roger Duvoisin (New York: Lothrop, 1951). Sights and smells of fall.

Thanksgiving Day by Gail Gibbons (New York: Holiday House, 1983). About the holiday.

Follow-up activities for home or school:
  Eat chicken or turkey soup.
  Visit a zoo or farm to see a live turkey.
  See also: "Feeling Glad," Program 58.

Hanukkah

53. Happy Hanukkah

Opening songs.

Read: *Happy Hanukkah Everybody* by Hyman and Alice Chan-over; illus. by Maurice Zembeck. (United Synagogue Commission on Jewish Education, 1954).

Read: *Potato Pancakes All Around* by Marilyn Hirsh (Bonim Books, 1978).

Fingerplay:

> Take a potato, pat pat pat. (pat)
> Take it and roll it flat flat flat. (roll and slap)
> Put it in a pan with fat fat fat. (put in pretend pan)
> Hanukkah latkes Clap Clap Clap! (clap hands)

Read: *Laughing Latkes* by M.B. Goffstein (New York: Farrar, 1981). Why do latkes laugh?

Poem: "Dreidl" from *Poems for Jewish Holidays* by Myra Cohn Livingston; illus. by Lloyd Bloom (New York: Holiday House, 1986), p. 12.

Show: A toy dreidel. Spin it and read off the answers a few times.

Sing: "I Have a Little Dreidel." For music and other verses, see "My Dreidel" in *The Book of Religious Holdiays and Celebrations* by Marguerite Icks (New York: Dodd, Mead, 1966), p. 16.

> I have a little dreidel.
> I made it out of clay.
> And when it's dry and ready,
> Oh dreidel I will play.
> Oh dreidel dreidel dreidel,
> Oh dreidel I will play.
> Oh dreidel dreidel dreidel,
> Oh dreidel I will play.

Play dreidel: Use Hanukkah *gelt* or pennies as money. Give each child five pennies or *gelt*. Put small pile in center of circle. Each child spins dreidel. If "Nun" comes up, you do nothing. If "Gimmel," you take all of the kitty. If "Hay," you take half kitty. If "Shin," you add one to kitty. If kitty becomes depleted, each adds one from own pile to restore it. Use this pattern to make paper dreidels. Poke a short pencil through holes to make the spinner. At end of game put all winnings back in center and divide equally. If your group is large, divide into two or three circles to play and ask parents to help organize the dreidel games.

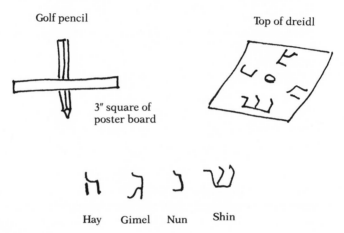

Golf pencil

Top of dreidl

3″ square of poster board

Hay   Gimel   Nun   Shin

Closing songs.

More books to read:

A Picture Book of Hanukkah by David A. Adler; illus. by Linda Heller (New York: Holiday House, 1982).

Follow-up activities for home or school:

Make a miniature menorah. Flatten a ball of clay into a circle an inch thick. Cut the circle in half and use one half for base. Stand the other up as backing. Stick eight candles into the base in a semicircle. Put one on top of the back piece for the shamus. For complete instructions and diagrams, see *A Pumpkin in a Pear Tree: Creative Ideas for Twelve Months of Holiday Fun* by Ann Cole, Carolyn Haas, Elizabeth Heller, and Betty Weinberger (Boston: Little, Brown, 1976). Make latkes and eat them! See *A Pumpkin in a Pear Tree* for recipe.

Christmas

54. Christmas Lullabies

Opening songs.

Read: *The Animal's Lullaby* by Trudi Alberti; illus. by Chiyako Nakatani (Cleveland: World, 1967). Each animal goes to sleep in his habitat.

Read: *Hush Little Baby*; illus. by Aliki (New York: Prentice-Hall, 1968). Poppa's gonna buy you a mockingbird. Encourage parents to sing or hum along.

Read: *On Mother's Lap* by Ann Herbert Scott; illus. by Glo Coalson (New York: McGraw-Hill, 1972). There's always room on mother's lap. Parents should hold children on their laps and rock back and forth with story.

Play, sing, and read: *The Little Drummer Boy* by Ezra Jack Keats (New York: Macmillan, 1968). Pass out a coffee can drum for each child. Decorate them ahead of time by wrapping Christmas foil around the cans and pasting a ribbon around top. They can be stored and used for several years. Or have the children bring you cans and use this as a craft. Teach the children to play on their drums when you hold up your hand and to *stop* when you lower it. Practice this until they are following you. Hold up your hand as a signal to *play* on the phrase "Rum-pa-pum-pum."

Sing and play: *Din Dan Don It's Christmas* by Janina Domanska (New York: Greenwillow, 1975). Speckled duck, turkey, and gander lead the procession to see Baby Jesus. This is a Polish carol. Since Domanska did not include the music for the carol, I made up a tune. See Appendix for tune. Let children play drums on the chorus "Din Dan Don it's Christmas."

Alternate sing and play: "Zumba Zumba." See Appendix for tune. Use drums.

Zumba Zumba play the cymbal;
Zumba Zumba play the drums;
Zumba Zumba play the cymbal;
Zumba Zumba play the drums.
Born on this night is a baby. (clap clap clap)
Everyone bring him a present. (clap clap clap)
Bring him some savory meat pies (clap clap clap)

Made out of partridge and pheasant. (clap clap clap)

Repeat refrain.

Read: *Bears Are Sleeping* by Yulya; illus. by Nonny Hogrogian (New York: Scribner's, 1967). Russian animals sleep in heavy snow. Sing this softly (the tune is at the end of the book). Let the children mime sleeping and hushing.

Craft: Make a baby in a walnut shell cradle. You will need one-half walnut shell per child. Small scraps of flannel or calico serve as covers for the babies. Buy tiny plastic baby dolls in bulk at a craft shop or pre-cut tiny babies from cardboard. The children tuck the babies into their shell cradles and glue on the cover. If you add a bit of ribbon, the cradle becomes a tree ornament.

Closing songs: Be sure to sing a lullaby to your new "baby" before you go.

See also related programs: "The Sleepy Storytime," Program 65.

More books to use:

Christmas by Dick Bruna; trans. of *Kerstmis*; English verse by Eve Merriam (New York: Doubleday, 1969). Biblical story in very brief verse with simple pictures.

The Friendly Beasts by Laura Nelson Baker; illus. by Nicolas Sidjakov (New York; Parnassus, 1958). Gentle carol of animals visiting Baby Jesus.

Follow-up activities for home or school:

Sing a lullaby to someone. Can you put them to sleep by singing?

Sing some Christmas carols which could be used as lullabies, "Silent Night," "Away in a Manger," for example.

Listen to *Lullabies Go Jazz* by John Crosse (Sunland, CA: Jazz Cat Productions, 1985; P.O. Box 4278, Sunland, CA 91040).

55. Christmas Bells

Opening songs.

Read: *A Bell for Ursli* by Selina Chonz; illus. by Alois Carigiet (New York: Walck, 1950). Ursli wants a big bell to lead the parade.

Play with bells: Pass out a variety of bells, one for each child. Ask children to bring a favorite bell from home as well.

Sing: "Christmas Bells" See Appendix for tune. Song by author.

Great big bells sing DING DONG DING. (slowly and
  deliberately)
Christmas bells sing DING DONG DING.
Tiny tiny Christmas bells sing ting-aling-a ting-aling-a.
  (quickly)
Tiny tiny Christmas bells sing ting-aling-a ting-aling-a.
In the middle Christmas bells sing Ring Ring Ring.
  (ringingly)
In the middle Christmas bells sing Ring Ring Ring.

Fingerplay: Put down your bells and say this first time through
  using only your fingers. Wiggle one finger for each bell,
  wiggle all fingers on last line. Then pick up your bells and
  say the poem again using the bells to ring "slow" and "fast."

> Five little bells hanging in a row,
> The first one says, "ring me slow."
> The second one says, "ring me fast."
> The third one says, "ring me last."
> The fourth one says, "ring me like a chime."
> The fifth one says, "ring us all at Christmas time."

Read: *Din Dan Don It's Christmas* by Janina Domanska (New
  York: Greenwillow, 1975). Have the children put their bells
  on the floor in front of them. Pick up the bells and play on
  the chorus lines "Din dan don it's Christmas!" See Appendix
  for tune, Program 54.
Sing: "Jingle Bells." Play your bells as you sing. Put the bells
  away: Let each child come up and return the bell to your
  basket. This gives them a chance to stretch.
Read: *Noël for Jeanne-Marie* by Françoise (New York: Scribner's, 1953). Jeanne-Marie awaits the arrival of Father Noël.
  She buys wooden shoes for her sheep Patapon so Patapon
  can receive a present too—a little golden bell.
Make a paper cup bell: Poke two holes in the bottom of a small
  paper cup. Thread ribbon or yarn through the holes and tie
  a jingle bell inside the cup (hanging down from the bottom).
  Dip snippets of colored paper in glue and paste onto outside
  of cup. Hang it on your tree.
More books to read:
The Bells of London by Ashley Wolff (New York: Dodd, Mead,
  1985). A chant about the church bells of London. Illustrations add a story of a boy, a girl and a dove passing the
  churches.

The Polar Express by Chris Van Allsburg (Boston: Houghton, Mifflin, 1985). The boy brings back one souvenir from the North Pole, a sleigh bell that only he can hear.

Follow-up activities for home or school:

Gather together all the bells you can find. Bells on shoes and hats? Dinner bells? Bells on toy animals? Decorative Christmas bells? Experiment with their different sounds. Notice the different way they produce sound. Touch a bell while it is ringing. What happens? Talk about sound vibrations.

Be alert to bells in your neighborhood. Are there church bells of different tones? A school bell? A bell choir?

56. Here Comes Santa Claus!

Opening songs.

Read: *Paddy's Christmas* by Helen Albee Monsell; illus. by Kurt Wiese (New York: Knopf, 1942).

Read: *Noël for Jeanne-Marie* by Françoise (New York: Scribner's, 1961).

Fingerplay:

> Here is the chimney. (squat, arms up)
> Here is the top. (close hands over head)
> Open the lid, (hands up)
> Out Santa will POP! (jump up)

Act out: Squat down and fold your hands over your head as a chimney. Pop up a santa.

Sing, then add action: "Up on the Housetop." See Appendix for tune.

Up on the housetop
reindeers pause, (lift feet delicately, like hooves)
Out jumps good old Santa Claus, (jump out)
Down through the chimney (hands over head and sink down)
With lots of toys,
All for the little one's Christmas joys. (hands up in amazement, big smiles)
Ho Ho Ho (hands pat tummy, laughing)
Who wouldn't go?
Ho Ho Ho (hands pat tummy, laughing)
Who wouldn't go?

Up to the house top
Click click click, (lift "hooves" delicately)
Down through the chimney (arms over head and sink
 down)
with good St. Nick.

Read: *The Night Before Christmas* by Clement Moore; designed by Paul Taylor; illus. by Marvin Brehm (New York: Random House, n.d.) I like the Random House Pop-Up version. Santa pops out of the chimney dramatically.

For older audiences also read: *How the Grinch Stole Christmas* by Dr. Seuss (New York: Random House, 1957). The grinch's heart grows on Christmas morn.

Make: Candy cane reindeer. A craft with more adult helpers' direction than child input, but a nice treat for the last program before Christmas. Paste onto a candy cane two goggle eyes in front of the crook. Cut one long red pipe cleaner in half. Cut one of these "deer horns" in half again. Twist the first piece around the crook of the cane. This forms the antlers. Twist a piece around each "prong" to complete. Paste a red pom-pom on the short end of the cane as a nose. Hang canes on the tree or eat.

More books to share:

Bah! Humbug? by Lorna Balian (Nashville, TN: Abingdon, 1977). Who believes in Santa Claus?

Peter Spier's Christmas by Peter Spier (New York: Doubleday, 1983). Lots of activities of a family Christmas are shown.

Birthdays

57. Happy Birthday to Me!

Opening songs.

Books about giving someone a happy birthday.

Read: *The Birthday* by Hans Fischer (New York: Harcourt, 1954). The two cats Mauli and Ruli join Bello the dog in planning a birthday party for Old Lisette.

Read: *Ask Mr. Bear* by Marjorie Flack (New York: Macmillan, 1932). Mr. Bear knows just the right present to give a mother on her birthday—a bear hug. Children can help you with the animal sounds in this one. Let every parent present get a nice bear hug at the story's end. This makes a good flannel board story.

Sing and play: "A Tisket A Tasket" For tune see *Singing Bee!* by Jane Hart; illus. by Anita Lobel (New York: Lothrop, 1982).

Make a circle. One child walks around the circle carrying a small wrapped present and drops it behind another child, then runs back to his or her place. That child is now "it."

> A tisket, a tasket,
> A green and yellow basket,
> Brought a present for my love
> and on the way I dropped it. (drop present)

Read: *Happy Birthday Sam* by Pat Hutchins (New York: Greenwillow, 1978). Sam cannot reach the light, the closet, and other places even though he is a year older. But with Grandpa's present, a chair to stand on, he can.

Read: *A Letter for Amy* by Ezra Jack Keats (New York: Harper & Row, 1968). Peter writes to invite Amy to his party, but fears she won't come.

Light candles, sing: "Happy Birthday to US!"

Eat a birthday cake!

Closing songs.

More books to read:

A Birthday for Frances by Russell Hoban; illus. Lillian Hoban (New York: Harper & Row, 1968).

The Birthday Wish by Chihiro Iwasaki (New York: McGraw-Hill, 1974). A special birthday wish.

Happy Birthday to You! by Dr. Seuss (New York: Random House, 1959). A silly birthday with the great Birthday Bird of Katroo. Lengthy, wordy, wacky for oldest preschoolers.

Jenny's Birthday Book by Esther Averill (New York: Harper, 1954). Jenny the cat has a birthday.

Little Bear by Else Holmelund Minarik; illus. by Maurice Sendak (New York: Harper & Row, 1957). "Birthday Soup" story. Little Bear makes birthday soup.

Tobias's Birthday by Ole Hertza; trans. by Tobi Tobias (Minneapolis: Carolrhoda Books, 1984). An Eskimo village makes a birthday visit to Tobias's house.

Follow-up activities for home or school:

Plan an unbirthday party for yourself. Plan decorations, games, food. Make decorations yourself. Everyone sing happy *unbirthday* to me.

Getting to
Know Yourself

Feelings

(For related programs, see "Making Faces," Program 69; "Copy Cats," Program 82; "Exploring Our Senses," Programs 20 and 24; "Feeling Foolish," Program 46.)

58. Feeling Glad

Opening songs.

Talk about: Things that make us feel happy. Help the children talk about why each character in these books feels glad.

Read: *The Carrot Seed* by Ruth Krauss; illus. by Crockett Johnson (New York: Harper & Row, 1945). A little boy plants a carrot seed. He faithfully waters it until it grows.

Read: *MA nDA LA* by Arnold Adoff; illus. by Emily McCully (New York: Harper & Row, 1971). An African family plant corn and joyously watch it grow, pound it into meal, make it into cornbread. I ask the children to repeat each line of this "poem" after me, turning it into a joyous choral reading.

Read and act out: *The Great Big Enormous Turnip* by Helen Oxenbury; from a story by Alexei Tolstoy (New York: Watts, 1968). When everyone in the family pulls together the enormous turnip finally comes up. Choose a heavy person to be the turnip—a parent works well. Add plenty of dogs, cats, and other creatures so that everyone can help pull.

Read: *Play With Me* by Marie Hall Ets (New York: Viking, 1955). Chipmunk, snake, and the others all flee from a little girl. But when she sits quietly they all come back and play with her.

Read: *On Mother's Lap* by Ann Herbert Scott; illus. by Glo Coalson (New York: McGraw-Hill, 1972). A small Eskimo boy feels content on mother's lap. There is room for baby and Michael too. Have the children rock with you on the refrains in this one. Be sure children are on their parents' laps, if you are including parents in the story time.

Sing: "If You're Happy and You Know It, Clap Your Hands."

Read and act out: "What Will Little Bear Wear?" from *Little Bear* by Else Holmelund Minarik; illus. by Maurice Sendak (New York: Harper & Row, 1957). Mother Bear makes something for Little Bear to wear. Each parent should be Mother Bear. In classes without parents you be mother bear.

Make a book of "pictures that make you feel good": Tape lots of book jackets to the wall. Let the children browse for pictures they like. When they find a picture that makes them feel good, they take it down and paste it on a piece of paper. Staple all together to form a book. This should be a gallery browsing experience. Encourage them to take their time. Avoid displaying a picture so attractive that everyone will want it.

Closing songs.

More books to read:

Hooray for Me! by Remy Charlip and Lillian Moore; illus. by Vera B. Williams (New York: Parents' Magazine Press, 1975). A celebration of relationships—I'm my mother's daughter, my cousin's cousin, etc.

Follow-up activities for home or school:

Talk with children about things that make them feel good. Look at pictures in a book or visit an art gallery with your child. Talk about which pictures make the child feel good. Give the child a sheet of sticky circles on which you have drawn smiling faces. Look through a magazine and paste smiling faces on any pictures that make the child feel good. You are teaching the child to get in touch with his or her feelings, to *think* about what is seen, and to develop a critical eye. When using this exercise in the library, I have to make do with the discarded magazines we have on hand. In working with my own child in the home, I would choose a magazine with fine illustrations, such as *Cricket*, or a handsomely illustrated adult magazine.

59. Feeling Mad

Opening songs.

Talk about: Bad, mad feelings.

Read: *The Temper Tantrum Book* by Edna Mitchell Preston; illus. by Rainey Bennett (New York: Viking, 1969). Elephant, tiger, and other animals are throwing tantrums for some of the same reasons children do—tangles in their hair, soap in the eyes, not being allowed to go out and play, etc.

Read: *Alexander and the Terrible, Horrible, No Good, Very Bad Day* by Judith Viorst; illus. by Ray Cruz (New York: Atheneum, 1984). Everything about Alexander's day goes wrong. Let the children repeat the refrain, "A terrible, horrible, no good, very bad day!" with you.

Read: *The Grouchy Ladybug* by Eric Carle (New York: Crowell, 1977). A grouchy ladybug challenges everyone encountered to a fight, then claims, "Oh you're not big enough," when they accept. Add action by letting the children "put up their fists" and challenge "Wanna fight!" Then they can wave the potential foe away saying, "Oh you're not big enough!" Act it out again afterwards if you like.

Sing: "If You're MAD and You Know It Stomp Your Feet." For tune, see *Making Music Your Own* by Mary Tinnin Jaye (Morris town, NJ: Silver Burdett, 1971). Form a circle for the song and use lots of actions.

Read: *The Elephant Who Liked to Smash Small Cars* by Jean Merrill and Ronnie Solbert (New York: Pantheon, 1967). The elephant *loves* smashing small cars, until he gets a taste of his own medicine.

Read: *A is for Angry* by Sandra Boynton (New York: Workman, 1983). One emotion for every letter of the alphabet. We discussed each and gave it a thumbs up or thumbs down. We liked "Jazzy"; gave "Ill" a thumbs down, and so forth.

Play with clay: Give each child a lump of play dough and a table top to pound on. Tell them to wait until they hear the music then pound the way the music tells them. I played a bit of Beethoven's *Fifth Symphony* for angry pounding; "The Dance of the Sugarplum Fairy" for delicate stroking, poking; the "Russian Dance" from the *Nutcracker Suite* for energetic, frenzied pounding. I let the record run on into the "Waltz of the Flowers" and allowed them free play with the clay during that cut.

Closing songs.

More books to read:

How Do I Feel? by Norma Simon; illus. by Joe Lasker (Chicago: Albert Whitman, 1979) Talking about feelings.

I Was So Mad by Norma Simon; illus. by Dora Leder (Niles, IL: Albert Whitman, 1974). Things that make me mad.

It's Mine: A Greedy Book by Crosby Bonsall (New York:

Harper & Row, 1964). Two friends fight over everything but maintain a friendship throughout.

The Little Brute Family by Russell Hoban; illus. by Lillian Hoban (New York: Macmillan, 1966). When baby brute catches a good feeling, it spreads to the whole family and they change their name to "Nice."

Osito Pardo Esta de Mal Humor by Daniele Bour (Madrid: Ediciones Altea, 1985). *Little Bear Is In a Bad Mood* by Daniele Bour (New York: Barron's, 1986).

The Quarreling Book by Charlotte Zolotow; illus. by Arnold Lobel (New York: Harper & Row, 1963). Anger is contagious, but so is kindness, as this family learns.

Follow-up activities for home or school:

Talk with your children about feeling mad, feeling bad. Find safe ways to express anger.

Talk about ways to *change* a mood. *The Quarreling Book* may help discuss this. See if you can change someone's mood from bad to better.

60. The Don't Be Scared Storytime

Opening songs.

Read: *The Night Book* by Mark Strand; illus. by William Pene du Bois (New York: Clarkson N. Potter/Crown, 1985). Moon teaches a little girl not to fear the night.

Read: *Poinsettia and the Firefighters* by Felicia Bond (New York: Crowell, 1984). Poinsettia fears the night but is comforted to know others, the firefighters, are awake, watching.

Talk about: Fears. Distinguish between imaginary fears and real fears. Fear helps us deal with danger at times. At other times it handicaps us by making us imagine danger which does not exist. Talk about real versus imaginary fears.

Read: *The Don't Be Scared Book* by Isle-Margaret Vogel (New York: Atheneum, 1964). Friendly approaches to scary visitors. All can act out the responses to scary things as you read.

Form a circle and sing: "If you're scared of a (supply fear) and you know it—just (supply solution)." Let kids supply fears and the ways of dealing with them. For example, "If you're scared of a dragon and you know it—invite it to tea." You may have to distinguish here also between real and imaginary fear. For example, "If you're scared of a friendly dog and you know it—pat its head." But, "If you're scared of an angry dog and you know it—leave it alone!" Sing to tune of "If you're happy and you know it."

Read: *Night in the Country* by Cynthia Rylant; illus. by Mary Zilagyi (New York: Bradbury, 1986). Sounds and sights of the dark country night.

Make a night picture: Pass out dark blue construction paper sheets. Paste night things onto your page. Photocopy several illustrations from books, pasted on one sheet. Cut up into small pasteable pictures for the children to select from.

Closing songs.

See also related programs: "The Sleepy Story," Program 65; "Monster Bash!" Program 85.

More books to read:

Bedtime for Frances by Russell Hoban; illus. by Garth Williams (New York: Harper & Row, 1960). Everything seems like a monster when the lights are out.

A Book of Scary Things by Paul Showers; illus. by Susan Perl (Garden City, NY: Doubleday, 1977). Discussion of various fears people have. Notes also the importance of legitimate fear as a warning for action to avoid danger.

Harriet and the Roller Coaster by Nancy Carlson (Minneapolis: Carolrhoda, 1982). George drags Harriet onto the roller coaster despite her fears. She loves it.

Only the Cat Saw by Ashley Wolff (New York: Dodd, Mead, 1985). Glowing, evocative illustrations of a cat's view of the night.

Follow-up activities for home or school:

Use Paul Showers *Book of Scary Things* (see above citation) to start a discussion of real versus imaginary fears. Help the child distinguish between these.

Learn more about some thing you are afraid of. Make up a story of an encounter between you and the scary thing, from the scary thing's point of view.

61. The Caring Day

Opening songs.

Read: *John Brown, Rose, and the Midnight Cat* by Jenny Wagner; illus. by Ron Brooks (New York: Bradbury, 1978). John Brown's caring for Rose overcomes his jealousy of the cat.

Read: *The Tomten and the Fox* by Astrid Lindgren; illus. by

Harald Wiberg (New York: Coward, 1965). The Tomten cares for the fox during the cold winter.

Read and act out: *Sam Who Never Forgets* by Eve Rice (New York: Greenwillow, 1977). Sam the zookeeper cares for all the animals. Let everyone be an animal and get fed.

Act out the recording: "Birds in the Nest" from *Cloud Journeys* by Anne Lief Barlin and Marcia Berman. (Van Nuys, CA: Learning Through Movement, 1982). Each parent can hold his or her brood in their own "nest." With older groups without parents you can be the parent and cuddle them all close in the group "nest."

Talk about: Ways to show someone you care.

Read: *No More Monsters for Me!* by Peggy Parish; illus. by Marc Simont (New York: Harper & Row, 1981). Even a monster needs caring.

Make: A bookmark to give someone as a present. Litter the table with small brightly colored paper shapes—squares, circles, triangles. Give each child a bookmark size strip of clear contact paper. Tape it to the table so child won't tangle it up. Child arranges colored shape on strip. An adult helps put second strip on top to seal in the "picture." Trim edges, if necessary.

Closing songs.

More books to read:

The Biggest Bear by Lynd Ward (Boston: Houghton Mifflin, 1952). Caring for a bear cub gets harder as he gets bigger!

Horton Hatches the Egg by Dr. Seuss (New York: Random House, 1940, 1968). An elephant cares for Mayzie Bird's egg.

The Lady and the Spider by Faith McNulty; illus. by Bob Marstall (New York: Harper & Row, 1986). A spider is returned to the native habitat.

The Plant Sitter by Gene Zion; illus. by Margaret Bloye Graham (New York: Harper & Row, 1959). Plants, too, need care.

A Salmon for Simon by Betty Waterton; illus. by Ann Blades (New York: Atheneum, 1980). Simon helps a stranded salmon.

Thy Friend, Obadiah by Brinton Turkle (New York: Viking, 1969). Obadiah helps a seagull and makes a friend.

Tiger is a Scaredy Cat by Joan Phillips; illus. by Norman (New York: Random House, 1986). Tiger is frightened but tries to be bold when a friend is scared.

Follow-up activities for home or school:

Choose a person or an animal that you care about. Think of ways to show them that you care.

Take care of a pet for a few days. What kind of care does a pet need?

Give someone a hug today. Is a hug a way to show caring?

62. Just Me!

Opening songs.

Read: *Arthur's Nose* by Marc Brown (Boston: Little, Brown, 1976). Arthur Anteater wants a different nose, but decides his own is best after all.

Read: *You Look Ridiculous Said the Rhinocerous to the Hippopotamus* by Bernard Waber (Boston: Houghton Mifflin, 1966). Hippopotamus wants a mane like a lion, ears like an elephant, and other characteristics. But when she gets them she decides her old self is best. It would be fun to retell this with flannel board pieces, letting the children put the ears, mane, and so forth on the figure.

Read: *Is It Hard? Is It Easy?* by Mary McBurney Green; illus. by Len Gittleman (New York; Young Scott, 1960).

Form a circle and talk about things that different people find hard and easy. Let children suggest skips and jumps that everyone can try. But don't limit it to actions. Try whistling, saying a hard word "supercalifragilistic." The aim is to point up *differences*, not to see who can excel.

Read some poems in celebration of being me: "At the Top of My Voice" by Felice Holman in *Surprises* by Lee Bennett Hopkins; illus. by Megan Lloyd (New York: Harper & Row, 1984), p. 27. "When I stamp the ground thunders."

"Changing" by Mary Ann Hoberman from *Best Friends* by Lee Bennett Hopkins; illus. by James Watts (New York: Harper & Row, 1986), p. 10–11.

"Beginning on Paper" from *Somebody Spilled the Sky* by Ruth Krauss; illus. by Eleanor Hazard (New York: Greenwillow, 1936, 1979), p. 30.

"The Frame" from *The Other Side of a Poem* by Barbara Abercrombie (New York: Harper & Row, 1977), p. 49.

Read: "At Evening" from *Grasshopper on the Road* by Arnold Lobel (New York: Harper & Row, 1978). Fireflies zip and zoom, grasshopper walks on the road. Both are happy with their lot.

Make a Just Me picture: Use your favorite colors. Color in your favorite way. Compare pictures to note our different tastes.

Closing songs.

See also related program: "Feeling Glad," Program 58.

More books to read:

The Big Orange Splot by Daniel Manus Pinkwater (New York: Hastings House, 1977). Mr. Plumbeam paints his house exotic colors. The neighbors criticize at first, then join him.

Clive Eats Alligators by Alison Lester (Boston: Houghton Mifflin, 1986). Celebrating the differences in kids lives— different breakfasts, different clothes and other differences.

The Importance of Crocus by Roger Duvoisin (New York: Harper & Row, 1980). Crocus crocodile can't do anything as well as the other animals, until he discovers his specialty.

A Little House of Your Own by Beatrice Schenk de Regniers; illus. by Irene Haas (New York: Harcourt, 1954). The need for a private place. Many ways to find that privacy.

Otto is Different by Franz Brandenberg; illus. by James Stevenson (New York: Greenwillow, 1985). Otto hates having eight arms. Why can't he be like other folks? Then he discovers advantages.

Where Wild Willie by Arnold Adoff; illus. by Emily Arnold McCully (New York: Harper & Row, 1978). Willie walks away, plays alone all day, but comes home to his loving family at night.

Follow-up activities for home or school:

Make a book called "My Favorite Things."

Make a list of ways *I* am special.

63. The New Baby

Opening songs.

Read: *On Mother's Lap* by Ann Herbert Scott; illus. by Glo Coalson (New York: McGraw-Hill, 1972). Sharing mother's lap. Have parents rock their children on their laps during the story. Older children can rock themselves back and forth.

Read: *Peter's Chair* by Ezra Jack Keats (New York: Harper & Row, 1967). Peter repaints his chair for baby sister.

Poem: "Little" by Dorothy Aldis in *Such Foolishness* by William Cole (Philadelphia: Lippincott, 1978), p. 72.

Poem: "A Little Lullaby" in *The Tamarindo Puppy* by Charlotte Pomerantz; illus. by Byron Barton (New York: Greenwillow, 1980). Pretend to feed your baby as you say it. Do it again and let everyone act it.

Make a circle and sing:"When I Was a Baby." See Appendix for tune. Program 12.

> When I was a baby, a baby, a baby;
> When I was a baby
> I kicked my feet like this. (kick)

Let children suggest motions: "Drank my bottle;" "played with my ball;" etc.

Read: *My Mama Needs Me* by Mildred Pitts Walter; illus. by Pat Cummings (New York: Lothrop, 1983). A new baby displaces big brother temporarily.

Fingerplay: Learn a song to use with a baby. This works best from the rear while holding baby on your lap. But for preschoolers facing the baby is a more practical approach. Stress gentle motions. See Appendix for tune to this original song by Margaret MacDonald and Baby Jennifer Skye MacDonald.

> Baby's little hands go clap clap clap, (hold baby's hand in yours and clap them)
> Clap clap clap and-a clap clap clap.
> Baby's little legs go slap slap slap, (slap baby's hands on baby's leg)
> slap slap slap and-a slap slap slap.
> Baby's little hand goes tap tap tap. (tap baby's hand lightly on baby's head)
> tap tap tap and-a tap tap tap.
> Baby's little eyes go peek-a-boo (baby's hands over eyes)
> and that-is-all. (put baby's hand back in baby's lap decisively)

Add more verses if you like such as "feet go stomp stomp stomp."

Film: *Smile for Auntie* (Weston Woods, 1974) 4 min. Read the book *Smile for Auntie* by Diane Paterson (New York: Dial, 1974).

Make: A picture book for baby. Cut pictures from old book jackets and magazines. Paste onto papers and staple the three or four sheets together.

Closing songs.

See also related programs: "Christmas Lullabies," Program 54; "The Sleepy Storytime," Program 65.

More books to read:

A Baby Sister for Frances by Russell Hoban; illus. by Lillian Hoban (New York: Harper & Row, 1970). Frances contemplates running away.

The Family of Tiny White Elephants: A Tale About a New Baby Bird and Her Jealous Brother by Alona Frankel (New York: Barron's, 1978, 1980).

101 Things to Do With a Baby by Jan Ormerod (New York: Lothrop, Lee & Shepard, 1984). Baby appreciation at its best. Great promo for doubtful siblings on the joys of acquiring a baby in the family.

When You Were a Baby by Ann Jonas (New York: Greenwillow, 1982). Big, bright pictures and very simple text.

Follow-up activities for home or school:

Learn several fingerplays to do with babies.

Learn a song to sing to a baby.

Think about the things a baby needs—food, warm clothing, dry diapers, sleep, to be held gently.

Look at photos of your family members as babies.

Listen to stories of things you did as a baby.

About You

64. Making Faces

Opening songs.

Read: *Frances Face-Maker* by William Cole; illus. by Tomi Ungerer (New York: Collins-World, 1963). Frances's father puts her to bed with a session of face-making. Lead your children in making faces along with Frances.

Read poem: "Timothy Grady" by Leroy F. Jackson in *Oh Such*

Foolishness by William Cole (Philadelphia: Lippincott, 1978), p. 45.

Read: *When the Wind Changed* by Ruth Park; illus. by Deborah Niland (New York: Coward, McCann & Geoghegan, 1980). Did you know that if you are making a face when the wind changes your face will stick that way forever? Hear what happened to Josh when the wind changed.

Play: Changing the wind. Give a huge fan to wave and have one child be the wind. Everytime the "wind" changes all faces must freeze. When the "wind" puts his or her fan down, everyone can relax again. The trick is to make the most horrendous faces possible without getting "frozen."

Sing: "If You're Happy and You Know It." For tune see *Making Music Your Own* by Mary Tinnan Jaye (Morristown, NJ: Silver Burdett, 1971). Exaggerate all facial expressions.

Read: *A is for Angry* by Sandra Boynton (New York: Workman, 1983). Make appropriate faces for Boynton's emotions.

Make: Paper plate faces. Give the children paper plates, tongue depressors, cut out mouths shaped in a crescent. Let them paste on the mouths in a happy or sad face.

Sing: "Show Me a Happy, Happy Face." See Appendix for tune. All happy face plates should be held up. Then sing "Show Me a Sad, Sad Face." All sad faces are held up.

Closing songs.

See also related programs: "Feeling Glad," Program 58; "Feeling Mad," Program 59; "Just Me," Program 62.

More books to share:

Face Talk, Hand Talk, Body Talk by Sue Castle; illus. by Frances McLaughlin Gill (New York: Doubleday, 1977).

Follow-up activities for home or school:

Practice making different faces.

Tell a simple story, such as "Three Bears." Make exaggerated faces to express the character's emotions.

Play the "Copy My Face" game described in the follow-up activities for "Copy Cats," Program 82.

65. Sleepy Storytime

Opening songs.

Read: *In the Night Kitchen* by Maurice Sendak (New York: Harper & Row, 1970). Mickey's night adventures.

Read: *Good Night, Good Night* by Sandra Boynton (New York: Random House, 1985).

Act out: Pantomine getting ready for bed, going to sleep. Let the children "sleep" for a few moments, then gently "wake them up." Keep the mood quiet as they sit up and stretch awake.

Read: *Dawn* by Uri Shulevitz (New York: Farrar, 1974). Dawn comes slowly over mountain and lake. You can create a remarkable mood piece from this book by reading it with the beginning of Strauss's "Blue Danube Waltz" as a background. It works best to tape exactly the cut you need beforehand so the music will stop at just the right point. It takes some practice to get this effect to come off just right but is well worth it. (Thanks to June Pinnell for this idea.)

Stand up and act out a day rapidly. Dress, play, lunch, nap, play, dinner, now bedtime story.

Read: *Goodnight Moon* by Margaret Wise Brown; illus. by Clement Hurd (New York: Harper & Row, 1947). Encourage the children to chime in with you on the refrains "Goodnight bears, goodnight chairs." Make your goodnights drowsy and wistful.

Film: *Lullaby* (International Film Bureau, 1975) 4 min. This is a very quiet film. The lullaby is sung in Hungarian. It shows bright pictures of simple objects floating on the screen as the mother's voice sings of them. This is a strange film for adults and seems boring to some, but preschoolers find the succession of objects interesting. Depending on the mood you want, you might encourage them to name the objects aloud as they see them. The text to this song has been translated for us by Veronika Embody Coyle, whose daughter Ilona attended these storytimes.

Lullaby by Jozsef Attila

> The sky closes its blue eye,
> The house closes its many eyes,
> The meadow sleeps under an eiderdown.
> You sleep, too, little Balazs.
> Putting his head down on his foot,
> The beetle, the wasp is sleeping.
> The buzzing bee sleeps with him too.
> You sleep, too, little Balazs.
> The jacket is sleeping on the chair.

The tear is slumbering, too.
Today it won't tear any further.
You sleep—
The tramcar is sleeping
And while its rumbling is taking a nap,
It tinkles a little in its sleep.
You sleep—
The ball and the whistle are asleep,
The woods, the outing,
The good candy is sleeping, too.
You sleep—
You can be a fireman, a soldier,
A shepherd herding wild beasts.
Only shut your little eyes
And sleep quietly, like Balazs.

Make a goodnight book: Choose pictures of objects from old magazines or book jackets. Cut them out and paste on sheets of paper. Staple the pages together to form a booklet. Let each child go through his or her own booklet saying goodnight to each object chosen.

Closing songs.

See also related programs: "Harvest Moon," Program 31; "Christmas Lullabies," Program 54; "The Don't Be Scared Storytime," Program 60.

More books to share:

A Child's Good Night Book by Margaret Wise Brown; illus. Jean Charlot (New York: Addison-Wesley, 1952). A soft goodnight to the animals.

Lisa Can't Sleep by Kaj Beckman; illus. by Per Beckman (New York: Watts, 1969).

Peace at Last by Jill Murphy (New York: Dial, 1980).

Sleepy People by M.B. Goffstein (New York: Farrar, Straus, Giroux, 1966). Tiny family goes to bed.

Winifred's New Bed by Lynn and Richard Howell (New York: Knopf, 1985). Too many toys in bed with Winifred.

Follow-up activities for home or school:

Plan a bedtime ritual which includes reading aloud. Visit a public library to choose books for a week's menu of bedtime stories.

Talk about bedtime stories. Encourage the children to bring

in their bedtime favorites to share with the class. Plan a "naptime" story for a few days.

66. New Shoes

Opening songs.

Read: *The Foot Book* by Dr. Seuss (New York: Random House, 1968). Foot nonsense.

Read: *Mister Magnolia* by Quentin Blake (London: Jonathan Cape, 1980). In this nonsense rhyme Mister Magnolia has only one boot.

Act out poem: "Happiness" from *When We Were Very Young* by A.A. Milne (New York: Dutton, 1927). "John had great big waterproof boots on."

Sing: "I'm putting on my sandals." See Appendix for tune. Program 12.

> I'm putting on my sandals,
> my sandals, my sandals.
> I'm putting on my sandals
> And walking on the beach.

Let the kids suggest footwear and add verses. "Putting on my boots and walking in big puddles;" "Putting on my snowshoes and walking over the snow." Sing about ballet slippers, high heels, jogging shoes, work boots.

Singing game: "Mmbera." See Appendix for tune and my transliteration of the words (I've seen three other printed versions, each different from the others.) Sit in a circle. Take off one shoe. Pound it on the floor as you sing the first part. Pass it to the right as you sing the chorus. Keep shoes moving to the right. One shoe moves on each beat during chorus for older groups. Just pass one shoe per chorus for smaller children. Stop when your own shoe gets back to you or you've had enough. I learned this song from a student who had studied under Dumisami Maraire, a Rhodesian ethnomusicologist who has studied and taught at the University of Washington. The game-song, apparently introduced by Maraire, is widely used in the Seattle area and like all good folk materials now exists in several different variations. According to my student, this game was played to pass time on trains in Rhodesia.

Read: *A Pair of Red Clogs* by Masako Matsuno; illus. by Kazue Mizumura (New York: Collins, 1960). A ruined pair of new red clogs and a lie.

Play: The "Weather Telling Game" as described in *A Pair of Red Clogs*. Take off one shoe each, line up, chant, and KICK your shoes into the air. Find out what the weather will be tomorrow.

Lace a slipper: Give each child a cut out of a shoe sole and toe with pre-punched holes to form a slipper. A yarn with end taped to a point can be used to "sew" the two pieces together. You might want to play the "weather telling game" again wearing your new slippers to kick into the air.

Closing songs.

More books to share:

How Do I Put It On? by Shigeo Watanabe; illus. by Yasuo Ohtomo (New York: Putnam's, 1979). Very simple text. Bear puts shoes on ears, etc.

New Blue Shoes by Eve Rice (New York: Macmillan, 1975). Desire for new blue shoes.

Follow-up activities for home or school:

Make a display of shoes. Compare them. What do they all have in common?

Imagine a pair of fantastic shoes. How do they look? How does it feel to walk in them? Put them on and pretend to walk, dance, skip in them.

67. Button, Button

Opening songs.

Read: *Corduroy* by Don Freeman (New York: Viking, 1968). A teddy bear loses a button and finds a little girl to love him.

Read: *Elephant Buttons* by Noriko Ueno (New York: Harper & Row, 1973). An elephant unbuttons his suit and out comes a lion, who unbuttons his suit . . .

Act out: *Elephant Buttons*. Unzip your suit each time and step out as the next animal. I end by moving into an action chant of the poem "An Elephant Moves Like This and That." (See program 73.)

Move to a standing circle and chant.

> Hello—my name is Joe.
> I work in a button factory.
> I've got a dog—a cat—and a family.
> One day—my boss came up to me.
> He said, 'Joe turn the lever with your right hand.'
> Begin making this motion and don't stop until chant is
> over. Repeat verses, singing
> "He said, 'Joe turn the lever with your *left* hand.' "
> Repeat verse adding new motion each time through:
> "He said, 'Joe push the button with your right foot;' 'Joe
> turn the lever with your nose;' 'Joe push the button with
> your hip.' " Keep this up until every appendage and
> movable part of your body is in action. The older the
> child, the farther you can carry this. End with "I said—I
> QUIT!"

Seated Circle Sing: "If You Have a Red Button, Please Stand
Up." For tune, see Appendix, Program 15.

> If you have a red button, please stand up.
> If you have a red button, please stand up.
> If you have a red button, please stand up.
> Then sit—back—down.

You could call for round buttons or various colored buttons.
End by calling for all buttons so everyone can stand on the
last verse. You may have to add in zippers and velcro fasten-
ers if someone in the group is totally buttonless.

Read: "The Button" from *Frog and Toad are Friends* by Arnold
Lobel (New York: Harper & Row, 1970). A tale of lost buttons. You might want to make a tiny felt jacket with buttons
sewn on like those lost. Show it after the story and let the
children point out the lost buttons.

Craft: Cut large cardboard "button" circles with four holes
punched in center. Let children thread these with a length
of bright colored yarn and wear them home as necklaces.
Or, provide a printed picture card with matching holes and
let the children "sew" the button onto the picture card. Be
sure you punch card and button at the same time so the
holes match properly, and keep each button paperclipped
to its matching card.

Closing songs.

More books to share:

I Can Dress Myself by Dick Bruna (New York: Methuen, 1977). Very simple dressing book.

The Philharmonic Gets Dressed by Karla Kuskin; illus. by Marc Simont (New York: Harper & Row, 1982). A long delightful tale of the intricacies of dressing for a concert. For older preschoolers under the guidance of an adult who enjoys the book's wry humor.

Follow-up activities for home or school:

Make a button mosaic.

Make a button necklace.

Play "Button, button, who's got the button." Children sit in a circle holding a string with a button on it. Children keep moving both hands back and forth touching their neighbor's hands. The button is passed surreptitiously around on the string. "It" tries to guess who has the button. "It" says, "Button, button, who's got the button? Jamie has it." If "It" guesses right, "It" changes places with Jamie.

68. My House, My Home

Opening songs.

Read: *A Very Special House* by Ruth Krauss; illus. by Maurice Sendak (New York: Harper & Row, 1953). Silly talk about an imaginary house.

Fingerplay:

Here is a nest for the robin, (form nest, etc. with hands)
Here is a hive for a bee,
Here is a hole for the bunny,
And here is a house for me.

Read: *The Little House* by Virginia Lee Burton (Boston: Houghton, Mifflin, 1942).

Sing and act out: "In a Cabin in a Wood." For tune, see Appendix.

In a cabin in a wood, (for cabin with peaked hands)
Little man by the window stood, (hands over eyes peering out)
Saw a rabbit, hopping by, (two fingers up, hand hops by)
Knocking at his door. (knock)
"Help me! Help me! Sir," he said. (flapping hands into air)

"Or the hunter shoot me dead!" (imitation shotgun
shooting)
"Rabbit come and live with me. (beckoning)
Happy we will always be." (one hand cuddles and strokes
rabbit hand with two fingers up)

Circle song: "Bluebird, Bluebird Fly Through My Window"
For tune, see Appendix, Program 26.

Read: *From King Bogen's Hall to Nothing at All A collection of
improbable houses and unusual places found in traditional
rhymes and limericks* illus. by Blair Lent (Boston: Little,
Brown, 1967). Delightfully illustrated nursery rhymes about
homes.

Read: *A House is a House is a House for Me* by Mary Ann
Hoberman; illus. by Betty Fraser (New York: Viking, 1978).

House visiting: Bring in sheets to drape over tables, large
boxes that a child can crawl into, and other materials for
making "houses". Set up enough houses to house all of the
children in family groups. Decide which children will go
visiting and which will stay home to be hosts. Act out this
play. (Practice call-response first):

Caller: Everybody home?
Children: Yes!
Caller: Visiting day!
"Visitors" leave their 'homes' and enter another 'home.'
Hosts make them welcome.
Caller: What do you say?
Guests and visitors: Hello.
Caller: Everybody hungry?
Children: Yes!
Caller: Teatime!
Guests and children sit down and have pretend tea.
Caller: Time to go home.
         What do you say?
Children: Goodbye.
Caller: What do you say?
Children: Goodbye.
Caller: Everybody go home.
Children go back to own homes.
Switch roles and repeat with hosts being visitors this time.

Closing songs.
More books to read:

Building a House by Ken Robbins (New York: Four Winds, 1984). Photos show the steps in building a house. For older children with curiosity about this process.

How a House Happens by Jan Adkins (New York: Walker & Co., 1972). Somewhat lengthy text and complicated drawings for the very mature preschooler and older. *You* will learn a lot.

I Can Build a House! by Shigeo Watanabe; illus. by Yasuo Ohtomo (New York: Philomel, 1982). Baby bear makes a house of blocks, cushions, and a box.

In Our House by Anne Rockwell (New York: Crowell, 1985). A very simple look at the rooms of a house, with tiny illustrations showing all the things we do there.

A Little House of Your Own by Beatrice Schenk de Regniers; illus. by Irene Haas (New York: Harcourt, 1954). The need for a private place, and many ways to find that privacy.

Pete's House by Harriet Langsam Sobel; illus. by Patricia Agee (New York: Macmillan, 1978). Pete visits the site where his new home is being built.

We Were Tired of Living in a House by Liesel Moak Skorpen; illus. by Doris Burn (New York: Harper & Row, 1969).

Follow-up activities for home or school:

Make a pretend house out of an old appliance box, a bedspread draped over a table, or a sheet over a clothesline.

Discuss the things you need to make a house a home. What makes your house feel like a home? Why is your room a special place to be?

Read *Come Over to My House* by Theo. Le Sieg; illus. by Richard Erdoes (New York: Random House, 1966). Talk about kinds of houses it might be fun to live in. Notice the different kinds of houses in your own neighborhood.

Read *It's Your Turn, Roger!* by Susanna Gretz (New York: Dial, 1985) and discuss varying lifestyles. Roger Pig finds his neighbor's suppers just aren't like his family's.

Using Your Imagination

Adventuring

69. Here Comes the Train!

Opening songs.

Read: *Freight Train* by Robert Crews (New York: Greenwillow, 1978). Images of a fast moving train.

Fingerplay:

> Here comes the choo choo train, (hands rotate around each in a rolling motion)
> Chugging down the track.
> First it goes forward,
> Then it goes back. (reverse motion)
> Now the bell is ringing. (Ding Ding Ding)
> Now the whistle blows. (Whooo Whooo Whooo)
> What a lot of noise it makes (hands over ears)
> Everywhere it goes!

Read: *Two Little Trains* by Margaret Wise Brown; illus. by Jean Charlot (New York: Addison-Wesley, 1949). A slow freight train and a streamlined train go west. Slightly dated.

Form a train and sing: "I'm a Little Train Going Down the Track." For tune, see Appendix.

> I'm a little train going down the track.
> See my engine shiny and black.
> I'm a little train going down the track,
> Clear to California and back.

Move your train and chant:

> This train is carryin' coal—Toot Toot
> With (number of kids) cars in line.
> Here comes a station, all cars STOP
> And leave one car behind.

This works nicely in a circle, with parents in an outside circle. Try to stop the train near the appropriate parent as you drop off each child. You may have to add some "chugs" before you "STOP" to reach the right parent.

Read: *The Little Engine That Could* by Watty Piper; illus. by George and Doris Hauman (New York: Platt, 1961). Little engine keeps chugging till it gets over the hill.

Make train picture: Pass out pre-cut engines and cabooses and lots of colored rectangles for cars. Let the children paste them together onto a long strip of paper. Ask them what their trains are carrying in their cars. Where is their train going?

Closing songs.

More books to share:

Choo Choo: The Story of a Little Engine Who Ran Away by Virginia Lee Burton (Boston: Houghton Mifflin, 1937).

Huck Scarry's Steam Train Journey by Huck Scarry (New York: Collins-World, 1979). Detailed illustrations; lots of trains.

The Little Train by Lois Lenski (New York: Oxford University Press, 1940). Engineer Small and his train.

The Train by David McPhail (Boston: Little, Brown, 1977)

Follow-up activities for home or school:

Find out when a train passes nearby and watch it go by. Count the cars and think about what might be in them. Where could this train be coming from? Where could it be going?

Discuss train safety if you are in an area where pedestrians or cars regularly have to cross train tracks.

Take a ride on a train if you can! If you can find a steam train to ride, do that. Most literature about trains evoke the image of the steam engine, but children seldom see that type of train these days.

70. Take Me Ridin' in Your Car!

Opening songs.

Read and act out: *Mr. Gumpy's Motor Car* by John Burningham (New York: Crowell, 1976). Mr. Gumpy takes his animals for a ride. Take everyone on board for your "drive."

Form a circle and sing: "Take You Ridin' in My Car, Car."

Words and music for this Woody Guthrie song are found in *Making Music Your Own* by Imogene Hilyard (Morristown, NJ: Silver Burdett, 1971), p. 157.

Pretend to drive your cars and make motions as your sing. Add other verses, such as "Windshield wipers go swish, swish."

Sing: "I'm a Big Tire" to the tune of "I'm a Little Teapot." For tune, see *Music For Ones and Twos* by Tom Glazer (New York: Doubleday, 1983), p. 52.

I'm a big tire, (make yourself big and round and "roll"
  back and forth)
Round and fat.
I rolled on a nail
and I got a flat. (deflate and sink to ground)
(patch your flat, blow yourself up again and sing:)
I'm a big tire,
round and fat,
I rolled away
and that was that.

Read: *The Little Old Automobile* by Marie Hall Ets (New York: Viking, 1948). Adventures of an old but determined car.

Film: *Alexander and the Car With the Missing Headlights* (Weston Woods, 1966) 13 min. Adventure with Alexander's magical car.

Make a truck: Paste together two rectangles and two circles to form a truck.

Closing songs.

See also related programs: "Wheels and Gears," Program 14.

More books to read:

Cars by Anne Rockwell (New York: Dutton, 1984). Bright Rockwell drawings of big, small, old, new cars.

Cars and How They Go by Joanna Cole; illus. by Gail Gibbons (New York: Crowell, 1983). Details of a car's engine, gears, and other mechanical parts. Could be used with older preschoolers.

The Little Auto by Lois Lenski (New York: Walck, 1934). Papa Small goes for a ride in his auto.

Lucky Chuck by Beverly Cleary; illus. by J. Winslow Higginbottom (New York: Morrow, 1984). Lots of technical details are given as Chuck rides his motorcycle. Chuck disobeys the traffic laws, crashes, is given a ticket and reforms.

Trucks by Anne Rockwell (New York: Dutton, 1984). Bright Rockwell drawings of many kinds of trucks.

Trucks You Can Count On by Doug Magee (New York: Dodd,

Mead, 1985). Black and white photos show the parts of a truck radiator, exhaust pipes, lug nuts, axles, and other parts.

Follow-up activities for home or school:

Go for a ride in a car. Note all the parts of the car—windshield wipers, horn, etc. Look under the hood and note parts of the engine. Look under the car and note the axles, tires, etc.

Other enjoyable films to screen are:

Mole and the Car (Phoenix, 1977) 16 min.

Suzie the Little Blue Coupe 8 min. (Disney, 1952).

71. On the High Seas!

Opening songs.

Read: *And I Must Hurry For the Sea Is Coming In* by George Mendoza; photos by DeWayne Dalrymple (New York: Prentice-Hall, 1969). A dream of the sea.

Read and act out: *Little Fox Goes to the End of the World* by Ann Tompert; illus. by John Wallner (New York: Crown, 1976). Little Fox's adventures include sailing away.

Act out: *Little Fox Goes to the End of the World*. Let some children be bears, crocodiles, and other animals, and hide under tables ready to roar as Little Fox passes by. You can use several Little Foxes and escort them from adventure to adventure as you retell the story.

Read: *Wynken, Blynken and Nod* by Eugene Field; illus. by Barbara Cooney (New York: Hastings House, 1964). Fanciful poem.

Film: *Captain Silas* by Ron McAdow (Yellow Bison, 1977) 14 min. Animated peanuts in an economics adventure on the sea.

Make peanut puppets: Adults will need to insert pipe cleaners for arms and legs. Cut one pipe cleaner into four pieces for two arms and two legs. Children can paint on hats and pants. Use felt markers for eyes. Tempera will work, but red nail polish makes excellent paint for these little critters and can sometimes be purchased cheap at sales.

Closing songs.

More books to share:

Boat Book by Gail Gibbons (New York: Holiday House, 1983). Simple illustrations.

Little Boat by Michel Gay (New York: Macmillan, 1985). Very brief text. Tiny book for youngest listeners.

The Maggie B. by Irene Haas (New York: Atheneum, 1983). Margaret and her little brother sail off on *The Maggie B*.

Me and My Captain by M.B. Goffstein (New York: Farrar, 1974). Wooden doll lady waits for sea-going captain to return.

The Sailor Dog by Margaret Wise Brown; illus. by Garth Williams (Racine, WI: Golden, 1953). Scuppers wants to go to sea, and he goes!

Wreck of the Zephyr by Chris Van Allsburg (New York: Houghton, Mifflin, 1983). A sailing ship flies away.

Follow-up activities for home or school:

Look at a globe and note the blue seas. Trace with your finger the routes a ship might travel across those oceans.

Visit a lake, sea, or riverport to see different kinds of ships.

Look at adult picture books of ships.

Get into an imaginary ship. What does it look like? Where will it take you?

Go someplace on a boat or a ship if you get the chance.

Animal Antics

(For related programs see: "Frog Songs," Program 96; "Spring Kittens," Program 38; "Black Cats," Program 33; "Owls in the Night," Program 32; "Snow Bears," Program 35; "Feathered Babies," Program 37.)

72. Happy Lions

Opening songs.

Read: *The Lion and the Rat* by La Fontaine; illus. by Brian Wildsmith (New York: Watts, 1963).

Read: *Andy and the Lion* by James Daugherty (New York: Viking, 1938). A thorn removed; a friend for life.

Read: *Roar and More* by Karla Kuskin (New York: Harper & Row, 1956). Animal noises. Everyone make the noises.

Activity: "Walking Through the Jungle." Make a circle, tiptoe around following each other and chanting:

Walking through the jungle
What did I see?

A big green crocodile
Was snapping at me!

Turn around and snap with your arms at the person behind
you. Repeat this as many times as you like, changing animals each time. You might see "a long green snake was
hissing at me," "A big brown bear was growling at me." I·
end with a lighter note such as "A little tiny bird was singing
just for me," or "a little brown monkey was chattering at
me."

Read: *Pierre* by Maurice Sendak (New York: Harper, 1962). A
boy who says only, "I don't care," is eaten by a lion.

Film: *The Happy Lion*. (Macmillan, n.d.) 7 min.

Or read: *The Happy Lion* by Louise Fatio; illus. by Roger
Duvoisin (New York: McGraw-Hill, 1954). Happy Lion escapes from the zoo and finds his former friends. All flee.

Make popsicle stick lion: Paste yellow circle on stick. Paste on
orange yarn for mane. Draw eyes, nose.

Holding popsicle stick lion, chant:

"A lion's knocking on my door." (Lion in right hand knocks,
left hand opens door)
"Hello Lion!" (left hand waves hello)
"ROAARRRR!" (popsicle lion roars)

Closing song: Let your lions all say *bon jour* to their parents
and to each·other. Sing *"Au revoir* happy lions—toodle-ay."
See "Goodbye Song" for tune.

More books to share:
Elsa by Joy Adamson; photos by author (New York: Pan-
theon, 1961). Photos of Joy Adamson's work with Elsa the
Lion.
Randy's Dandy Lions by Bill Peet (New York: Houghton
Mifflin, 1964). A lion tamer and some cowardly lions.

Follow-up activities for home or school:
Go to the zoo and watch the lion family. How do the mother
and father lion differ? Do they seem like a family? Why?
Find pictures of lions in books. How do artists portray the
lion? What poses does the photographer show in lion photographs?
Watch the movie or video *Pierre*. (Weston Woods, 1976) 6
min.

73. Elephants, Babies, and Elephant Babies

Opening songs.

Read: *Where is My Friend?* by Betsy Maestro; illus. Giulio Maestro (New York: Crown, 1976). Harriet climbs ON a chair and falls OFF again while looking for her friend.

Read: *The Circus Baby* by Maud and Miska Petersham (New York: Macmillan, 1950). Baby elephant is too big for clown's tent.

Fingerplay:

> An elephant goes like this and that.
> (rocking sideways, hands stiff out to sides)
> He's terribly big and he's terribly fat.
> (Continue rocking motion taking stiff steps)
> He has no fingers. (wiggle fingers)
> He has no toes. (wiggle toes)
> But OH MY GOODNESS WHAT A NOSE!
> (make trunk with arms clasped and walk around
>   swinging it)

Read: *The Elephant and the Bad Baby* by Elfrida Vipont; illus. by Raymond Briggs (New York: Coward, 1969). Elephant takes the bad baby for a ride. Adults should hold kids on laps and "rumpeta rumpeta" them. Older kids can bounce themselves. All say "YES" with the bad baby, stre-e-tch out trunks and taste all of the foods with the elephant and baby.

Action song: "One Elephant." For tune, see Appendix.

Form a circle. One elephant child goes to the middle and chooses another to join after song. Each can then choose another until only parents are left as the circle.

> One elephant went out to play
> On a spider's web one day.
> He had such enormous fun,
> He asked another elephant to come.

Or, put a piece of masking tape on the floor and have children walk the tightrope as you sing:

> One little elephant balancing,
> Step by step on a piece of string.
> He had such enormous fun,
> He asked another elephant to come.

For other variations see *Sally Go Round the Sun* by Edith Fowke (Garden City, NY: Doubleday, 1969), p. 42; or *Dancing Games for Children of All Ages* by Esther L. Nelson (New York: Sterling, 1973), p. 14.

Read: *Elephant in a Well* by Marie Hall Ets (New York: Viking, 1972). Elephant falls into a well and it takes all of the animals to pull her out. You can make a flannel board for this by tracing the animals onto white paper and using a piece of string for the clothesline.

Act out: *Elephant in a Well*. Bring in a real cloth clothesline and let everyone help pull the elephant out. Use a heavy parent for elephant in the well.

Read and act out: *Elephant Buttons* by Noriko Ueno (New York: Harper & Row, 1973). An elephant unbuttons his suit and out comes a lion. The lion unbuttons his suit and . . . Become each animal as you unbutton your suits and step out. End with another rendition of the rhyme "An Elephant Goes Like This and That."

Make an elephant mask: Pre-cut ears, eyes, and eyeballs to paste onto a paper plate face. Accordion fold a long strip of grey construction paper for the trunk. Accordion folding is a difficult task for younger children; encourage the parents to turn the paper for the children and show them how to press down the folds.

Play: Try out your masks. Holding them in front of your faces (there are no eye holes, you are pretending to be an elephant) rumpeta around the room a bit, then all recite your "An Elephant Goes Like This and That" one more time, waggling your paper trunks.

Closing songs: "Goodbye to the Elephants"

More books to share:

The Blind Men and the Elephant by Lillian Fox Quigley; illus. by Janice Holland (New York: Scribner's, 1959). Each man feels a different part of the elephant and comes up with a different conclusion as to what an elephant is like.

The Elephant's Child by Rudyard Kipling; illus. Tim Raglin (New York: Knopf, 1986). An excellent tape read by Jack Nicholson with music by Bobby McFerrin accompanies book. The classic story of the elephant's child who was filled with "satiable curtiosity." This picture book replaces that phrase with "insatiable curiosity" but *you* should read it the way Kipling wrote it. Otherwise delightful.

The Life Cycle of the Elephant by Paula Z. Hogan; illus. (Milwaukee: Raintree, 1979).

The Little Elephant by Ylla and Arthur S. Gregor; photos by Ylla (New York: Harper & Row, 1956). Fine black-and-white photos of a baby elephant with story.

Follow-up activities for home or school:

Go to a circus and watch the elephants perform, or visit a zoo to watch them. How do they use their trunks?

Watch the film *Niok*. (Walt Disney, 1959) 29 min. A Cambodian boy with a baby elephant pet. The film includes scenes of Angkor Wat.

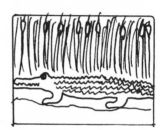

74. Crocodiles and Alligators

Opening songs.

Read: *La Petite Famille* by Sesyle Joslin. Retell this story in English. It is very simple. We see a room, a mama, a papa, a *bébé*, then a crocodile. Adieu petite famille!

Read: *Crocodile and Hen* by Jean M. Lexau; illus. by Joan Sandin (New York: Harper & Row, 1969).

Poem: "The Crocodile" by Lewis Carroll in *The Random House Book of Poetry* by Jack Prelutsky; illus. by Arnold Lobel (New York: Random House, 1983).

Fingerplay:

Five little monkeys, (hold up five fingers)
sitting on a tree,
teasing the crocodile,
"You can't catch meeee." (taunting hands wagged by ear)
Along came the crocodile (slither with arms)
Quiet as can be—
(loud handclap) (arms form jaws, open and SNAP)
Four little monkeys,
sitting on a tree.

Repeat until no monkeys are left.

Action chant:

Walking through the jungle
What did I see?
A big green crocodile
Was snapping at me!

Form a circle and walk through the jungle chanting. Turn and snap at person behind you on last line. Change to other animals and continue: "a yellow striped tiger was snarling at me", "a big, brown bear was growling at me."

Read: *The Monkey and the Crocodile* by Paul Galdone (New York: Seabury, 1969). Crocodile tries to trick monkey into his clutches. You may have to shorten this for the youngest children.

Film: "Alligators All Around" (Weston Woods, 1976) 2 min. From the book *Alligators All Around* by Maurice Sendak (New York: Harper & Row, 1962).

Make an envelope crocodile: Seal an envelope. Cut along the sealed flap and down one side to middle (cut through entire envelope). Cut along seam coming up from bottom of envelope to meet this point. Hold envelope by the end which is still uncut. Squish it here and the "mouth" will open and close. Add stick-on dots for eyes. Color green and attach triangles as teeth if you like.

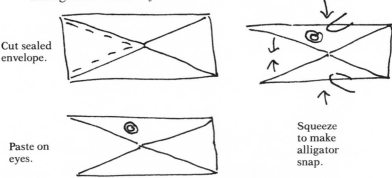

Cut sealed envelope.

Paste on eyes.

Squeeze to make alligator snap.

Closing songs: "Goodbye to the Crocodiles."
More books to share:

The Life Cycle of the Crocodile by Paula Z. Hogan; illus. by Larry Mikec (Milwaukee: Raintree, 1979). Color illustrations and text present the life cycle of the crocodile.

Lyle, Lyle, Crocodile by Bernard Waber (Boston: Houghton Mifflin, 1965). A crocodile's life in the big city.

Follow-up activities for home and school:

Visit a zoo to see a real crocodile. Notice the camouflaging of his skin. Does his stillness help him hide, too?

Watch for imitation or real alligator belts, purses, and other items. Touch them and examine the grain carefully.

75. Mice Are Nice

Opening songs.

Read: *Mouse* by Sara Bonnett Stein; illus. by Manuel Garcia (New York: Harcourt, 1985). A brightly colored look at a mouse's life.

Poem: "Mice" by Rose Fyleman in *The Random House Book of Poetry for Children*, comp. by Jack Prelutsky (New York: Random House, 1983).

Read: *Alexander and the Wind-Up Mouse* by Leo Lionni (New York: Pantheon, 1969). Alexander the mouse wishes he were a wind-up toy mouse like Willy so he would be loved too.

Fingerplay: "Five Lttle Mice." For text see "Black Cats," Program 33.

Sing and Play: "The Old Grey Cat is Sleeping." See "Black Cats," Program 33.

Read: *Whose Mouse Are You?* by Robert Kraus; illus. by Jose Aruego (New York: Macmillan, 1970). A small mouse and his family.

Make a mouse: Pass out grey pom-poms, snippets of grey felt paper for ears and tail, tiny goggle eyes. Paste together.

Closing songs.

See also related programs: "Black Cats," Program 33.

More books to share:

I Love You Mouse by John Graham; illus. by Tomie de Paola (New York: Harcourt, 1976). Friendship with a mouse.

The Story of a Little Mouse Trapped in a Book by Monique Felix (La Jolla, CA: Green Tiger, 1980). Mouse tries to escape pages of the book.

The Tale of Two Bad Mice by Beatrix Potter (New York: Warne, 1904, 1934). Two mice wreak havoc in a doll house.

The Tale of Mrs. Tittle-Mouse by Beatrix Potter (New York: Warne, 1910). Adventures of a lady fieldmouse.

Follow-up activities for home or school:
> Visit a pet store to see mice for sale as pets. Note how they move, the delicacy of their feet, how they eat.
> Do mice live in your house? Talk about their habits.

76. Portly Pigs

Opening songs.

Read: *Yummers!* by James Marshall (Boston: Houghton Mifflin, 1973). Emily Pig eats and eats and eats, then wonders why she's sick.

Read: *The Old Woman and Her Pig* by Paul Galdone (New York: McGraw-Hill, 1960). Mother Goose rhyme.

Sing and play: "There Was an Old Woman and She Had a Little Pig." For tune, see Appendix.

> There was an old woman and she had a little pig.
> Oink oink oink—oink oink oink.
> There was an old woman and she had a little pig.
> It didn't cost much cause it wasn't very big.
> Oink oink oink—oink oink oink.

Sit "pigs" in circle center on the floor as you sing.

Verse 2: Those little pigs curled up in a log. (pigs curl up)
> They shut their eyes and went to sleep.

Verse 3: They slept and slept and slept and slept. (pigs sleep)

Verse 4: The farmer woke them one by one. (touching each pig to wake it)

Verse 5: They rolled and they rolled and they rolled and they rolled. (pigs roll)

Verse 6: Those pigs rolled right back to their pen,
> And then they went to sleep again.

Read: *Pig Pig Rides* by David McPhail (New York: Dutton, 1982). Pig Pig dreams of wild rides.

Make paper pig: Cut circles—large for body, small for nose. Paper punch for eyes. Cut two triangles for ears, two strips for legs. Children paste together. If you like, put a construction paper "puddle" on your bulletin board and let the children stick their pigs in the puddle. This makes a nice display and advertises your storytimes, too. This pig is simple enough so that the children can make two if they like, one to take home and one to leave on display.

More books to read:

Pigs at Christmas by Arlene Dubanevich (New York: Bradbury, 1986). An insider's look at the pig family's goings-on at Christmas. Cartoon-like drawings.

Pigs from A to Z by Arthur Geisert (Boston: Houghton Mifflin, 1986). Seven little pigs build a treehouse. An engaging book for the older alphabetizer. Pen and ink drawings show the pigs' elaborate construction. Hidden letters to search for on every page.

Pig William by Arlene Dubanevich (New York: Bradbury, 1985). Pig William dawdles behind his older siblings and misses the picnic—or does he?

The Tale of Little Pig Robinson by Beatrix Potter (New York: Warne, 1930).

The Tale of Pigling Bland by Beatrix Potter (New York: Warne, 1913, 1941).

Follow-up activities for home or school:

Take a trip to a children's zoo or farm to visit a real hog. How does he use his snout? How heavy do you think he is? How would it feel to be a pig and lie in the mud all day?

See film: *Pigs*. (Churchill, 1967) 11 min. Close-ups of snouts, tails, and other piggly parts.

Make a collection of pig pictures, pig dolls, pig statues. How do different artists portray the pig? Why do you think people like piggy things?

77. Problem Pups

Opening songs.

Read: *Angus and the Ducks* by Marjorie Flack (New York: Doubleday, 1930). Involve the younger listeners in the story by letting them "quack" with the ducks, "woof" with Angus, sip the water, and so forth. Older groups don't need such participation.

Read: *Where's Spot?* by Eric Hill (New York: Putnam's, 1980).

Read and act out: *Old Mother Hubbard and Her Dog* by Sarah Catherine Martin; illus. by Paul Galdone (New York: Mc-

Graw-Hill, 1960). Form a circle to act this out. Let the parents be "Old Mother Hubbard." The kids are the dog. In groups without parents, you can be "Old Mother Hubbard." Sing: "Rags." For tune, see Appendix. Sing with motions.

> I have a dog his name is Rags.
> Eats so much that his tummy sags.
> Ears flip flop and his tail wig wags,
> When he walks—he zig zag zags.
> My little dog he likes to play.
> Rolls himself in the grass all day.
> When I call he won't obey.
> Always walks the other way.
> Flip flop—wig wag—zig zag.
> Flip flop—wig wag—zig zag.

Bark a poem: "Littlekid Opera: Bow Wow Wow" from *Somebody Spilled the Sky* by Ruth Krauss; illus. by Eleanor Hazard (New York: Greenwillow, 1976, 1979), p. 4.

Pup poems: From *Something Sleeping in the Hall* by Karla Kuskin (New York: Harper & Row, 1985) read: "The Running Dogs Begin to Bark," "My Dog Runs Down the Hall," and "I Would Like to Have a Pet."

Read: *Harry the Dirty Dog* by Gene Zion; illus. by Margaret Bloye Graham (New York: Harper & Row, 1954). Harry hates a bath.

Read: *Poofy Loves Company* by Nancy Winslow Parker (New York: Dodd, Mead, 1980). A huge dog and a small girl.

Film: *Angus Lost* by John Sturner and Gary Templeton (Phoenix, 1987) 1 min. Angus gets lost, then finds his way home.

Make a dog-and-bone bulletin board: Put a large cutout dog on your bulletin board. Give each child two cutout paper bones to color. Write the child's name on each. Let one be taken home, put the other up on the bulletin board for the dog. Let each child decide where he or she wants the bone stapled to the bulletin board. Label the board "Book Hounds." This makes a nice activity for the first storytime of a series since it advertises storytime to other families.

Closing songs.

More books to read:

The Biggest, Meanest, Ugliest Dog in the Whole Wide World by Rebecca C. Jones; illus. by Wendy Watson (New York: Macmillan, 1982). The terrifying, next door dog becomes a friend.

The Comic Adventures of Old Mother Hubbard and Her Dog illus. by Tomie de Paola (New York: Harcourt, 1950). Another delightfully illustrated version.

A Dog I Know by Barbara Brenner; illus. by Fred Brenner (New York: Harper & Row, 1983). Mood book about a boy's pet. "I know this dog so well, how he feels, his look, even his doggy smell."

Go Away, Dog by Joan L. Nodset; illus. by Crosby Bonsall (New York: Harper & Row, 1963). A boy doesn't like dogs, but this persistent pup wins his affection.

Pinkerton Behave! by Stephen Kellogg (New York: Dial, 1974). A very large and feisty dog.

Follow-up activities for home or school:

Invite a friendly dog to visit you. Find out how to make him happy. How does he like to play? What does he like to eat? Look at pictures of dogs and watch for dogs in your community. Learn the names of different breeds.

Dreams and Nonsense

78. Freaky Food

Opening songs.

Read: *The Little Mouse, the Red Ripe Strawberry, and THE BIG HUNGRY BEAR* by Don and Audrey Wood; illus. by Don Wood (Singapore: Child's Play, 1984). A mouse is induced to share his strawberry with the storyteller.

Read: *The Elephant and the Bad Baby* by Elfrida Vipont; illus. by Raymond Briggs (New York: Coward-McCann, 1969). An elephant gives a bad baby a ride and offers him lots of goodies to eat along the way. Have children in their parents' laps for this one. Parents should bounce their kids on the "rumpeta rumpeta" lines. Older kids can bounce themselves. Let everyone join in the Bad Baby's "YES!" Also stre-e-etch out your trunks and take a bite of each goody with the elephant and the Bad Baby. A fun participation story.

Read and act out: "Yellow Butter" by Mary Ann Hoberman. A nice illustration for the piece is in *Oh, Such Foolishness!* by William Cole; illus. by Tomie de Paola (New York: Lippincott, 1978). Say the poem several times, spreading your butter and jelly as you speak. Kids love the admonishment at the end, "Don't talk with your mouth full!"

Funny food poem roundelay: Give one poem to each parent-child group. Have the parents share the poems quietly with their own children. Then call out each food and let the appropriate parent-child group share their poem with everyone. For groups without parent involvement, give a poem to each child. Have that child come to the front of the group while you read that child's poem.

Suggested poems for "Funny Food":

From *The Random House Book of Poetry for Children* comp. by Jack Prelutsky; illus. by Arnold Lobel (New York: Random House, 1983) "My Mouth" by Arnold Adoff; "This is Just to Say" by William Carols Williams; "Egg Thoughts" by Russell Hoban (you might give each verse to a different child); "Oodles of Noodles" by Lucia and James L. Hymes, Jr.; "Meg's Egg" by Mary Ann Hoberman; "Pie Problem" by Shel Silverstein; "Celery" by Odgen Nash; "Chocolate Cake" by Nina Payne; "Chocolate Chocolate" by Arnold Adoff; "My Little Sister" by William Wise; "I Eat My Peas With Honey" by Anonymous; "I Raised a Great Hullabaloo" by Anonymous; "Sneaky Bill" by William Cole.

From *Oh, Such Foolishness* by William Cole; illus. by Tomie de Paola (Philadelphia: Lippincott, 1978) try "The Sausage" by Anonymous; "Spaghetti" by Shel Silverstein; "Bad and Good" by Alexander Resnikoff.

From *If I had a Paka; Poems in Eleven Languages* by Charlotte Pomerantz; illus. by Nancy Tafuri (New York: Greenwillow, 1982). Use "Rice and Beans—Arroz y Habichuelas"; "Where Do These Words Come From"; and "Toy Tik Ka."

Don't miss *Eats* by Arnold Adolf; illus. by Susan Russ (New York: Lothrop, 1979). Several entries here are great. Poems are illustrated.

Also see *Munching: Poems About Eating* sel. by Lee Bennett Hopkins; illus. by Nelle Davis (Boston: Little, Brown, 1985). A tiny, illustrated collection.

From *Days Are Where We Live and Other Poems* comp. by Jill Bennett, illus. by Maureen Roffey (New York: Lothrop, Lee & Shepard, 1981). "Toaster Time."

Action Song: "Peanut Butter." Stand and dance out the peanut butter sandwich song. It is very like Mary Ann Hoberman's poem and kids may like to end the song as well with a shout "Don't Talk With Your Mouth Full!" Words for song can be found in Program 21. Music in Appendix, Program 21.

Film: *Peanut Butter and Jelly* by Eliot Noyes (Unifilms, 1976) 2 min. Humorous look at the making of a peanut butter and jelly sandwich.

Read: *Green Eggs and Ham* by Dr. Seuss (New York: Random House, 1960). "Green eggs and ham are TASTY, if you will just *try* them." Older groups enjoy supplying the ending rhymes as this progresses, "I will not eat them with a fox, I will not eat them in a (kids supply "box")."

Make a green applesauce picture: Provide green cake coloring in tins on the table. Spread the applesauce in a thin layer over bottom of small bowl. Use swizzle sticks to dip in cake coloring and drop dots of color onto the applesauce. After you have had fun making a picture, EAT IT.

Closing songs.

See also related programs: "Taste It," Program 21; "Smell It," Program 24; "Apple Day," Program 30; "Blueberry, Strawberry, Jamberry," Program 87.

More books to read:

"Birthday Soup" from *Little Bear* by Else Homeland Minarik; illus. by Maurice Sendak (New York: Harper, 1957). "Carrots, tomatoes, peas and potatoes" make a birthday soup.

Cloudy With a Chance of Meatballs by Judi Barrett; illus. by Ron Barrett (New York: Atheneum, 1979). It precipitates food!

The Giant Vegetable Garden by Nadine Bernard Westcott (Boston: Little, Brown, 1981). Giant vegetables pose a problem. How do you *eat* them?

Follow-up activities for home or school:

Make up "silly food" poems about the things you munch for lunch or snack. Try using the onomatopoeic sounds of the food in your poem.

For more food ideas, see: *Mudluscious: Stories and Activities Featuring Food for Preschool Children* by Jan Irving and Robin Currie (Boulder: Libraries Unlimited, 1986).

79. Foolish Furniture

Opening songs.

Read: *A Very Special House* by Ruth Krauss; illus. by Maurice

Sendak (New York: Harper & Row, 1953). A silly house inside MY head. Let the children repeat key phrases such as "ME ME ME!" and "OOOOOIE OOOIE OOOIE!" with you. The rhyme's the thing. Keep it moving.

Read: *Amanda and the Mysterious Carpet* by Fernando Krahn (New York: Clarion, 1985). A wordless picture book. You may have to take time to show the book around to everyone if the group is large. A magic carpet arrives and "upsets" a little girl.

Read: *Ugbu* by Ora Ayal; trans. by Naomi Low Nakao (New York: Harper & Row, 1977). A little girl pretends her chair is a dog.

Poems: "Chairs" by Valerie Worth in *Oh Such Foolishness!* by William Cole; illus. by Tomie de Paola (Philadelphia: Lippincott, 1978), p. 189. Stand up and act out being various chairs—straight-backed, overstuffed, reclining lawn chairs, and other types. Conclude with "The Perfect Reactionary" by Hugh Mearns in *A New Treasury of Children's Poetry* by Joanna Cole (Garden City, NY: Doubleday, 1984), p. 100. "As I was sitting on my chair, I knew the bottom wasn't there." Pretend sitting on a nonexistent chair.

Film: *The Chairy Tale* by Norman McLaren (International Film Board, 1957) 10 min. Ravi Shankar sitar accompaniment. A chair refuses to let its owner sit.

Play with a chair: Give each child or family group a chair to experiment with. How many things can you think of to do with a chair? What can you pretend with a chair? Return to circle and share ideas for things to do with a chair. Group might try some of these things all together with their own chairs. Could continue into group chair activities if you have time—trains, etc.

Closing songs: "Goodbye to Chairs."

More books to read:

Amelia Bedelia by Peggy Parish; illus. by Fritz Siebel (New York: Harper & Row, 1963). Foolish household antics by a maid who takes all commands literally.

A Chair For My Mother by Vera B. Williams (New York: Greenwillow, 1982). Joyful story of saving enough coins to buy a new easy chair after fire destroyed the apartment.

Funny Bone Read-Alongs: Does My Room Come Alive at Night? read by Sandy Duncan (New York: Caedmon, 1986). Cassette and book. Furniture dances at night.

The Man Who Took the Indoors Out by Arnold Lobel (New York: Harper & Row, 1974). A man takes his furniture outdoors.

Follow-up activities for home or school:
Play with your furniture. Make a train of chairs. Hang a sheet over a table to make a tent. Turn a table upside down to make a boat. Use your imagination.

80. Dream Time

Opening songs.

Read: *In the Night Kitchen* by Maurice Sendak (New York: Harper & Row, 1970). Mickey's night adventures with three bakers.

Read: *When the Sky is Like Lace* by Elinor Lander Horwitz; illus. by Barbara Cooney (New York: Lippincott, 1975). Not really a dream, but a dream-like fantasy of dancing with the otters on a bimulous night.

Talk about: Dreams you have had.

Dream a while: Lie down on the floor, close your eyes, and dream while you listen to music. Talk about images you saw in your dreams while the music played.

Read: *Night Story* by Nancy Willard; illus. by Ilse Plume (San Diego: Harcourt, 1981). A dream sequence, brief and whimsical.

Film: *Lullaby* (International Film Bureau, 1975) 4 min. See "The Sleepy Storytime," program 65 for translation of song's text. Name the objects the child "dreams" of as they appear on the screen.

Closing songs.

See also related program: "Monster Bash!", Program 85.

More books to read:
Ben's Dream by Chris Van Allsburg (Boston: Houghton Mifflin, 1982).

Come Out to Play by Jeanette Winter (New York: Knopf, 1986). An elf invites city children to nightime frolic.

Fergus and the Snow Deer by Yasuko Kimura (New York: McGraw-Hill, 1978). Hibernating Fergus wakes and plays with the snow deer, or is it all a dream?

The Polar Express by Chris Van Allsburg (Boston: Houghton Mifflin, 1985). A dreamlike fantasy. Train ride to the North Pole and return in Santa's sleigh.

The Silver Pony by Lynd Ward (Boston: Houghton Mifflin, 1973). A boy sees a flying horse but no one believes him.

When Everyone Was Fast Asleep by Tomie de Paola (New York: Holiday House, 1976). Nightime fantasy, dreamlike.

Follow-up activities for home or school:

Talk about dreams you have had. How did they feel? Discuss both frightening dreams and pleasant dreams.

Make up a dream that is pleasant. Remember you can do anything you want in a dream!

81. Teddy Bears Go Dancing

Opening songs.

Invite the children to bring bears to this class. Introduce everyone's teddy bear.

Read: *Teddy Bears One to Ten* by Susanna Gretz (Chicago: Follett, 1969). A counting book.

Read: *Corduroy* by Don Freeman (New York: Viking, 1968). Corduroy wanders the department store at night searching for his lost button.

Action Song: "Teddy Bears Go Dancing." See Appendix for tune.

> Teddy bears go dancing, Hop Hop Hop.
> See the teddies prancing, Hippity Hippity Hop.
> Now they stumble.
> Now they fumble.
> Now they tumble in a jumble,
> Flip Flip Flop.
> Now they're getting up again,
> Hippity Hop Hippity Hop
> Hippity Hippity Hop Hop Hop!

Action Chant:

> Teddy bear, teddy bear turn around.
> Teddy bear, teddy bear touch the ground.
> Teddy bear, teddy bear shine your shoes.

Teddy bear, teddy bear read the news.
Teddy bear, teddy bear go upstairs.
Teddy bear, teddy bear say your prayers.
Teddy bear, teddy bear turn out the light.
Teddy bear, teddy bear say good night.
Good night!

Read: *The Teddy Bear's Picnic* by Jimmy Kennedy; illus. by Alexandra Day (La Jolla, CA: Green Tiger, 1983). Text and illustrations to accompany the familiar song. A recording is included. Play the recording and act out a teddy bear picnic.

Have a teddy bear picnic: Spread out picnic cloths and seat yourselves and your teddy bears around them. Provide a simple picnic snack such as crackers and apple slices.

Closing songs. "Goodbye to the Teddy Bears."

More books to read:

Alphabears: An ABC Book by Kathleen Hague; illus. by Michael Hague (New York: Holt, 1984).

Archie and the Strict Baptists by John Betjeman; illus. by Phillida Gile (New York: Lippincott, 1977). Very British tale of teddy bear Archie's attempts to go to chapel.

Teddy Bear Gardener by Phoebe and John Worthington (New York: Warne, 1983). One of a British series of simple occupation stories. Includes *Teddy Bear Baker* (Warne, 1980) and *Teddy Bear Coalman* (Warne, 1980).

Follow-up activities for home or school:

Invite a number of teddy bears to tea. Compare their features, size, colors, type of fur, and other characteristics.

Make up a story about a day in the life of a teddy bear. Share it with someone else.

82. Copy Cats

Opening songs.

Read: *The Chick and the Duckling* by Mirra Ginsburg; illus. by Jose Aruego and Ariane Dewey (New York: Macmillan, 1972).

Read and act out: *Caps for Sale* by Esphyr Slobodkina (New York: Addison-Wesley, 1940). All the kids are monkeys. You or a parent can be the peddler.

Sing: "The Monkey Stamp, Stamp, Stamps His Feet." For tune, see Appendix.

The monkey stamp, stamp, stamps his feet.
The monkey stamp, stamp, stamps his feet.

Monkey see and monkey do.
Monkey just the same as you.

Make up other verses as "The monkey claps, claps, claps his hands. "For variation, see *Sally Go Round the Sun* by Edith Fowke (Garden City, NY: Doubleday, 1969), p. 17.

Read: *Cora Copycat* by Helen Lester (New York: Dutton, 1979). Cora copycats once too often.

Read this riddle: "Ten little copycats were sitting in a boat, and one jumped out. How many were left?" There is an illustrated version of this riddle in *Ten Copycats in a Boat and Other Riddles* by Alvin Schwartz; illus. by Marc Simont (New York: Harper & Row, 1980).

Play: "Simon Says." Leader says "Simon says 'Arms in the air.'" Everyone follows leader's actions. Let children take turns being leader.

Make: Stamp art pictures. Use a variety of rubber stamps. Or precut potatoes or carrots for the children to use.

Closing songs.

More books to read:

Goat's Trail by Brian Wildsmith (New York: Knopf, 1986). Following a goat gets the animals in trouble.

The Importance of Crocus by Roger Duvoisin (New York: Knopf, 1980). Crocus crocodile tries to imitate other farm animals.

Follow-up activities for home or school:

Play follow the leader. First person in the line walks a certain way, makes a certain action, etc. Everyone follows in line behind, imitating.

Play "Copy My Face." One child says "I feel sad" and makes a sad face. Everyone imitates. Try happy, mad, mean, scary, scared, and so on.

83. Rhyme, Rhyme, Rhyme

Opening songs.

Read: *Bears* by Ruth Krauss; illus. by Phyllis Rowand (New York: Harper & Row, 1948). Rhymes with "ears."

Read: *Mister Magnolia* by Quentin Blake (London: Jonathan Cape, 1980). Words that rhyme with "oot."

Read: *This Is* . . . by Gloria Patrick; illus. by Joan Hanson (Minneapolis: Carolrhoda, 1970). Lots of rhymes.

Form a circle and sing:

> I will jump jump jump jump jump. (jump)
> (make up a rhyme to go with it)
> And I'll bump bump bump bump bump. (bump)

Sing it again and do the motions. Make up another one. Let the kids supply the rhymes and starting lines. See Appendix for possible tune.

Read: *Mig the Pig* by Colin and Jacqui Hawkins (New York: Putnam's, 1984). Rhymes with "ig."

Read: *Old Mother Hubbard and Her Dog* by Paul Galdone (New York: McGraw-Hill, 1960). Let the kids guess the rhyming words as you read.

Make rhyming cards to take home: Give each child a cutout shape with "AT" printed on it. Litter the table with multicolored cutouts on which the child can print, or have printed letters to combine with "AT" to form words. Younger children can think up "at" words and an adult helper will write the letters down for them. The shape used to print on could be a dog bone, valentine, boot, or any shape.

Closing songs.

Additonal activity: From a teacher I learned a delightful flannel board story for rhyming at Easter. You need to make several eggs of white felt on one side, backed with different bright colors on the other. Make a cutout Easter Bunny if you like, but it is not necessary. Tell how the Easter Bunny woke up one Easter morning to find he had forgotten to dye his eggs. He sat down, held an egg in his hand and said, "Think think think—I wish this egg were pink." The egg turned PINK. If he could think of a rhyme to go with each color, he could turn all of the eggs into colored eggs. Cover each egg with your whole hand and flip it surreptitiously as you say the rhyme and it will seem like a magic color change to the children. Have them suggest rhymes for each color and all repeat them together as a magic chant.

More books to read:

Father Fox's Pennyrhymes by Clyde Watson; illus. by Wendy Watson (New York: Crowell, 1971). Delightful rhymes of a rural fox family.

Pop Corn and Ma Goodness by Edna Mitchell Preston; illus. by Robert Andrew Parker (New York: Viking, 1969). Silly rhythmic tale of wedded bliss.

Where Have You Been? by Margaret Wise Brown; illus. by
Barbara Cooney (New York: Hastings House, 1981). Small
book in simple rhyme asking each animal where it has been.
Follow-up activities for home or school:
  Make a rhyme book. Write a word on the first page, for
  example, "Fox." Think of rhyming words to write on following pages. Draw a simple illustration for the child or cut out
  pictures to illustrate the book, for example "a box," "socks,"
  "clocks." For a school setting photocopied pictures can be
  used.

84. Wonderful Words

Opening songs.
Read: *The Camel Who Took a Walk* by Jack Tworkov; illus. by
  Roger Duvoison (New York: Dutton, 1951). A very beautiful
  camel goes for a walk. Talk about the sound of the story
  repeating certain phrases from the story and noting their
  imagery; "turning her pretty head this way—and that," "the
  sun shone like brass in the sky."
Read: *In a Spring Garden* by Richard Lewis; illus. by Ezra Jack
  Keats (New York: Dial, 1945). Talk about Haiku and the way
  just a few words can make us "see" a thing.
Act out a Haiku:
  Pass out one haiku to each family unit. Let the parents and
  children plan how to act out their haiku. Make a circle. Let
  each family act out a haiku. Repeat it, acting it out as a
  group using their actions, if this seems appropriate. Select
  poems from collections such as: *Cricket Songs* by Harry Behn
  (New York: Harcourt, Brace, Jovanovich, 1964); *More Cricket
  Songs* by Harry Behn (New York: Harcourt, Brace, Jovanovich, 1971); *A Few Flies and I: Haiku by Issa* by Jean Merrill
  and Ronni Solbert; illus. by Ronni Solbert (New York: Pantheon, 1969).
Read: *Rain Makes Applesauce* by Julian Scheer and Marvin
  Bileck; illus. by Marvin Bileck (New York: Holiday House,
  1964). Let everyone join in the refrain, "Rain Makes Applesauce." Admonish them "Oh you're just talking silly talk."
Make a candy poem: Let each child select a candy from a tray.
  Give the child another identical candy, one to paste one on
  a card, and one to eat. Tell an adult some words to describe
  the candy or the way you feel when you eat it. Adults write

these words on the appropriate card and read the "candy poem" back to the child. Have some sugarless items available for those who can't eat candy. Return to the story circle and share your candy poems.

Closing songs.

More books to read:

In the Night Kitchen by Maurice Sendak (New York: Harper & Row, 1970). "Milk in the batter, milk in the batter. We bake cake and nothing's the matter."

When the Sky is Like Lace by Elinor Lander Horwitz; illus. by Barbara Cooney (New York: Lippincott, 1975). "On bimulous nights, . . . the trees eucalyptus back and forth."

Follow-up activities for home or school:

Make a "word" collection. Listen for scrumptious words and write them down on a poster or bulletin board. Say them once in a while for a treat.

85. Monster Bash!

Opening songs.

Read: *There's a Nightmare in My Closet* by Mercer Mayer (New York: Dial, 1968). Boy befriends the nightmare in his closet.

For older groups, read: *I'm Coming to Get You!* by Tony Ross (New York: Dutton, 1984). A monster zooms through space devouring planets and threatens little Tommy Brown. Really scary, until the last page reveals the monster's size as two inches tall.

Read: *No More Monsters for Me!* by Peggy Parish; illus. by Marc Simont (New York: Harper & Row, 1981). A pet monster GROWS!

Read: *Where the Wild Things Are* by Maurice Sendak (New York: Harper & Row, 1963). Max sails off to visit the monsters.

Do a monster dance.

Make a monster puppet: Use styrofoam hamburger containers. MacDonalds and other fast food restaurants will usually give you some for your program if you ask. They can also be purchased at bulk quantity stores. Paste large eyes on the top lid, paste a tongue inside the container. Add yarn or curled paper hair if you like.

Closing songs: "Goodbye to the Monsters." Let the puppets sing.

See also: "The Don't Be Scared Storytime," Program 60.

More books to read:

The Judge: An Untrue Tale by Harve Zemach; illus. by Margot Zemach (New York: Farrar, 1969). The judge doesn't believe any reports of monsters coming, until too late. This can be fun to act out with older children.

Monster Tracks? by A. Delaney (New York: Harper & Row, 1981). Boy lets his imagination get the best of him. Finally he must face his fear.

Patrick's Dinosaurs by Carol Carrick; illus. by Donald Carrick (New York: Clarion, 1983). Patrick imagines dinosaurs everywhere he looks.

Follow-up activities for home or school:

Make a monster mask from a paper bag, use curled paper, yarn, raffia, unraveled rope for hair. Cut eye holes so it can be worn. Wear it and do a monster dance.

Create an imaginary monster. Create an imaginary trick to make it disappear. Talk about the fact that monsters are only as real as we THINK they are.

Plan a Be-Kind-To-Monsters Day. Everyone bring an imaginary monster and introduce it. Decide what kind of "monster food" would be appropriate to feed your guests.

86. A Visit to the King and Queen

Opening songs.

Read and act out: *May I Bring a Friend?* by Beatrice Schenk de Regniers; illus. by Beni Montresor (New York: Atheneum, 1964). The king and queen invite me for tea and I bring all of the animals in the zoo.

Read: *One Monday Morning* by Uri Shulevitz (New York: Scribner's, 1967). Attempted visits every day of the week.

Read: *The Princess and the Pea* by Hans Christian Andersen; illus. by Paul Galdone (New York: Seabury, 1978). The real princess is discovered by placing a pea under her mattresses.

Film: "The Tender Tale of Cinderella Penguin" by Janet Perlman (National Film Board of Canada, 1981) 10 min. Cinderella is a penguin.

Craft: Pre-cut crowns from construction paper and let the children decorate them. Tape finished crowns to fit each head.

Closing songs.

More books to read:

The Duchess Bakes a Cake by Virginia Kahl (New York: Scribner's, 1955). A marvelous confection is stirred up.

Hector Protector and *As I Went Over the Water* illus. by Maurice Sendak (New York: Harper & Row, 1965). Elaborate Sendak interpretations of two foolish nursery rhymes, first is "Hector Protector was sent to the queen."

How Does a Czar Eat Potatoes? by Anne Rose; illus. by Janosch (New York: Lothrop, Lee & Shepard, 1973). A peasant father's life is contrasted with that of the Czar. But a happy peasant dancing to a balalaika is happier than any czar!

Follow-up activities for home or school:

Make up a story about a pretend king or queen.

Design a kingly or queenly costume. Put it on and pretend you are king or queen for a day. What kind of royal food will you eat? What royal activities will you take part in?

87. Blueberry, Strawberry, Jamberry!

Opening songs.

Read: *Blueberries For Sal* by Robert McCloskey (New York: Viking, 1948). Little Sal and little bear get their mothers mixed up!

Read: *The Grey Lady and the Strawberry Snatcher* by Molly Bang (New York: Four Winds, 1980). The strawberry snatcher is thwarted by a fast moving "grey lady."

Read: *Jamberry* by Bruce Degen (New York: Harper & Row, 1983).

Display berries: Show several kinds of berries. You could use berry jams here if berries are hard to obtain. Compare their color, shape, texture, and taste if possible.

Read: *The Little Mouse, the Red Ripe Strawberry, and the BIG HUNGRY BEAR* by Don and Audrey Wood; illus. by Don Wood (Singapore: Child's Play, 1984). Mouse tries to hide his strawberry, saves it by giving half to the storyteller.

Share a berry: Cut strawberries in half to share.

Decorate a berry basket: Use plastic baskets from the supermarket.

Closing songs.

More books to read:

If I Had a Paka: Poems in Eleven Languages by Charlotte Pomerantz; illus. by Nancy Tafuri (New York: Greenwillow, 1982). Read berry poem.

Mama's Secret by Maria Polushkin; illus. by Felicia Bond (New York: Four Winds, 1984). Mama tiptoes off to pick berries.

Follow-up activities for home or school:

Take a trip to a berry patch and pick your own berries.

Sample several kinds of berries. Eat them with cream, in a pie, as juice.

Find the seeds in berries and talk about what the berry does for its plant.

Ethnic Programs

There is some risk in presenting ethnic programs for the very young child. Because the material presented is so brief, there is a tendency to leave the child with a set of stereotypes: Eskimos live in igloos; Japanese wear kimonos, etc. There is, on the other hand, fascination and a certain magic inherent in the stories of other cultures. Even small children experience this sense of wonder. Certainly it is never too early to start opening windows into other ways of life for all children.

European Travelers

88. Highland Fling

Opening songs.

Read: *All in the Morning Early* by Sorche Nic Leodhas; illus. by Evaline Ness (New York: Holt, 1963). Sandy with his sack of corn meets all sorts of folks on the way to the mill in this counting rhyme. Let the children say the chant with you and make "down the road and over the hill" motions. Make turning motion for "clickety-clickety."

I make a simple "flannel board" for this story by photocopying the characters from the book and backing the cutout photocopies with posterboard. I use a sheet of colored poster board as my flannel board, put a masking tape loop behind each figure and stick them up. I color the photocopied pictures with felt tip markers.

Read: *Always Room for One More* by Sorche Nic Leodhas; illus. by Nonny Hogrogian (New York: Holt, 1965). More folks keep squeezing into the little house.

Act out: *Always Room for One More.*

Listen to bagpipe music: Play a bit of a recording.

Read: *Wee Gillis* by Munro Leaf; illus. by Robert Lawson (New York: Viking, 1938). Wee Gillis can't decide whether to live in the lowlands and call the cows or in the highlands and stalk stags. His lungs develop in any case until he is the finest bagpiper in Scotland.

Show: Scottish tartans and discuss Wee Gillis's kilt. Talk about the way the different colored threads are woven through the fabric.

Color your own tartan plaid: Pass out papers lined for plaid creation and let the children select colors and create their own plaid. I included a photocopied picture of Wee Gillis in his own kilt on the same page with the tartan coloring strip, making a coloring page for them to take home.

Closing songs.

More books to read:

> *Kellyburn Braes* by Sorche Nic Leodhas; illus. by Evaline Ness (New York: Harcourt, 1968). Nagging wife is not wanted by the devil. A folk rhyme.
>
> *The Wee Wee Mannie and the Big Big Coo: A Scottish Folk Tale* by Marcia Sewall (Boston: Little, Brown, 1977). Folk rhyme.

Follow-up activities for home or school:

> Listen to bagpipe music. Perhaps you can hear live pipers in a parade or attend a Highland Games event. If you listen to piping on a recording, you must turn the volume up to get the full effect. Bagpipers make loud music.
>
> Watch for Scottish plaids in the clothing and fabric you encounter. Which tartans do you like best? If you have Scottish heritage, find out about your clan tartan.

89. Russian Winter

Opening songs.

Show Russia on a globe and talk about the cold, snowy winters there.

Read: *Bears Are Sleeping* by Yulya; illus. by Nonny Hogrogian (New York: Scribner's, 1967). A Russian lullaby. Music included. Sing it softly, and let the snowy countryside of the pictures seep in. A mood book.

Read: *The Neighbors* by Marcia Brown (New York: Scribner's, 1967). Hare builds a house of bark, Fox of ice. In the spring Fox's house melts and he takes over Hare's house. Wolf, Bear fail to rout Fox, but Cock intimidates and succeeds.

Act out: *The Neighbors*. With younger classes, let five children assume the main roles. Let all of the children help Bear GROWL and help repeat Fox's chant, Cock's "Coo coo ree coo." With older classes, you may want to repeat the play several times to let everyone have a chance to act. Or use several hares, foxes, and other animals at once.

Tell as a fingerplay: "The Mitten." See "Who Lives in the Skull" in MacDonald, *When the Lights Go Out* (New York: H.W. Wilson, 1988) for instructions on using this as a fingerplay. Right hand simulates mitten, fingers on left hand are animals who enter. Change the skull in MacDonald's text to a mitten. Show selected illustrations from *The Mitten* by Alvin Tresselt; illus. by Yaroslava (Lothrop, Lee & Shepard 1964) after the story is over and explain that this is another version of the Russian folktale.

Let two-and-a-half to three-and-a-half year-old groups stand to do this fingerplay story. They need the stretch. For fours to fives, move this activity to the end of the program, after the film. They will be too hyper after acting out *The Neighbors* for another active story.

Read: *The Little Girl and the Big Bear* by Joanna Galdone; illus. by Paul Galdone (New York: Houghton Mifflin/Clarion, 1960). Little Girl tricks Bear into carrying her home by hiding in a basket of pies which he is carrying to her grandparents.

Show a Russian nested doll: Take each successively smaller doll out of the larger one, then nest them again. (Toy and East European import stores might have them.)

Show film: *Matrioska* animation by Co Hoedeman. (National Film Board of Canada, 1979) 5 min. Nested Russian dolls dance.

Sing Fingerplay: "Matrioska!" For tune by author, see Appendix.

> Matrioska Matrioska Matrioska Dance Dance.
> Matrioska Matrioska Matrioska Dance Dance.

Start by folding left hand over right. Remove left hand—this is the mother doll. Lift up one by one—thumb, first, second, third, fourth fingers—these are the sisters. Little finger is the baby sister. Hold hands upright and move them around each other in a "dance" as you sing first chorus. Hold hand upright and turn them with palms front then back as you sing second chorus. Put fingers (dolls) back into their nest and cover again with left hand.

Closing songs.

Note: For my oldest group (four to five) I follow the high activity level of our creative dramatics adaptation of *The Neighbors* with a very quiet reading of *Varenka* by Bernadette

(New York: Putnam's, 1971). It tells of a woman who takes in refugees from the war and prays to God for her hut to be hidden from the marauding soldiers. A snowfall answers her prayers. Her hut is hidden, and the soldiers pass by. This quiet, somewhat lengthy picture book is very well received. If you use *Varenka* you may want to drop the *Little Girl and the Big Bear* from the program and move directly into the movie, since the quiet mood of *Varenka* flows nicely into *Matrioska*.

More books to read:

At Home: A Visit in Four Languages by Esther Hautzig; illus. by Aliki (New York: Macmillan, 1969). English, French, Spanish, and Russian text.

Baboushka and the Three Kings by Ruth Robbins; illus. by Nicolas Sidjakov (Berkeley: Parnassus, 1960). Baboushka searches for the Christ Child.

The Bun: A Tale from Russia by Marcia Brown (New York: Harcourt, 1972). Folktale of a runaway bun.

The Great Big Enormous Turnip by Alexei Tolstoy; illus. by Helen Oxenbury (New York: Franklin Watts, 1968).

Follow-up activities for home or school:

Learn a few words in Russian. Use them in your daily life.

Visit a Russian restaurant or try your hand at Russian cuisine. Borscht, a delicious beet soup is not hard to make. Children love piroshkis (a sort of deep fried hamburger-in-bun).

90. Voici Paris!

Opening songs.

Read: *Madeline* by Ludwig Bemelmans (New York: Viking, 1939). A Parisian boarding school and a bold little girl.

Read: *The Happy Lion* by Louise Fatio; illus. by Roger Duvoisin (New York: McGraw-Hill, 1954). The Happy Lion escapes from the zoo. Teach the children to say "Bonjour" to the Happy Lion on his jaunt.

Film: "The Red Balloon," by Albert Lamorisse (Macmillan Films, 1956) 34 min. A Parisian schoolboy and a magic balloon.

Make a "balloon over rooftops" picture: Pass out a picture of city rooftops and packets of red dot labels. Let the children stick red labels on as balloons in the sky above their pictures and draw on the dangling strings. I photocopied the title page scene from David McCauley's *Castle* (Boston: Houghton Mifflin, 1977) and gave each child a copy of this for their rooftop scene. Older children seemed to find this illustration very evocative. One boy pointed out to me the exact spot in the labyrinth streets where he imagined the little boy with the red balloon to be hiding.

Closing songs. "Bonjour, Happy Lion."

More books to read:

The Glorious Flight Across the Channel With Louis Bleriot by Alice and Martin Provensen (New York: Viking, 1983). A citizen of Cambrai, France invents an airplane.

Jeanne-Marie in Gay Paris by Françoise (New York: Scribner's, 1956).

Minou by Françoise (New York: Scribner's, 1962). Jeanne-Marie loses her cat Minou in Paris.

La Petite Famille by Sesyle Joslin; illus. by John Alcorn (New York: Harcourt, 1964). Four short stories in French. Quite delightful even if you don't speak a work of the language!

This is Paris by Sasek (New York: Macmillan, 1959). Brief text and colorful sketches of Parisian scenes.

Follow-up activities for home or school:

Read several picture books written in the French language. Can you guess what the words mean? Try *La Petite Famille* by Seysle Joslin for starters. Learn a few French words and use them daily.

Read Sasek's *This is Paris* or look at photographs in books about Paris. What would you like to see if you were to visit there? Where would you like to walk?

Visit a French restaurant or bakery and sample some foods. Older children may enjoy the video *Bon Voyage Charlie Brown* (Paramout Home Video, 1980) 76 min. Charlie Brown visits the French countryside and learns several French phrases as well as much about life there.

Show film *The Happy Lion* (Macmillan Films,) 7 min.

Art Concepts Series

Even very young children can begin to distinguish between various kinds of art, can understand differences in art techniques, and begin to recognize the styles of various artists. When dealing with the twos and threes, this series of programs is probably most useful in encouraging the *parents* to think about art and its techniques. They can then help their children to look at illustrations more intelligently. Fours and fives pick up on ideas readily and are eager to discuss techniques with you.

This series introduces the children to several different artistic methods. It was cut down and simplified from an eight-week series which I offer for school-age children.

Focus on Art

91. Print It!

Opening songs.

Read: *Once a Mouse* by Marcia Brown (New York: Scribner's, 1961). Show a piece of wood with grain and point out that the pictures were made by cutting pictures into a piece of wood, inking it, and pressing this onto paper.

Activity: Turn everyone into mice, then cats, dogs, tigers, and mice again.

Read: *How Hippo!* by Marcia Brown (New York: Scribner's, 1954). Practice "Howing" like a hippo first. Let the children join you in repeating hippo's various "Hows." After the story point out the wood grain in pictures.

Activity: Form a circle and go for a walk through the jungle, saying:

> Walking through the jungle,
> What did I see?
> A big yellow lion
> was roaring at me!

Everyone turns to the person behind them and roars. Let the children suggest animals to meet as you continue your walk. End with a huge hippo "HOWING" at me. And all say "HOW HIPPO."

Read: *A Story A Story* by Gail E. Haley (New York: Atheneum, 1970). Let the children join in the Sky God's laugh, "Twe twe twe," and in Ananse's, "Yiridi yiridi yiridi," and "Sora sora sora." Pat hands on knees for "Yiridi"; rub hands together for "Sora." After the story, show again the hornet picture and point out that the hornet has been stamped repeatedly on the page. Act out stamping the hornet onto the picture.

Sing: "The Monkey Stamp Stamp Stamps His Feet." For tune, see Appendix, Program 82.

> The monkey stamp stamp stamps his feet.
> The monkey stamp stamp stamps his feet.
> The monkey stamp stamp stamps his feet.
> chorus: Monkey see (point to eyes)
> and Monkey do, (extend both hands toward audience)
> Monkey's just the same as you. (point to audience members)

Read: *Swimmy* by Leo Lionni (New York: Pantheon, 1963). Point out that the little red fish are stamped repeatedly to make the picture. Older groups can also note that Lionni used paper doilies to print seaweed. Speculate on Lionni's other techniques.

Make a print picture: This can be executed very simply by using library stamp pads and a variety of stamps. A small selection of interesting stamps, such as dinosaurs or bears, can be supplemented with cut carrots which make nice circular blotches, potatoes, etc. Or use only vegetables for your art work. In order to pick up ink from a stamp pad, you need a hard object. Carrots work well.

Closing songs.

More books to read:

Drummer Hoff adapted by Barbara Emberley; illus. by Ed Emberley (Englewood Cliffs, NJ: Prentice-Hall, 1967). Intricately cut prints illustrate a rhythmic tale of assembling a cannon.

See and Say: Guarda e Parla; Mira y Habla; Regarde et Parle by Antonio Frasconi (New York: Harcourt, 1955). Woodcuts by Antonio Frasconi illustrate this four-language word book.

This is . . . by Gloria Patrick; illus. by Joan Hanson (Minneapolis: Carolrhoda, 1970). Single block prints illustrate a primer text. "A dog—on a log."

Follow-up activities for home or school:

Look for fabrics, paper products, and other objects in your home that were decorated with a repeated motif.

Experiment with various objects and a stamp pad to see how many different prints, textures you can create.

Make a picture using only fingerprints to create a design.

92. Looking at a Line

Opening songs.

Read: *A Very Special House* by Ruth Krauss; illus. by Maurice Sendak (New York: Harper & Row, 1953). A boy describes the pretend house full of monkeys, "skunkeys," and a lion "right in the middle of his head head head!" Let the smaller children say the refrains with you; "snore snore snore," "more more more." After the story, talk about pretend things "inside your head." Point out that Maurice Sendak drew this pretend house. He used just lines to make his picture, and no colors except the boy's blue overalls.

Draw: Some lines on a paper, magic slate, or chalkboard while the children watch. See what kind of picture you can make from simple lines. Let the children make suggestions. Example: draw a line. Add two lines and it becomes a table. Add a roof and floor and it's a house. Draw a curve and two dots, it's a happy face. Could just a single line make a picture? It does in the next book.

Read: *The Missing Piece* by Shel Silverstein (New York: Harper & Row, 1976). A circle rolls along looking for its missing piece. Point out the simplicity of the drawings. The first picture is a simple line crossing the page. Hold the interest of small children by letting them sing the circle's song with you and perhaps repeating it a few times more than the story calls for.

Circle song: "The Wheels on the Bus." For tune, see Appendix.

> The wheels on the bus go round and round,
> Round and round, round and round.
> The wheels on the bus go round and round.
> All around the town.

Make circular hand motions for wheels on the bus, steering

wheel. Be sure and include something that goes "back and forth" (windshield wipers) and something that goes "up and down" (bouncing people).

Read: *Cricter* by Tomi Ungerer (New York: Harper & Row, 1958). Madame Bodot receives a pet boa constrictor. The delicate line drawings here are a bit difficult to see from any distance.

Craft: Stick two round colored labels together on the end of a piece of yarn to make a crictor. Pencil on eyes if you like. These can be made quickly while still seated in the story circle.

Experiment with crictors: Let the children experiment with making their crictors into "O", "S", "L", "2", "6", etc.

Draw an abstract picture: Explain that you are going to all draw pictures together. Then each child can draw his own picture. Show two paintings or reproductions in books, one representational and one abstract. Talk about the difference between the pictures.

Set the children at tables in such a way that they can all watch you. Have crayons in brown, blue, orange, yellow, and green in front of each place. Now:

Each child selects a crayon. Sing "Wheels on the bus go round and round" and make "round" motions with hands. Begin to make circles on paper.

Select another crayon. Sing "people on the bus go up and down." Make "up and down" motions with your crayon.

Select another crayon. Sing "windshield wipers go back and forth." Make left-right horizontal motions with your crayon. Admire your "abstract" drawing.

Pass out more paper and let the children make drawings of their own. I sometimes add a second "directed drawing" activity. Using the drawing motions we practiced we can create a representational picture. At Thanksgiving I asked the children to use their brown crayons to make a big circle, then a little one. We connected the two with a line. With our orange and yellow crayons we made back-and-forth and up-and-down lines most of the way around the big circle. With our green crayon we made up and down lines across the bottom of the page for grass. This resembled a turkey, more or less, in even the most wobbly efforts.

Closing songs.

More books to read:

Harold and the Purple Crayon by Crockett Johnson (New York: Harper & Row, 1955). Harold's "line" creates whatever he imagines.

What's in a Line? by Leonard Kessler (New York: Scott, 1951).

Follow-up activities for home or school:

Paste lines of string onto a sheet of colored paper to make pictures. Play with the strings a while first. What can you do with string?

Provide a variety of drawing instruments and play at drawing lines. Have pens to make wide lines, thin lines. Notice the lines in a picture. Trace them with your finger.

93. Paste a Collage

Opening songs.

Read: *Alexander and the Wind-up Mouse* by Leo Lionni (New York: Pantheon, 1969). Alexander wishes he were a wind-up toy mouse like Willy, until Willy gets tossed in the trash. After you have read this, point out the illustrative technique. Alexander is made of torn and cut paper. Show his hideout filled with torn newspaper.

Read: *Whistle for Willie* by Ezra Jack Keats (New York: Viking, 1964). Peter tries and tries and finally learns to whistle. Point out the cut paper technique in the illustrations after you have finished reading the book.

Make a collage together: Put a sheet of paper up on the wall. Pasting it against a contrasting color will enhance the yarn, stickers, etc. Let each child come up and select something to paste onto the collage.

Sing a collage song: Form a circle and sing about pasting up an imaginary collage. Get silly and paste all sorts of things on your picture. Our group pasted up a robot tiger, a birthday present, and a purple shiny paper cat among other things. Sing to the tune of "This is the way we wash our clothes."

> This is the way we paste our collage,
> paste our collage,
> paste our collage.
> This is the way we paste our collage.
> PASTE! PASTE! PASTE!

"This is the way we paste our purple, shiny paper cat," and so on. At the end remind them of all the marvelous things on their imaginary collage and admire it.

Read: *Inch by Inch* by Leo Lionni (New York: Astor-Honor, 1960). An inch worm measures the bigger animals. Point out the cut paper grasses.

Make a grass collage: Litter the work tables with strips and squares of green paper. Construction paper and old blotters tear into rough leaflike shapes. Add a few bright circles for flowers if you like. Provide glue and white paper sheets on which to paste up collages. A green strip can be pasted down at both of its ends with a humpy loop in the middle to make an inchworm.

Closing songs.

More books to read:

Home in the Sky by Jeannie Baker (New York: Greenwillow, 1984). A rooftop coop pigeon gets separated from its owner. Intricate collage construction by an Australian artist.

How Summer Came to Canada by William Toye; illus. by Elizabeth Cleaver (New York: Walck, 1969). Real pine needles and cedar are used to enhance this paint and collage artwork. Glooskap travels south to bring back Queen Summer with her flowers.

Let's Make Rabbits by Leo Lionni (New York: Pantheon, 1982). A pencil-drawn rabbit and a cutout rabbit and friends.

The Man Whose Mother Was a Pirate by Margaret Mahy; illus. by Brian Froud (New York: Atheneum, 1972). A man whose pirate mother dreams of the sea pushes her there in a wheelbarrow. Collage illustration uses fabric, sandpaper, real shells.

Follow-up activities for home and school:

Look at other pictures created with collage.

Set aside a "collage treasures" box. Have the children watch for interesting textured materials which could be pasted in a collage. Toss them in the box as you discover them. Then bring the box out some rainy day and create a collage.

94. Mold It!

Opening songs.

Read: *Don't Touch*! by Suzy Kline; illus. by Dora Leder (Nile, IL: Albert Whitman, 1985). Clay is pounded, pummeled, pulled. It is the one thing a preschooler is *allowed* to touch.

Play with pretend clay: Pound it, roll it, make a pancake, poke holes in it, make it into a ball.

Read: *Sand Castle* by Ron Wegen (New York: Greenwillow, 1977). A sand castle is built, then crumbles.

Film: *The Sand Castle*. by Co Hoedeman (National Film Board of Canada, 1977) 14 min. Sandman emerges from sand and fashions creatures to populate his world. A sandstorm obliterates all.

Clay play: Pass out Playdough for creative play. Talk about the way it feels, the ways it can be molded.

Closing songs.

More books to read:

Our Family by Shay Rieger (New York: Lothrop, Lee & Shepard, 1972). In clay, bronze, and plaster sculpture the artist depicts members of his family, revealing a tale of Jewish immigrant life in America.

Follow-up activities for home or school:

Find a beach or sandbox and build a sand castle.

Visit a gallery or shop selling hand molded clay objects and look at things created from molded clay.

Music Time Program

Using rhythm instruments is fun, but producing anything other than a cacophony with small children requires considerable direction. Rather than use the rhythm instruments every week, I save them for a once-a-year music series. This is very popular with parents and always draws many families who have never come to the regular storytime. This series is offered in late spring so that my regular preschoolers have had a full season of storytime experience before I try the music program. They already know the routines and can cope with the distraction of extra adults and unfamiliar children, and also with the added directions for handling the instruments.

As a part of this I try to teach simple musical concepts: distinctions between high and low tones, use of rests in a rhythm, dynamics (loud and soft). We hear a variety of musical styles in the course of the series: symphonic, jazz, folk, music for square dancing, and marching bands.

Each musical program is built around one very strong book from my "too good to miss" list. Sometimes an excellent musical film is included. Since the playing of instruments by the children themselves takes about a third of our session time, the program element in this series is much shorter than it is in a regular storytime. I include samples of special music programs here, but you can create a music program from many of the other storytime programs given in this book, following the same pattern. Select one favorite story from the program you plan and focus the music portion of the program around it. Replace the other books with rhythm instrument play. Keep the singing games, and perhaps a craft or film as part of the music program. Obviously, this program places less emphasis on the books than I would ordinarily like, but it is great fun and draws a lot of positive attention to the children's programming in our branch. A three- or four-week "music time" series each spring seems to work well.

Using Rhythm Instruments

There are several excellent recordings designed to facilitate the use of rhythm instruments with children. These usually assume a higher level of group activity than my twos and threes are ready for, so I have devised a very simple rhythm instrument activity sequence that works well for the young groups.

First, insist that all instruments be kept on the floor in front of each child *untouched* until the leader (you) gives the signal to raise them. Practice this. You may want to let your participants pound freely for a few minutes before going into your instruction mode, but once they begin working (playing) as a group, everyone must follow the rules. When you say, "Ready, set, play," or "One, two, three, play," all should begin playing together. It does take practice, and patience, but it is very satisfying for everyone when it begins to happen. Playing an instrument yourself helps the group a great deal, because they have a model. Rhythm sticks are good because they clearly demonstrate the beat.

To begin with, I let them play any way they want as long as they play together. I raise my arms to indicate that they should play louder, lower them to indicate softer. Next, I introduce a beat and demonstrate it, "One, two, three, four," and we all try it together. Later sessions will explore three-fourths time, and other musical elements. We try playing the beat louder and softer. I introduce rests, and we say them, "One, two, three, rest."

Then we sing a simple song and play along with it. Ella Jenkins's "Play Your Instruments and Make a Pretty Sound" is a good one to try. (*Play Your Instruments and Make a Pretty Sound* by Ella Jenkins. Recordings. New York: Folkways, 1968.)

We stand up in a circle and play our instruments in time to a recording. Hap Palmer's track for "Happy Mechanical Man" is especially good. (*Modern Tunes for Rhythms and Instruments* by Hap Palmer. Recording. Free port, NY: Educational Activities, 1969.) Children like to mimic the mechanical man's movements. The piece can be used each week, introducing the use of rests on the second week, and even using instruments in two parts later in the series.

After our instrument play, we return to the seated circle and each child comes as I call the instrument name and replaces that instrument in a basket.

We are now ready for our story, which will be followed by a singing game, film, or craft carrying out the story's theme. This is, of course, an oversimplification of the musical activity we engage in, but it will give you a procedure to start with. The key to success is that the leader must stay in complete control at all times. This takes a lot of energy and patience during the first session, but after that things usually go smoothly. I do discourage "drop-ins" from joining us after the first session because with every new child you have to go over the rules of the game again and this is disruptive.

95. A Little Schubert

Opening songs.

Rhythm instrument play.

Read: *A Little Schubert* by M.B. Goffstein (New York: Harper & Row, 1972). Schubert lives in a cold, bare room in Vienna but composes music and dances to keep warm.

Act out: Play the selections on the record accompanying the book and pretend to be Schubert. Play the piano. Write out musical scores. Dance to keep warm and make your coat tails fly. (If your book lacks a record you could substitute other short classical piano segments for your creative dramatics movement.)

Play the piano: If there is a piano in your room, stand the children by it four at a time and let them play a concert for the others. If you put stick-on dots on the notes of one chord (C, E, G for example) and ask them to play only those notes, the result should at least not be discordant. Have them follow your directions to play, soft, loud, slow, fast. The rest of the group forms the audience and applauds. Change players until all have had a turn.

Closing songs.

More books to read:

> *The Philharmonic Gets Dressed* by Karla Kuskin; illus. by Marc Simont (New York: Harper & Row, 1982). The members of the Philharmonic at home getting ready for their concert.

Follow-up activities for home or school:

> Listen to recordings of Schubert's piano compositions or other classical piano.
>
> Play on a piano.

96. Frog Songs

Opening songs.

Rhythm instrument play.

Read and sing: *Frog Went A 'Courtin'* by John Langstaff and Feodor Rojankovsky (New York: Harcourt, 1967). Have audience join on the "umhums."

Craft: Have each child bring a small box or shoebox lid, or visit your local shoe store ahead of time for a supply. Fold in half one green, cardboard circle approximately three and one-half inches in diameter. Paste one half of folded circle to inside of lid. Stick two, gummed hole reinforcers onto the top of this folded circle for frog eyes. Put rubber bands around the box lid. Use two or three rubber bands of different sizes to make different notes. Strum your frog guitar and sing.

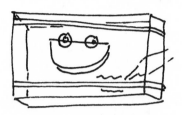

Sing: "The Frog Song." For tune, see Appendix.

> Glack Goong! Went the little green frog one day!
> Glack Goong! Went the little green frog one day!
> Glack Goong! Went the little green frog one day!
> And his eyes went Glack Glack Goong!

Blink your eyes on the "glack glack goong"; make his "glack goongs" way back in your throat, frog-like.

Talk about stringed instruments. How do they produce sound? Show some.

Poem: "The Sound of a Toad." from *Something Sleeping in the Hall* by Karla Kuskin (New York: Harper & Row, 1985).

Film: *A Boy, a Dog and a Frog* by John Sturner and Gary Templeton (Phoenix, 1980) 9 min. Live action as a boy tries to catch a frog. Listen for the stringed instruments in the sound track. With older groups you might want to watch it twice, paying special attention to the sound track a second time. From the book, *A Boy, a Dog and a Frog* by Mercer Mayer (New York: Dial, 1967).

More books to read:

The Old Banjo by Dennis Haseley; illus. by Stephen Gammell (New York: Macmillan, 1983). Forgotten instruments in an attic begin to play. A quiet book.

Follow-up activities for home or school:

Listen to recordings of stringed instruments. Children respond exuberantly to the vibrancy of baroque music.

Watch *The Foolish Frog* by Gene Deitch (Weston Woods, 1973) 8 min. Sing along with Pete Seeger and strum your own"guitars." See also, *The Foolish Frog* by Pete Seeger and Charles Seeger; illus. by Miloslav Jagr (New York: Macmillan, 1973).

97. Barnyard Dance

Opening songs.

Rhythm instrument play.

Read: *Rosie's Walk* by Pat Hutchins (New York: Macmillan, 1968). Fox chases Rosie but she struts on uncaring.

Film: *Rosie's Walk* by Gene Deitch (Weston Woods, 1970) 5 min. Rosie struts in time to fiddle music!

Creative play: Rewind the film and show it again. This time everyone get up and strut around with Rosie. Lunge to the floor with the fox, etc. Act this out as the movie rolls. Be sure the projector is adjusted to shoot over their heads.

Square dance: Make a circle. Choose a simple cut from any square dance record. It should not be too long, with a clear firm beat. You give the calls while the children and parents execute them. Keep the calls simple; "Circle to the left," "Circle to the right," "Swing your partner," "Bow to your partner," "Bow to the center," "Go into the center." Older kids can manage a "do-si-do" if you show them how first. Never mind that this isn't *real* square dancing—it *feels* like square dancing and the music makes it great fun. Just keep them moving—any old call will do. Clap your hands and stomp your feet.

Closing songs.

More books to read:

Clementine by Robert Quackenbush (Philadelphia: Lippincott, 1974).

Ol' Dan Tucker by John M. Langstaff; illus. Koe Krush (New York: Harcourt, 1963).

She'll Be Comin' Round the Mountain by Robert M. Quackenbush (Philadelphia: Lippincott, 1973).

Skip to My Lou by Robert M. Quackenbush (Philadelphia: Lippincott, 1975).

Sweet Betsy from Pike by Glen Rounds (Chicago: Children's 1973).

Follow-up activities for home or school:

Listen to a recording of a fiddler.

Continue to play at square dancing.

Watch folks square dancing. Why does it look like fun?

98. Chicken Soup

Opening songs.

Rhythm instrument play.

Read: *Chicken Soup With Rice* by Maurice Sendak (New York: Harper & Row, 1962). Through the year with chicken soup. Encourage the group to invent motions for each month's activities.

Sing and act out: "Chicken Soup With Rice" from *Really Rosie*. The Broadway Cast Album of Maurice Sendak's Really Rosie. Music by Carole King (Caedmon, 1981).

Play and sing: "Now the Chicken is A-boiling." For tune, see Appendix, Program 24.

> Now the chicken is a-boiling,
> In the steamy pot he bubbles.
> Out he pops his head and asks us,
> "Don't you know I need some onions!"

One child is the chicken in middle of circle. The child jumps up and calls, "Don't you know I need some onions!" on cue. Everyone throws "onions" at the child.

Eat: A cup of chicken soup, with crackers.

Closing songs.

See also related programs: "Thanksgiving Turkeys," Program 52.

More books to read:

"Birthday Soup" from *Little Bear* by Else Homelund Minarik (New York: Harper & Row, 1957). Little Bear puts in peas and tomatoes, carrots and potatoes.

Watch Out For the Chicken Feet in Your Soup by Tomie de Paola (Englewood Cliffs, NJ: Prentice-Hall, 1974). A visit to a friend's chicken soup cooking family.

Follow-up activities for home or school:

Watch the video or movie *Really Rosie* (Weston Woods, 1976) 26 min. Sing along. *Really Rosie* includes all four of Sendak's

Nutshell Library books set to music. Also each is available as single film, i.e. *Chicken Soup With Rice*, (Weston Woods, 1976) 5 min.

99. Drummer Hoff

Opening songs.
Rhythm instrument play.
Talk about drums: Show some. How is the sound produced?
Read: *Drummer Hoff* by Barbara Emberley; illus. by Ed Emberley (Englewood Cliffs, NJ: Prentice-Hall, 1967). Drummer Hoff fires off the cannon after the others assemble it. Let children say refrain with you. "Drummer Hoff—fired it off." This line should be drawn out like a drum roll.
Make coffee can drums: Ask everyone to bring a coffee can. Have plenty of extras on hand for those who forgot. Wrap bright paper around them, color with crayons if you like.
Reread and play drums for: *Drummer Hoff*. Everyone should play drums on the refrain this time.
March: Hold drums under one arm and play to marching music. A recording of Sousa marches would be good.
Closing songs.
See also related program: "Fourth of July Parade," Program 48.
More books to read:
Hand, Hand, Fingers, Thumb by Al Perkins; illus. by Eric Gurney (New York: Random House, 1969). Read and drum this ditty—dum-ditty—dum-ditty—dum-ditty-dum.
Follow-up activities for home or school:
Collect pots and pans, cardboard boxes, and other possible "musical instruments." Arrange them in some order according to the tone they produce. Make up a drumming routine to perform on them.
Go to hear a band or orchestra playing. Watch the drummers and notice how they contribute to the whole performance.

100. Dancing Dolls

Opening songs.
Rhythm instrument play.
Read: *The Wedding Procession of the Rag Doll and the Broom*

Handle and Who was in It by Carl Sandburg; illus. by Harriet Pincus (New York: Harcourt, 1922, 1950, 1967).

Act out: Put on some music to march to, not too stirring, and walk around in a circle forming a "procession" and "licking your spoons," etc.

Action Record: "The Wooden Doll" from *Dance-a-story, Sing-a-song* by Marcia Berman and Anne Lief Barlin. B/B Records #B/B 110 (Learning Through Movement, 5757; Ranchito, Van Nuys, CA 91401). This recording is long and is high energy. You may want to either cut the rhythm play short today or omit the march after the *Wedding Procession* book.

Closing songs.

See also related programs: "Teddy Bears Go Dancing," Program 81.

More books to read:

The Lonely Doll by Dare Wright (New York: Doubleday, 1957).

Follow-up activities for home and school:

Encourage imaginative play with dolls.

Play tea party with your children and a group of dolls.

Continue the rhythmic, body awareness exercises begun in "The Wooden Doll" by dancing like rag dolls or wooden dolls to other recordings.

If Carl Sandburg's use of language appeals to you, share stories from his *Rootabaga Stories* (New York: Harcourt, Brace & World, 1922). This is for older preschoolers.

101. May Day

Opening songs.

Rhythm instrument play.

A Maypole dance: A free-standing flagpole such as those found in meeting rooms makes an excellent Maypole. Remove the flag. Lay the pole on the floor and run crepe paper streamers over its top, letting them hang to the floor on both sides. Use several streamers of bright spring colors, like yellow, pink and green. Use masking tape to secure your bundle of streamers to the top of the pole. Put it back in its standard and arrange the streamers so that they fall on all sides of the pole. Have the children circle the Maypole. Hand a streamer to each child. Ask them to hold it lightly and not to pull on it. Show them how to let it drape in toward the pole. When everyone has a streamer, sing "We're Winding Up the May-pole." For tune, see Appendix.

> We're winding up the Maypole,
> the Maypole, the Maypole.
> We're winding up the Maypole
> on May Day.

Circle the pole slowly as you sing. Make up more verses; "We're dancing round the Maypole," "Round and round the Maypole," "Let's go round the Maypole." When it becomes nearly wound up, stop. Call the children's attention to the altered pole. It will have the streamers twisted around it now. Then turn and circle in the other direction.

Sing:"Let's Unwind the Maypole."

When you have completely unwound the pole, stop. Perhaps bow to the pole, singing, "We're bowing to the Maypole." Ask the children to hold their streamers as high over their heads as they can, and on the count of three, everyone let go. They flutter down gently, a pleasant sight.

Make May baskets: These can be made simply by rolling a sheet of paper into a cone and stapling on a handle. Let the children decorate the papers with crayons before you and the parents begin to staple them together.

Hold your baskets and sing: "A May Day Song." For tune, see Appendix.

> On May day,
> On May day,
> I woke up at day break
> And went out to gather a basket of May.

Take the baskets home to fill with flowers.

Closing songs.

Follow-up activities for home or school:

Make more May baskets.

Fill your baskets with flowers and give it to someone you know.

Bibliography

Since it is not possible to include poetry text and complete musical notation within this book, I refer to additional sources. To locate poetry texts and music for these programs it would be useful for you to have on hand: *The Random House Book of Poetry*, edited by Jack Prelutsky (New York: Random House, 1983), and *Making Music Your Own* by Mary Tinnan Jaye (Morristown, NJ: Silver Burdett, 1971).

In the following bibliography the name of the program citing each item is given. Programs using the item as a program element are starred.

Abercrombie, Barbara. *The Other Side of a Poem*. New York: Harper & Row, 1977. *Just Me! 62.

Adams, Adrienne. *A Woggle of Witches*. New York: Scribner's, 1971. *Ghosts and Witches, 50.

Adamson, Joy. *Elsa*; photos by author. New York: Pantheon, 1961. *Happy Lions, 72.

Adelson, Leone. *Please Pass the Grass*; illus. by Roger Duvoisin. New York: McKay, 1960. Habitat: the Field, 1.

Adkins, Jan. *How a House Happens*. New York: Walker, 1972. My House, My Home, 68.

Adler, David A. *A Picture Book of Hanukkah*; illus. by Linda Heller. New York: Holiday House, 1982. Happy Hanukkah, 53.

Adoff, Arnold. *Eats*; illus. by Susan Russo. New York: Lothrop, 1979. *Freaky Food, 78.

Adoff, Arnold. *Ma nDa La*; illus. by Emily McCully. New York: Harper & Row, 1971. *Feeling Glad, 58.

Adoff, Arnold. *Where Wild Willie*; illus. by Emily McCully. New York: Harper & Row, 1979. Just Me!, 62.

Alberti, Trude. *The Animals' Lullaby*; illus. by Chiyoko Nakatani. Cleveland: World, 1967. *Christmas Lullabies, 54.

Alexander and the Car With the Missing Headlight. 11 min. Weston Woods, 1966. *Take Me Ridin' in Your Car, 70.

Aliki. *Fossils Tell of Long Ago*. New York: Crowell, 1972. Dinosaurs, 17.

Aliki. *Hush Little Baby*. Englewood Cliffs, NJ: Prentice-Hall, 1968. *Christmas Lullabies, 54.

Aliki. *The Story of Johnny Appleseed*. Englewood Cliffs, NJ: Prentice-Hall, 1963. Apple Day, 30.

Alligators All Around. 2 min. Weston Woods, 1976. Crocodiles and Alligators, 74.

Andersen, Hans Christian. *The Princess and the Pea*; illus. by Paul Galdone. New York: Seabury, 1978. *A Visit to the King and Queen, 86.

Anderson, Lonzo. *The Halloween Party*; illus. by Adrienne Adams. New York: Scribner's, 1974. Ghosts and Witches, 50.

Angus Lost. 11 min. Filmmaker: John Sturner and Gary Templeton. Phoenix, 1987. *Problem Pups, 77.

Anno, Mitsumasa. *Anno's Counting House*. New York: Philomel, 1982. Number Rhumba, 25.

Arbuthnot, May Hill. *Time for Poetry*. Chicago: Scott, Foresman, 1952. *Habitat: the Garden, 2.

Aruego, Jose, and Ariane Dewey. *We Hide, You Seek*. New York: Greenwillow, 1979. *Take a Closer Look! 16.

Asayama, Eiichi. *Dandelions*; illus. by Ryo Ooshita. East Sussex, England: Wayland, 1976. *A Seed Grows, 7.

Averill, Esther. *Jenny's Birthday Book*. New York: Harper & Row, 1954. Happy Birthday to Me! 57.

Ayal, Ora. *Ugbu*; trans. by Naomi Low Nakao. New York: Harper & Row, 1977. *Foolish Furniture, 79; Classifying Chairs, 15.

Baker, Jeannie. *Home in the Sky*. New York: Greenwillow, 1984. Paste a Collage! 93.

Baker, Laura Nelson. *The Friendly Beasts*; illus. by Nicolas Sidjakov. New York: Parnassus, 1958. Christmas Lullabies, 54.

Balian, Lorna. *Bah! Humbug?* Nashville, TN: Abingdon, 1977. Here Comes Santa Claus! 56.

Balian, Lorna. *Humbug Witch*. Nashville, TN: Abingdon, 1965. *Ghosts and Witches, 50.

Balian, Lorna. *Sometimes It's Turkey, Sometimes It's Feathers*. Knoxville, TN: Abingdon, 1980. *Thanksgiving Turkeys, 52.

Bang, Betsy. *The Old Woman and the Red Pumpkin: A Bengali Folktale*; illus. by Molly Garrett Bang. New York: Macmillan, 1975. Pumpkin Magic, 49.

Bang, Molly. *The Grey Lady and the Strawberry Snatcher*. New York: Four Winds, 1980. *Blueberry, Strawberry, Jamberry! 87.

Bang, Molly. *Ten, Nine, Eight*. New York: Greenwillow, 1983. *Number Rhumba. 25.

Barlin, Anne Lief. *Teaching Your Wings to Fly: The Nonspecialist's*

Guide to Movement Activities for Children. Santa Monica: Goodyear, 1979. *Rainy Day, 40.

Barrett, Judi. *Cloudy With a Chance of Meatballs*; illus. by Ron Barrett. New York: Atheneum, 1979. Freaky Food, 78.

Bartoli, Jennifer. *Snow on Bear's Nose: A Story of a Japanese Moon Bear Cub*; illus. by Takeo Ishida. Chicago: Albert Whitman, 1972. Snow Bears, 35.

Barton, Byron. *Airport*. New York: Crowell, 1982. But Will It Fly? 11.

Barton, Byron. *Building a House*. New York: Greenwillow, 1981. *Tools Work For Us! 13.

Barton, Byron. *Hester*. New York: Greenwillow, 1975. *Trick or Treat, 51.

Barton, Byron. *Wheels*. New York: Crowell, 1979. Wheels and Gears, 14.

Bauer, Caroline Feller. *Celebrations*. New York: H.W. Wilson, 1985.

Baylor, Byrd. *Everybody Needs a Rock*; illus. by Peter Parnall. New York: Scribner's, 1974. *Your Own Special Rock, 18.

Baylor, Byrd. *The Way to Start a Day*; illus. by Peter Parnall. New York: Scribner's, 1978. Sun! 41.

Beall, Pamela Conn and Susan Hagen Nipp. *Wee Sing and Play*. Los Angeles: Price/Stern/Sloan, 1981. *Feeling Foolish, 46.

Beckman, Kaj. *Lisa Can't Sleep*; illus. by Per Beckman. New York: Watts, 1969. Sleepy Storytime, 65.

Behn, Harry. *Cricket Songs*. New York: Harcourt, 1964. *Wonderful Words, 84.

Behn, Harry. *More Cricket Songs*. New York: Harcourt, 1971. *Wonderful Words, 84.

Bemelmans, Ludwig. *Madeline*. New York: Viking, 1939. *Voici Paris! 90.

Bennett, Jill. *Days Are Where We Live and Other Poems*; illus. by Maureen Raffey. New York: Lothrop, 1981. *Freaky Food, 78.

Berenstain, Stan, and Jan Berenstain. *Bears in the Night*. New York: Random House, 1971. *Owls in the Night, 32.

Berenstain, Stan, and Jan Berenstain. *Bears on Wheels*. New York: Random House, 1969. Wheels and Gears, 14.

Berenstain, Stan, and Jan Berenstain. *Old Hat, New Hat*. New York: Random House, 1970. *Spring Hats, 39.

Bernadette. *Varenka*. New York: Putnam's, 1971. Russian Winter, 84.

Betjeman, John. *Archie and the Strict Baptists*; illus. by Phillida Gili. New York: Lippincott, 1977. Teddy Bears Go Dancing, 81.

Bileck, Marvin. See Julian Scheer.

Birnbaum, Abe. *Green Eyes.* New York: Golden, 1953. *All Falling Down, 29; *Spring Kittens, 38.

Blake, Quentin. *Mister Magnolia.* London: Jonathan Cape, 1950. *New Shoes, 66; *Rhyme, Rhyme, Rhyme, 83.

Blegvad, Erik. See Ruth Craft.

Boden, Alice. *Field of Buttercups: An Irish Story.* New York: Walck, 1974. St. Patrick's Day Parade, 45.

Bon Voyage Charlie Brown. 76 min. Paramount Home Video, 1980. Voici Paris! 90.

Bond, Felicia. *Poinsettia and the Firefighters.* New York: Crowell, 1984. *The Don't Be Scared Storytime, 60.

Bonsall, Crosby. *It's Mine: A Greedy Book.* New York: Harper & Row, 1964. Feeling Mad, 59.

Borton, Helen. *Do You Hear What I Hear?* New York: Abelard-Schuman, 1963. Hear It! 20.

Borton, Helen. *Do You See What I See?* New York: Abelard-Schuman, 1969. See It! 23.

Bos, Bev. *Don't Move the Muffin Tins: A Hands-Off Guide to Art for the Young Child.* Roseville, CA: Turn the Page Press, 1978.

Bour, Daniele. *Osito Pardo Esta de Mal Humor.* Madrid: Editiones Altea, 1985. Feeling Mad, 59.

Bour, Daniele. *Little Bear Is In a Bad Mood.* New York: Barrons, 1986. Feeling Mad, 59.

Bour, Daniele. *Osito Pardo Va de Vacaciones.* Madrid: Editiones Altea, 1985. Snow Bears, 35.

A Boy, a Dog, and a Frog. 9 min. Phoenix, 1980. *Habitat: the Pond, 5.

Boynton, Sandra. *A is for Angry.* New York: Whitman, 1983. *Making Faces, 64; Feeling Mad, 59.

Boynton, Sandra. *Good Night, Good Night.* New York: Random, 1985. *Sleepy Storytime, 65.

Bramblett, Ella. *Shoots of Green: Poems for Young Gardeners.* New York: Crowell, 1986. *Habitat: the Garden, 3.

Brandenberg, Franz. *Otto is Different;* illus. by James Stevenson. New York: Greenwillow, 1985. Just Me! 62.

Brandenburg, Aliki. See Aliki.

Branley, Franklyn M. *The Moon Seems to Change;* illus. by Helen Borten. New York: Crowell, 1960. Harvest Moon, 31.

Branley, Franklyn M. *Volcanoes;* illus. by Marc Simont. New York: Crowell, 1985. Volcanoes Erupt! 19.

Brenner, Barbara. *A Dog I Know*; illus. by Fred Brenner. New York: Harper & Row, 1983. Problem Pups, 77.

Brenner, Barbara. *Faces*; photos by George Ancoma. New York: Dutton, 1970. Smell It! 24.

Brenner, Barbara. See May Garelick.

Brett, Jan. *Annie and the Wild Animals*. Boston: Houghton Mifflin, 1985. Spring Kittens, 38.

Bright, Robert. *Georgie*. New York: Doubleday, 1944. *Ghosts and Witches, 50; *Owls in the Night, 32.

Bright, Robert. *I Like Red*. New York: Doubleday, 1955. Color Me Red!, 26.

Brown, Marcia. *Arthur's Nose*. Boston: Little, Brown, 1976. *Just Me! 62.

Brown, Marcia. *The Bun: A Tale from Russia*. New York: Harcourt, 1972. Russian Winter, 89.

Brown, Marcia. *How Hippo!* New York: Scribner's, 1954. *Print It! 91.

Brown, Marcia. *The Neighbors*. New York: Scribner's, 1967. *Russian Winter, 89.

Brown, Marcia. *Once a Mouse*. New York: Scribner's, 1961. *Print It! 91.

Brown, Margaret Wise. *A Child's Good Morning Book*; illus. by Jean Charlot. New York: Addison-Wesley, 1952. *Sleepy Storytime, 65.

Brown, Margaret Wise. *A Child's Good Night Book*; illus. by Jean Charlot. New York: Addison-Wesley, 1952. Sleepy Storytime, 65.

Brown, Margaret Wise. *The Golden Egg Book*; illus. by Leonard Weisgard. New York: Simon & Schuster, 1947. *Easter Rabbits, 47; *Feathered Babies, 37.

Brown, Margaret Wise. *Goodnight Moon*; illus. by Clement Hurd. New York: Harper, 1947. *Harvest Moon, 31; *Sleepy Storytime, 65.

Brown, Margaret Wise. *Home for a Bunny*; illus. by Garth Williams. Racine, WI: Western, 1983. *Easter Rabbits, 47.

Brown, Margaret Wise. *The Indoor Noisy Book*. New York: Harper & Row, 1942. Hear It! 20.

Brown, Margaret Wise. *Nibble, Nibble*; illus. by Leonard Weisgard. New York: Addison-Wesley, 1945. *Down in the Grass, 6.

Brown, Margaret Wise. *The Runaway Bunny*; illus. by Clement Hurd. New York: Harper & Row, 1942. *Easter Rabbits, 47; *What Then? 28.

Brown, Margaret Wise. *The Sailor Dog*; illus. by Garth Williams. Racine, WI: Golden, 1953. On the High Seas, 71.

Brown, Margaret Wise. *Shhhhhh . . . Bang. A Whispering Book*. New York: Harper & Row, 1943. Hear It! 20.

Brown, Margaret Wise. *Two Little Trains*; illus. by Jean Charlot. New York: Addison-Wesley, 1949. *Here Comes the Train! 69.

Brown, Margaret Wise. *Where Have You Been?*; illus. by Barbara Cooney. New York: Hastings House, 1981. Rhyme, Rhyme, Rhyme, 81.

Bruna, Dick. *I Can Dress Myself*. Methuen, 1977. Button Button, 67.

Bunting, Eve. *St. Patrick's Day in the Morning*; illus. Jan Brett. Boston: Houghton Mifflin, 1980. St. Patrick's Day, 45.

Burningham, John. *The Friend*. New York: Crowell, 1975. Be My Friend, 43.

Burningham, John. *Mr. Gumpy's Motor Car*. New York: Crowell, 1976. *Wheels and Gears; 14; *Take Me Ridin' in Your Car, 70.

Bursill, Henry. *Hand Shadows to be Thrown Upon the Wall*. New York: Dover, 1967. Shadow Play, 42.

Burton, Virginia Lee. *Choo Choo: The Story of the Little Engine Who Ran Away*. Boston: Houghton Mifflin, 1937. Here Comes the Train! 69.

Burton, Virginia Lee. *Katy and the Big Snow*. Boston: Houghton Mifflin, 1943. The Snowy Day, 34.

Burton, Virginia Lee. *The Little House*. Boston: Houghton Mifflin, 1942. *My House, My Home, 68.

Busch, Phyllis S. *Once There Was a Tree: The Story of the Tree, A Changing Home for Plants and Animals*. Cleveland: World, 1968. *Habitat: the Tree, 2.

Calhoun, Mary. *The Hungry Leprechaun*; illus. by Roger Duvoisin. New York: Harper & Row, 1962. St. Patrick's Day Parade, 45.

Captain Silas Filmmaker: Ron Mcadow. Yellow Bison, 1977. *On the High Seas, 71.

Carle, Eric. *The Grouchy Ladybug*. New York: Crowell, 1977. *Feeling Mad, 59.

Carle, Eric. *The Tiny Seed*. New York: Crowell, 1970. A Seed Grows, 7.

Carle, Eric. *The Very Hungry Caterpillar*. New York: Philomel, 1979. *Taste It! 21.

Carlson, Nancy. *Harriet and the Roller Coaster*. Minneapolis: Carolrhoda, 1982. The Don't Be Scared Storytime; 60, Feeling Foolish, 46.

Carlson, Nancy. *Harriet's Halloween Candy*. Minneapolis: Carolrhoda, 1982. *Trick or Treat, 71.

Carrick, Carol. *A Rabbit for Easter*; illus. by Donald Carrick. New York: Greenwillow, 1979. Easter Rabbits, 47.

Carrick, Carol. *Patrick's Dinosaurs*; illus. by Donald Carrick. New York: Clarion, 1983. Monster Bash! 55; *Dinosaurs, 17.

Castle, Sue. *Face Talk, Hand Talk, Body Talk*; illus. by Frances McLaughlin-Gill. Garden City, NY: Doubleday, 1977. Making Faces, 64.

Cendrars, Blaise. *Shadow*; trans. and illus. by Marcia Brown. New York: Scribner's, 1982. Shadow Play, 42.

The Chairy Tale. International Film Board, 1957. *Foolish Furniture, 74.

Chanover, Hyman, and Alice Hyman. *Happy Hanukkah Everybody*; illus. by Maurice Sendak. United Synagogue Commission on Jewish Education, 1954. *Happy Hanukkah, 53.

Charlie Needs a Cloak. 7 min. Weston Woods, 1977. *What Then? 28.

Charlip, Remy. *Fortunately*. New York: Four Winds, 1964. *What Then? 28.

Charlip, Remy, and Lillian Moore. *Hooray for Me!*; illus. by Vera B. Williams. New York: Parents', 1975. Feeling Glad! 58.

Chicken Soup With Rice. 5 min. Weston Woods, 1976. Chicken Soup, 98.

Child, Lydia Maria. *Over the River and Through the Woods*; illus. by Brinton Turkle. New York: Coward, 1974. *Thanksgiving Turkeys, 54.

Chönz, Selina. *A Bell for Ursli*; illus. by Alois Carigiet. New York: Walck, 1950. *Christmas Bells, 55.

Chönz, Selina. *The Snowstorm*; illus. by Alois Carigiet. New York: Walck 1958. The Snowy Day, 34.

Christini, Ermanno and Luigi Puricelli. *In the Pond*. Natick: Picture Book Studio, 1984. *Habitat: the Pond, 5.

Cleary, Beverly. *Lucky Chuck*; illus. by J. Winslow Higginbottom. New York: Morrow, 1984. Take Me Ridin' in Your Car, 70.

Clifton, Lucille. *The Boy Who Didn't Believe in Spring*; illus. by Brinton Turkle. New York: Dutton, 1973. It's Spring! 36.

Cloud Journeys. Van Nuys, CA: Learning Through Movement, 1982. *Feathered Babies, 37.

Coatsworth, Elizabeth. *Under the Green Willow*; illus. by Janina Domanska. New York: Macmillan, 1971. *Habitat: the Pond, 5.

Cobbs, Vicki. *Lots of Rot*; illus by Brian Schatell. Philadelphia: Lippincott, 1981. *Lots of Rot, 10.

Cole, Ann, Carolyn Haas, Elizabeth Heller, and Betty Weinberger. *A Pumpkin In a Pear Tree: Creative Ideas for Twelve Months of Holiday Fun*. Boston: Little, Brown, 1976. Happy Hanukkah, 53.

Cole, Joanna. *Cars and How They Go*; illus. by Gail Gibbons. New York: Crowell, 1983. Take Me Ridin' in Your Car, 70.

Cole, Joanna. *A Frog's Body*; photos by Jerome Wexler. New York: Morrow, 1980. Habitat: the Pond, 5.

Cole, Joanna. *A New Treasury of Children's Poetry*. Garden City, NY: Doubleday, 1984. *Habitat: the Pond, 5; *Foolish Furniture, 79; *Your Own Special Rock, 18.

Cole, Peter. See Doug Kincaid.

Cole, William. *Dinosaurs and Beasts of Yore*; illus. Susan Watt. New York: Philomel, 1979. *Dinosaurs, 17.

Cole, William. *Frances Face-Maker*; illus. by Tomi Ungerer. New York: Collins-World, 1963. *Making Faces, 64.

Cole, William. *I Went to the Animal Fair*; illus. by Colette Rosselli. Cleveland: World, 1958. *Feathered Babies, 37.

Cole, William. *Oh, Such Foolishness!*; illus. by Tomie de Paola. New York: Lippincott, 1978. *Freaky Food, 78; *Foolish Furniture, 79; *Making Faces, 64; *The New Baby, 63.

Colter's Hell. 14 min. Filmmaker: Robin Lehman. Phoenix, 1973.

Cooney, Barbara. *Miss Rumphius*. New York: Viking, 1982. Habitat: The Garden, 3.

Craft, Ruth and Erik Blegvad. *The Winter Bear*. New York: Atheneum, 1978. Snow Bears, 35.

Crews, Donald. *Flying*. New York: Greenwillow, 1986. But Will It Fly? 11.

Crews, Donald. *Harbor*. New York: Greenwillow, 1982. *Fourth of July Parade, 48.

Crews, Donald. *Parade*. New York: Greenwillow, 1983. *Fourth of July Parade, 48.

Crews, Robert. *Freight Train*. New York: Greenwillow, 1978. *Here Comes the Train, 69; Color Me Red! 26.

Cristini, Ermanno, and Luigi Puricelli. *In My Garden*. New York: Alphabet Press, 1981. Down in the Grass, 6.

Dabcovich, Lydia. *Sleepy Bear*. New York: Dutton, 1980. Snow Bears. 35.

Dance-A-Story, Sing-A-Song by Marcia Berman and Anne Lief Barlin. B/B Records #B/B 110. Van Nuys, CA: Learning Through Movement. *Dancing Dolls, 100.

Darling, Lois, and Louis Darling. *Worms*. New York: Morrow, 1973. *Meet a Worm, 8.

Daugherty, James. *Andy and the Lion*. New York: Viking, 1938. *Happy Lions, 72.

Dayrell, Elphingstone. *Why the Sun and Moon Live in the Sky*; illus. by Blair Lent. New York: Houghton Mifflin, 1968. *Sun! 41.

Degen, Bruce. *Jamberry*. New York: Harper & Row, 1983. *Blueberry, Strawberry, Jamberry! 87.

Delany, A. *Monster Tracks?* New York: Harper & Row, 1981. Monster Bash! 85.

De Paola, Tomie. *Charlie Needs a Cloak*. Englewood Cliffs, NJ: Prentice-Hall, 1973. *What Then? 28.

De Paola, Tomie, illus. *The Comic Adventures of Old Mother Hubbard and Her Dog*. New York: Harcourt, 1981. Problem Pups, 77.

De Paola, Tomie. *Fin McCoul: The Giant of Knockmany Hill*. New York: Holiday, 1981. *Saint Patrick's Day Parade, 45.

De Paola, Tomie. *Watch Out for the Chicken Feet in Your Soup*. Englewood Cliffs, NJ: Prentice-Hall, 1974. Chicken Soup, 98.

De Paola, Tomie. *When Everyone Was Fast Asleep*. New York: Holiday House, 1976. Dream Time, 80.

De Regniers, Beatrice Schenk. *A Little House of Your Own*; illus. by Irene Haas. New York: Harcourt, 1954. Just Me! 62; My House, My Home, 68.

De Regniers, Beatrice Schenk. *May I Bring a Friend?*; illus. by Beni Montresor. New York: Atheneum, 1964. *A Visit to the King and Queen, 86; Mailman, Mailman, Bring Me a Letter! 44.

De Regniers, Beatrice Schenk. *The Shadow Book*; photos by Isobel Gordon. New York: Harcourt, 1960. Shadow Play, 42.

Dewey, Ariane. See Jose Aruego.

Dinosaur. 14 min. Filmmaker: Will Vinton. Pyramid, 1981. *Dinosaurs, 17.

Domanska, Janina. *Din Dan Don It's Christmas*. New York: Greenwillow, 1975. *Christmas Bells, 55.

Domanska, Janina. *What Do You See?* New York: Macmillan, 1974. Down in the Grass, 6.

Dubanevich, Arlene. *Pigs at Christmas*. New York: Bradley, 1986. Portly Pigs, 76.

Dubanevich, Arlene. *Pig William*. New York: Bradley, 1985. Portly Pigs, 76.

Duvoisin, Roger. *The Importance of Crocus*. New York: Knopf, 1980. Just Me!, 62.

Emberley, Barbara, adapter. *Drummer Hoff*; illus. by Ed Emberley.

Englewood Cliffs, NJ: Prentice-Hall, 1967. *Hear It! 20; *Drummer Hoff, 99; Print It! 91.

Emberley, Ed. *The Parade Book*. Boston: Little, Brown, 1962. Fourth of July Parade, 48.

Emberley, Edward. *Green Says Go*. Boston: Little, Brown, 1968. Color me Red! 26.

Ernst, Kathryn. *Mr. Tamarin's Trees*; illus. by Diane de Groat. New York: Crown, 1976. *All Falling Down, 29.

Ets, Marie Hall. *Another Day*. New York: Viking, 1953. Fourth of July Parade, 48.

Ets, Marie Hall. *Elephant in a Well*. New York: Viking, 1972. *Elephants, Babies, and Elephant Babies, 73.

Ets, Marie Hall. *Gilberto and the Wind*. New York: Viking, 1963. *But Will It Fly? 11; *Wind Power, 12.

Ets, Marie Hall. *In the Forest*. New York: Viking, 1944. Fourth of July Parade, 48.

Ets, Marie Hall. *Play With Me!* New York: Viking, 1955. *Feeling Glad! 58.

Ets, Marie Hall. *The Little Old Automobile*. New York: Viking, 1948. *Take Me Ridin' in Your Car, 70.

Evans, Mel. *The Tiniest Sound*; illus. by Ed Young. Garden City, NY: Doubleday, 1969. Hear It! 20.

Fatio, Louise. *The Happy Lion*; illus. by Roger Duvoisin. New York: McGraw-Hill, 1954. *Voici Paris! 90; *Happy Lions, 72.

Felix, Monique. *The Story of a Little Mouse Trapped in a Book*. La Jolla, CA: Green Tiger, 1980. Mice Are Nice, 75.

Field, Eugene. *Wynken, Blynken, and Nod*; illus. by Barbara Cooney. New York: Hastings House, 1964. *On the High Seas, 71; Harvest Moon, 31.

Fischer, Hans. *The Birthday*. New York: Harcourt, 1954. *Happy Birthday to Me! 57.

Fischer, Hans. *Pitschi*. New York: Harcourt, 1953. Black Cats, 33.

Fish, Helen Dean. *When the Root Children Wake Up*; illus. by Sibylle Von Olfers. New York: Lippincott, 1930. It's Spring! 31.

Fisher, Aileen. *Once We Went on a Picnic*; illus. by Tony Chen. New York: Crowell, 1975. *Habitat: the Field, 1.

Fitzpatrick, Julie. *In the Air*. Morristown, NJ: Silver Burdett, 1984. But Will It Fly?, 11.

Flack, Marjorie. *Angus and the Cat*. Garden City, NY: Doubleday, 1971. *Black Cats, 33.

Flack, Marjorie. *Angus and the Ducks*. New York: Doubleday, 1930. *Problem Pups, 77.

Flack, Marjorie. *Angus Lost*. New York: Doubleday, 1932. *Problem Pups, 77.

Flack, Marjorie. *Ask Mr. Bear*. New York: Macmillan, 1932. *Happy Birthday to Me! 57.

Foolish Frog. 8 min. Filmmaker: Gene Deitch. Weston Woods, 1973. Frog Songs, 96.

Foster, John. *A First Poetry Book*. London: Oxford University Press, 1979. *Down in the Grass, 6.

Fowke, Edith. *Sally Go Round the Sun*. Garden City, NY: Doubleday, 1969. Elephants, Babies, and Elephant Babies, 73.

Fox Went Out on a Chilly Night. See Peter Spier.

Françoise (Seignobosc). *The Big Rain*. New York: Scribner's, 1961. The Rainy Day, 40.

Françoise (Seignobosc). *Jeanne-Marie Counts Her Sheep*. New York: Scribner's, 1951. *Number Rhumba, 25.

Françoise (Seignobosc). *Jeanne-Marie in Gay Paris*. New York: Scribner's, 1956. Voici Paris! 90.

Françoise. *Minou*. New York: Scribner's, 1962. Voici Paris! 90.

Françoise. *Noel for Jeanne-Marie*. New York: Scribner's, 1961. *Here Comes Santa Claus! 56; *Christmas Bells, 55.

Françoise (Seignobosc). *Springtime for Jeanne-Marie*. New York: Scribner's, 1955. *It's Spring! 36.

Frankel, Alona. *The Family of Tiny White Elephants*. New York: Barron's, 1978, 1980. The New Baby, 63.

Frasconi, Antonio. *See and Say; Guarda e Parla; Mira y Habla; Regarde et Parle*. New York: Harcourt, 1955. Print It! 91.

Freeman, Don. *Corduroy*. New York: Viking, 1968. *Teddy Bears Go Dancing, 81; *Button, Button, 67.

Freeman, Don. *A Rainbow of My Own*. New York: Viking, 1966. Color Me Red, 26.

Friskey, Margaret. *Seven Diving Ducks*; illus. by Jean Morey. Chicago: Children's Press, 1965. Feathered Babies, 37.

Frost, Robert. *Stopping By Woods on a Snowy Evening*; illus. by Susan Jeffers. New York: Dutton, 1978. *The Snowy Day, 34.

Funny Bone Read-Alongs: Does My Room Come Alive at Night? Read by Sandy Duncan. Caedmon. Cassette and Book. Foolish Furniture, 74.

Gag, Wanda. *Millions of Cats*. New York: Coward, 1928. *Spring Kittens, 38.

Galdone, Joanna. *The Little Girl and the Big Bear*; illus. by Paul Galdone. New York: Houghton Mifflin/Clarion, 1960. *Russian Winter, 89.

Galdone, Paul. *King of the Cats*. Adapted and illus. by Paul Galdone. Written by Joseph Jacobs. New York: Houghton Mifflin, 1980. Black Cats, 33.

Galdone, Paul. *The Monkey and the Crocodile*. New York: Seabury, 1969. *Crocodiles and Alligators, 74.

Galdone, Paul. *Old Mother Hubbard and Her Dog*. New York: McGraw-Hill, 1960. *Rhyme, Rhyme, Rhyme, 83.

Galdone, Paul. *The Old Woman and Her Pig*. New York: McGraw-Hill, 1960. *Portly Pigs, 76.

Gans, Roma. *Rock Collecting*; illus. by Holly Keller. New York: Crowell, 1984. Your Own Special Rock, 18.

Gantos, Jack. *Rotten Ralph*; illus. by Nicole Rubel. New York: Houghton Mifflin, 1976. Black Cats, 33.

Gantschev, Ivan. *Otto the Bear*; trans. by Karen M. Klockner. Boston: Little, Brown, 1985. Snow Bears, 35.

Garelick, May. *Down to the Beach*; illus. by Barbara Cooney. New York: Four Winds, 1973. *Habitat: The Sea, 4.

Garelick, May. *Sounds of a Summer Night*; illus. by Beni Montressor. New York: Young Scott, n.d. Hear It! 20.

Garelick, May, and Barbara Brenner. *The Tremendous Tree Book*; illus. by Fred Brenner. New York: Four Winds, 1979. Habitat: the Tree, 2.

Gay, Michel. *Little Boat*. New York: Macmillan, 1985. On The High Seas, 71.

Geisel, Theodore. See Theo. Le Sieg; Dr. Seuss.

Geisert, Arthur. *Pigs from A to Z*. Boston: Houghton Mifflin, 1956. Portly Pigs, 76.

Gerstein, Mordicai. *Roll Over*. New York: Crown, 1984. Number Rhumba, 25.

Getz, Arthur. *Hamilton Duck's Springtime Story*. New York: Golden Press, 1974. *Smell It! 24; *It's Spring! 36.

Gibbons, Gail. *Boat Book*. New York: Holiday House, 1983. On the High Seas, 71.

Gibbons, Gail. *Halloween*. New York: Holiday House, 1984. Ghosts and Witches, 50.

Gibbons, Gail. *The Post Office Book: Mail and How It Moves*. New York: Crowell, 1982. Mailman, Mailman, Bring Me a Letter, 44.

Gibbons, Gail. *The Seasons of Arnold's Apple Tree*. San Diego: Harcourt, 1984. Apple Day, 30.

Gibbons, Gail. *Thanksgiving Day*. New York: Holiday House, 1983. Thanksgiving Turkeys, 52.

Ginsburg, Mirra. *The Chick and the Duckling*; illus. by Jose Aruego and Ariane Dewey. New York: Macmillan, 1972. *Feathered Babies, 37; *Copy Cats, 82.

Ginsburg, Mirra. *How the Sun Was Brought Back to the Sky*; illus. by Jose Aruego and Ariane Dewey. New York: Macmillan, 1975. Sun! 41.

Ginsburg, Mirra. *Mushroom in the Rain*; illus. by Jose Aruego and Ariane Dewey. New York: Macmillan, 1974. *The Rainy Day, 40; *A Mushroom Is Growing, 9.

Ginsburg, Mirra. *The Strongest One of All*; illus. by Jose Aruego and Ariane Dewey. New York: Greenwillow, 1977. *Sun! 41.

Ginsburg, Mirra. *Three Kittens*; trans. by V. Suteyev; illus. by Giulio Maestro. New York: Crown, 1973. *Spring Kittens, 38.

Ginsburg, Mirra. *Where Does the Sun Go at Night?*; illus. by Jose Aruego and Ariane Dewey. New York: Greenwillow, 1977. *Sun! 41.

Glazer, Tom. *Do Your Ears Hang Low? Fifty More Musical Fingerplays*. Garden City, NY: Doubleday, 1980. *Feeling Glad, 58.

Glazer, Tom. *Music for Ones and Twos*. Garden City, NY: Doubleday, 1983. *Take Me Ridin' in Your Car! 70; *Sun! 41.

Goffstein, M. B. *A Little Schubert*. New York: Harper & Row, 1972. *A Little Schubert, 95.

Goffstein, M. B. *Fish for Supper*. New York: Dial, 1976. *What Then? 28

Goffstein, M. B. *Laughing Latkes*. New York; Farrar, 1981. *Happy Hanukkah, 53.

Goffstein, M. B. *Me and My Captain*. New York: Farrar, 1974. On the High Seas, 71.

Goffstein, M. B. *Sleepy People*. New York: Farrar, 1966. Sleeping Storytime, 65.

Goodall, John S. *Paddy's New Hat*. New York: Atheneum, 1980. What Then? 28.

Goudey, Alice E. *The Day We Saw the Sun Come Up*; illus. by Adrienne Adams. New York: Scribner's, 1961. Sun! 41.

Goudey, Alice E. *Houses from the Sea*; illus. by Adrienne Adams. New York: Scribner's, 1959. *Habitat: The Sea, 4.

Graham, John. *I Love You Mouse*; illus. by Tomie de Paola. New York: Harcourt, 1976. Mice Are Nice, 75.

Graham, Margaret Bloy. See Gene Zion

Gray, William D. *What We Find When We Look at Molds*; illus. by Howard Berelson. New York: McGraw-Hill, 1970. Lots of Rot, 10.

Green, Mary McBurney. *Is It Hard? Is It Easy?*; illus. by Len Gittlemen. New York: Young Scott, 1960. Just Me! 62.

Gregor, Arthur S. See Ylla.

Gretz, Susanna. *It's Your Turn, Roger!* New York: Dial, 1985. My House, My Home, 68.

Gretz, Susanna. *Teddy Bears One to Ten.* Chicago: Follett, 1969. Teddy Bears Go Dancing, 81; Number Rhumba, 25.

Grifalconi, Ann. *Village of Round and Square Houses.* Boston: Little, Brown, 1986. Volcanoes Erupting, 19.

Haas, Irene. *The Maggie B.* New York: Atheneum, 1983. On the High Seas, 71.

Hague, Kathleen. *Alphabears: An ABC Book*; illus. by Michael Hague. New York: Holt, 1984. Teddy Bears Go Dancing, 81.

Haley, Gail E. *A Story A Story.* New York: Atheneum, 1970. *Print It! 91.

Haller, Dorcas Woodbury. See Virginia Allen Jensen.

Halloween. Golden LP 242. Port Washington, New York: Den-Lan Music, 1969. *Pumpkin Magic, 49; *Ghosts and Witches, 50; *Trick or Treat, 51.

The Happy Lion. 7 min. Macmillan, n.d. *Happy Lions, 72; *Voici Paris! 90.

Harlow, Joan Hiatt. *Shadow Bear*; illus. by Jim Arnosky. Garden City, NY: Doubleday, 1981. Snow Bears, 35; Shadow Play, 42.

Hart, Jane. *Singing Bee!*; illus. by Anita Lobel. New York: Lothrop, Lee & Shephard, 1982. Happy Birthday to Me! 57.

Haseley, Dennis. *The Old Banjo*; illus. by Stephen Gammell. New York: Macmillan, 1983. *Frog Songs, 96.

Hautzig, Esther. *At Home: A Visit in Four Languages*; illus. by Aliki. New York: Macmillan, 1969. Russian Winter, 89.

Hawkins, Colin and Jacqui Hawkins. *Jen the Hen.* New York: Putnam's, 1985. *Mailman, Mailman, Bring Me a Letter, 44.

Hawkins, Colin and Jacqui Hawkins. *Mig the Pig.* New York: Putnam's, 1984. *Rhyme, Rhyme, Rhyme, 83.

Hefter, Richard. *El Libro de la Fresa de Los Colores: Un Libro de la Fresa*; Trad. Enric Monforte. Barcelona: Editorial Juventud, S.A. Provenca, 101, 1975. Color Me Red!, 26.

Heller, Ruth. *The Reason for a Flower.* New York: Grosset & Dunlop, 1983. *Habitat: the Garden, 3.

Hertza, Ole. *Tobias Has a Birthday*; trans. Tobi Tobias. Minneapolis: Carolrhoda, 1984. Happy Birthday to Me! 57.

Heyward, DuBose. *The Country Bunny and the Little Gold Shoes*; illus. Marjorie Flack. New York: Houghton Mifflin, 1939. Easter Rabbits, 47.

Hill, Eric. *Where's Spot?* New York: Putnam's, 1980. *Problem Pups, 77.

Hirsh, Marilyn. *Potato Pancakes All Around.* *Happy Hanukkah.

Hoban, Russell. *A Baby Sister for Frances*; illus. by Lillian Hoban. New York: Harper & Row, 1970. The New Baby, 63.

Hoban, Russell. *A Birthday for Frances*; illus. by Lillian Hoban. New York: Harper & Row, 1968. Happy Birthday to Me! 57.

Hoban, Russell. *Bedtime for Frances*; illus. by Garth Williams. New York: Harper & Row, 1960. The Don't Be Scared Storytime, 60; *See It! 23.

Hoban, Russell. *Bread and Jam for Frances*; illus. by Lillian Hoban. New York: Harper & Row, 1964. *Taste It! 21.

Hoban, Russell. *The Little Brute Family*; illus. by Lillian Hoban. New York: Macmillan, 1966. Feeling Mad, 59.

Hoban, Tana. *Is It Red, Is It Yellow, Is It Blue?* New York: Greenwillow, 1978. Color Me Red! 26.

Hoban, Tana. *Is It Rough, Is It Smooth? Is It Shiny?* New York: Greenwillow, 1984. Touch It! 22.

Hoban, Tana. *Take Another Look.* New York: Greenwillow, 1981. *Take a Closer Look! 16.

Hoberman, Mary Ann. *A House is a House is a House for Me*; illus. by Betty Fraser. New York: Viking, 1978. *My House, My Home, 68.

Hogan, Paula Z. *The Life Cycle of the Crocodile*; illus. by Larry Mikec. Milwaukee: Raintree, 1979. Crocodiles and Alligators, 74.

Hogan, Paula Z. *The Life Cycle of a Dandelion*; illus. by Yoshi Miyake. Milwaukee: Raintree, 1979. *Habitat: the Field, 2; *A Seed Grows, 7.

Hogan, Paula Z. *The Life Cycle of the Elephant*; illus. by Milwaukee: Raintree, 1979. Elephants, Babies, and Elephant Babies, 73.

Hogan, Paul Z. *Life Cycle of the Frog*; illus. by Geri K. Strigenz. Milwaukee: Raintree, 1979. Habitat: the Pond, 5.

Hogan, Paula Z. *The Life Cycle of the Oak Tree*; illus. Kinuko Craft. Milwaukee; Raintree, 1979. All Falling Down, 29.

Hogrogian, Nonny. *Apples.* New York: Macmillan, 1972. Apple Day, 30.

Holl, Adelaide. *The Runaway Giant*; illus. by Mamoru Funai. New York: Lothrop, 1968. *The Snowy Day, 34.

Holling, C. *Pagoo.* New York: Houghton Mifflin, 1957. Habitat: The Sea, 4.

Homan, Dianne. *In Christina's Toolbox*; illus. by Mary Heine. Chapel Hill, NC: Lollipop Power, 1981. Tools Do Work For Us! 13.

Hopkins, Lee Bennett. *Best Friends*; illus. by James Watts. New York: Harper & Row, 1986. Be My Friend, 43; Just Me! 62.

Hopkins, Lee Bennett. *Hey-How for Halloween!*; illus. by Janet McCoffery. New York: Harcourt 1974. *Pumpkin Magic, 49.

Hopkins, Lee Bennett. *Munching: Poems About Eating*; illus. by Nelle Davis. Boston: Little, Brown, 1985. *Freaky Food, 78.

Hopkins, Lee Bennett. *Surprises*; illus. by Megan Lloyd. New York: Harper, & Row, 1984. *But Will It Fly? 11; *The Snowy Day, 34; Just Me! 62.

Horwitz, Elinor Lander. *When the Sky is Like Lace*; illus. by Barbara Cooney. New York: Lippincott, 1975. Dream Time, 80.

House Cats. 5 min. Phoenix, 1986. *Black Cats, 33.

Howell, Lynn, and Richard Howell. *Winifred's New Bed*. New York: Knopf, 1985. Sleeping Storytime, 65

Hurd, Thacher. *The Quiet Evening*. New York: Greenwillow, 1978. *Hear It! 20.

Hutchins, Pat. *Good-night Owl!* New York: Macmillan, 1972. *Owls in the Night, 32.

Hutchins, Pat. *Happy Birthday Sam*. New York: Greenwillow, 1978. *Happy Birthday to Me! 57; *Classifying Chairs, 15.

Hutchins, Pat. *Rosie's Walk*. New York: Macmillan, 1968. *Thanksgiving Turkeys, 52; *Touch It! 22; *Barnyard Dance, 97.

Hutchins, Pat. *Titch*. New York: Macmillan, 1971. *A Seed Grows! 7.

Hutchins, Pat. *The Wind Blew*. New York: Macmillan, 1974. Wind Power, 12.

Icks, Marguerite. *The Book of Religious Holidays and Celebration*. New York: Dodd, Mead, 1966. *Happy Hanukkah, 53.

Irving, Jan and Robin Currie. *Mudluscious: Stories and Activities Featuring Food for Preschool Children*. Boulder: Libraries Unlimited, 1986. Freaky Food, 78.

Isadora, Rachel. *I Hear*. New York: Greenwillow, 1985. Hear It! 20.

Isadora, Rachel. *I Touch*. New York: Greenwillow, 1985. *Touch It! 22.

Iwamure, Kazuo. *Tan Tan's Hat*. New York: Bradbury, 1983. Spring Hats, 39.

Iwasaki, Chihiro. *The Birthday Wish*. New York: McGraw-Hill, 1974. Happy Birthday to Me! 57.

Jackson, Kathryn. *Dinosaurs*; illus. by Jay H. Matternes. National Geographic Society, 1972. *Dinosaurs, 17.

Jacobs, Joseph. See Paul Galdone.

Janice. *Little Bear Marches in the St. Patrick's Day Parade*; illus. by

Mariana. New York: Lothrop, 1967. *St. Patrick's Day Parade, 45.

Jaye, Mary Tinnin. *Making Music Your Own*. Morristown, NJ: Silver Burdett, 1971.

Joasse, Barbara M. *Fourth of July*; illus. by Emily Arnold McCully. New York: Knopf, 1985. *Fourth of July Parade, 48.

Johnson, Crockett. *Harold and the Purple Crayon*. New York: Harpers, 1955. *Looking at a Line, 92.

Johnson, LaVerne. *Night Noises*; illus. by Martha Alexander. New York: Parents' 1968. Hear It! 20.

Johnston, Hannah Lyons. *From Seed to Jack-O-Lantern*; photos by Daniel Dorn. New York: Lothrop, 1974. Pumpkin Magic, 49.

Jonas, Ann. *The Trek*. New York: Greenwillow, 1975. Take a Closer Look! 16.

Jonas, Ann. *When You Were a Baby*. New York: Greenwillow, 1982. The New Baby, 63.

Jones, Rebecca C. *The Biggest, Meanest, Ugliest Dog in the Whole Wide World*; illus. by Wendy Watson. New York: Macmillan, 1982. Problem Pups, 77.

Jordon, Helene J. *Seeds by Wind and Water*. New York: Crowell, 1962. A Seed Grows, 7.

Joslin, Sesyle. *La Petite Famille*; illus. by John Alcorn. New York: Harcourt, 1964. *Wheels and Gears, 14.; *Voici Paris! 90.; *Crocodiles and Alligators, 74.

Kahl, Virginia. *The Duchess Bakes a Cake*. New York: Scribner's, 1955. A Visit to the King and Queen, 86.

Kalan, Robert. *Blue Sea*; illus. by Donald Crews. New York: Greenwillow, 1979. *Habitat: The Sea, 4.

Keats, Ezra Jack. *A Letter to Amy*. New York: Harper, 1968. *Mailman, Mailman Bring Me a Letter, 44; *Happy Birthday to Me! 57.

Keats, Ezra Jack. *Dreams*. New York: Collier, 1974. *Shadow Play, 42.

Keats, Ezra Jack. *Jennie's Hat*. New York: Harper & Row, 1966. *Spring Hats, 39.

Keats, Ezra Jack. *Peter's Chair*. New York: Harper, 1967. *Classifying Chairs, 15; *The New Baby, 63.

Keats, Ezra Jack. *The Little Drummer Boy*. New York: Macmillan, 1968. *Christmas Lullabies, 54.

Keats, Ezra Jack. *The Snowy Day*. New York: Viking, 1962. *The Snowy Day, 34.

Keats, Ezra Jack. *The Trip*. New York: Greenwillow, 1978. *Trick or Treat, 51.

Keats, Ezra Jack. *Whistle for Willie*. New York: Viking, 1964. *Paste a Collage! 93.

Keith, Eros. *Rr——aah*. New York: Bradbury, 1969. Habitat: the Pond, 5.

Kellogg, Steven. *Pinkerton Behave!* New York: Dial, 1979. Problem Pups, 77.

Kennedy, Jimmy. *The Teddy Bear's Picnic*; illus. by Alexandra Day. La Jolla, CA: Green Tiger, 1983. *Teddy Bears Go Dancing, 81.

Kessler, Leonard. *What's In a Line?* New York: Scott, 1951. *Looking at a Line, 92.

Kettlekamp, Larry. *Shadows*. New York: Morrow, 1957. Shadow Play, 42.

Key, Francis Scott. *The Star Spangled Banner*; illus. by Peter Spier. New York: Doubleday, 1963. *Fourth of July Parade, 48.

Kimura, Yasuko. *Fergus and the Snow Deer*. New York: McGraw-Hill, 1978. *Snow Bears, 35.; Dream Time, 80.

Kincaid, Doug and Peter Cole. *Ears and Hearing*. Read and Do Series. New York: Rourke, 1983. Hear It! 20.

Kincaid, Doug and Peter Cole. *Eyes and Looking*. Read and Do Series. Windermere, FL: Rourke, 1983. See It! 23.

Kincaid, Doug and Peter Cole. *Taste and Smell*. Read and Do Series. Windermere, FL: Rourke, 1983. Taste It! 21.

Kincaid, Doug and Peter Cole. *Touch and Feel*. Read and Do Series. Windermere, FL: Rourke, 1983. Touch It! 22.

Kipling, Rudyard. *The Elephant's Child*; illus. by Tim Raglin. New York: Knopf, 1979. Elephants, Babies, and Elephant Babies, 73.

Kline, Suzy. *Don't Touch*; illus. by Dora Leder. Nile, IL: Albert Whitman, 1985. *Touch It! 22; *Mold It! 94.

Kohl, Herbert. *The View From the Oak: The Private World of Other Creatures*; illus. by Roger Bayless. San Francisco/New York: Sierra Club/Scribner's, 1977. Habitat: the Tree, 2.

Krahn, Fernando. *Amanda and the Mysterious Carpet*. New York: Clarion, 1985. Foolish Furniture, 79.

Kraus, Robert. *Whose Mouse Are You?*; illus. by Jose Aruego. New York: Macmillan, 1970. *Mice Are Nice, 75.

Krauss, Ruth. *Bears*; illus. by Phyllis Rowand. New York: Harper & Row, 1948. *Rhyme, Rhyme, Rhyme, 83.

Krauss, Ruth. *The Carrot Seed*; illus. by Crockett Johnson. New York: Harper & Row, 1945. *Feeling Glad! 58; *A Seed Grows, 7.

Krauss, Ruth. *The Happy Day*; illus. by Marc Simont. New York: Harper, & Row, 1949. *It's Spring! 36.

Krauss, Ruth. *The Happy Egg*; illus. by Crockett Johnson. Merrick, NY: O'Hara, 1967. *Feathered Babies, 37.

Krauss, Ruth. *Somebody Spilled the Sky*; illus. Eleanor Hazard. New York: Greewillow, 1976, 1979. *Problem Pups, 77; Just Me! 62.

Krauss, Ruth. *A Very Special House*; illus. by Maurice Sendak. New York: Harper & Row, 1953. *Looking at a Line, 92.; Foolish Furniture, 79; *Classifying Chairs, 15; *My House, My Home, 68.

Krieger, David L. *Too Many Stones*. New York: Young Scott, 1970. *Your Own Very Special Rock, 18.

Krum, Charlotte. *The Four Riders*; illus. by Katharine Evans. Chicago: Follett, 1953. *Thanksgiving Turkeys, 52.

Kumin, Maxine. *The Microscope*; illus. by Arnold Lobel. New York: Harper & Row, 1984. *Take a Closer Look! 16.

Kunhart, Dorothy. *Pat the Bunny*. Racine, WI: Western, 1942. Touch It! 22.

Kuskin, Karla. *All Sizes of Noises*. New York: Harper & Row, 1962. *Hear It! 20.

Kuskin, Karla. *The Philharmonic Gets Dressed*; illus. by Marc Simont. New York: Harper & Row, 1982. Button, Button, 67.; *A Little Schubert, 95.

Kuskin, Karla. *Roar and More*. New York: Harper & Row, 1956. *Happy Lions, 72.

Kuskin, Karla. *Something Sleeping in the Hall*. New York: Harper & Row, 1985. *Problem Pups, 77.; *Frog Songs, 96.

La Fontaine, Jean de. *The Hare and the Tortoise*; illus. by Brian Wildsmith. New York: Oxford University Press, 1966. *Is It Fast? Is It Slow?, 27.

La Fontaine, Jean de. *The Lion and the Rat*; illus. by Brian Wildsmith. New York: Watts, 1963. *Happy Lions, 72.

La Fontaine, Jean de. *The North Wind and the Sun*; illus. by Brian Wildsmith. New York: Watts, 1963. *Wind Power, 12.

Landeck, Beatrice. *More Songs to Grow On*. Edward B. Marks, 1954. Habitat: The Sea, 4.

Langstaff, John M. *Ol' Dan Tucker*; illus. by Joe Krush. New York: Harcourt, 1963. *Barnyard Dance, 97.

Langstaff, John M. *Over in the Meadow*; illus. by Feodor Rojankovsky. New York: Harcourt, 1957. *Number Rhumba, 25.

Langstaff, John, and Feodor Rojankovsky. *Frog Went A-Courtin'*. New York: Harcourt, 1967. *Frog Songs, 96.

Larrick, Nancy. *Piping Down the Valleys Wild*. New York: Delacorte, 1968. *It's Spring! 36.

Lauber, Patricia. *Volcano: The Eruption and Healing of Mount St. Helens*. New York: Bradbury, 1986. Volcanoes Erupt! 19.

Leaf, Munro. *Wee Gillis*; illus. by Robert Lawson. New York: Viking, 1938. *Highland Fling, 88.

Lear, Edward. *Hilary Knight's The Owl and the Pussy-Cat*. New York: Macmillan, 1983. *Be My Friend, 43.

LeClair, Alger. See Sorche Nic Leodhas.

Legend of Johnny Appleseed. Walt Disney, 1948.

Lenski, Lois. *The Little Airplane*. New York: Walck, 1938. But Will It Fly? 11.

Lenski, Lois. *The Little Auto*. New York: Walck, 1934. Take Me Ridin' in Your Car, 70.

Lenski, Lois. *The Little Train*. New York: Oxford, 1940. Here Comes the Train! 69.

Lent, Blair. *From King Bogen's Hall to Nothing at All: A Collection of Improbable Houses and Unusual Places Found in Traditional Rhymes and Limericks*; illus. by Blair Lent. Boston: Little, Brown, 1967. *My House, My Home, 68.

Leodhas, Sorche Nic. *All In the Morning Early*; illus. by Evaline Ness. New York: Holt, 1963. *Highland Fling, 88.

Leodhas, Sorche Nic. *Always Room For One More*; illus. by Nonny Hogrogian. New York: Holt, 1965. *Highland Fling, 88.

Leodhas, Sorche Nic. *Kellyburn Braes*; illus. Evaline Ness. New York: Harcourt, 1968. Highland Fling, 88.

Le Sieg, Theo. *Come Over to My House*; illus. by Ricard Erdoes. New York: Random House, 1966. My House, My Home, 68.

Lesikin, Joan. *Down the Road*. Englewood Cliffs, NJ: Prentice-Hall, 1978. *Down in the Grass, 6.

Lesikin, Joan. *In My Garden*. Englewood Cliffs, NJ: Prentice-Hall, 1979. *Down in the Grass, 6.

Lester, Alison. *Clive Eats Alligators*. Boston: Houghton Mifflin, 1986. Just Me! 62.

Lester, Helen. *Cora Copycat*. New York: E.P. Dutton, 1979. *Copy Cats, 82.

LeTord, Bijou. *Rabbit Seeds*. New York: Four Winds, 1984. A Seed Grows, 7.

Levine, Joseph. See Tillie S. Pine.

Lewis, Richard. *In a Spring Garden*; illus. by Ezra Jack Keats. New York: Dial, 1965. *Wonderful Words, 84; *Habitat: the Pond, 5; *It's Spring! 36.

Lewis, Thomas. *Hill of Fire*; illus. by Joan Sandin. New York: Harper & Row, 1971. *Volcanoes Erupt! 19.

Lexau, Joan M. *Crocodile and Hen*; illus. by Joan Sandin. New York: Harper & Row, 1960. Crocodiles and Alligators, 74.

Lindgren, Astrid. *The Tomten and the Fox*; illus. by Harald Wiberg. New York: Coward, 1965. *The Caring Day, 61; *The Snowy Day, 34.

Lionni, Leo. *Alexander and the Wind-Up Mouse*. New York: Pantheon, 1969. *Mice Are Nice, 75; *Paste a Collage! 93.

Lionni, Leo. *Inch by Inch*. New York: Astor-Honor, 1960. *Paste a Collage! 93; *Habitat: the Field, 1.

Lionni, Leo. *Let's Make Rabbits*. New York: Pantheon, 1982. Paste a Collage! 93.

Lionni, Leo. *Little Blue and Little Yellow*. New York: Obolensky, 1959. *Color Me Red! 26.

Lionni, Leo. *On My Beach are Many Pebbles*. New York: Astor-Honor, 1961. *Your Own Special Rock, 18.

Lionni, Leo. *Swimmy*. New York: Pantheon, 1963. *Habitat: The Sea, 4; *Print It! 91.

Littlefield, William. *The Whiskers of Ho Ho*; illus. by Vladimir Bobri. New York: Lothrop, 1958. *Easter Rabbits, 47.

Livingston, Myra Cohn. *Celebrations*; illus. by Leonard Everett Fisher. New York: Holiday House, 1985. *Fourth of July Parade, 48.

Livingston, Myra Cohn. *Earth Songs*; illus. by Leonard Everett Fisher. New York: Holiday House, 1986. *Your Own Special Rock, 18.

Livingston, Myra Cohn. *Poems for Jewish Holidays*; illus. by Lloyd Bloom. New York: Holiday House, 1986. *Happy Hanukkah, 53.

Lloyd, Errol. *Nini at Carnival*. New York: Crowell, 1978. Fourth of July Parade, 48.

Loasse, Barbara M. *Fourth of July*; illus. by Emily Arnold McCully. New York: Knopf, 1985. Fourth of July Parade, 48.

Lobel, Arnold. *Frog and Toad Are Friends*. New York: Harper & Row, 1970. Button, Button, 67.

Lobel, Arnold. *Grasshopper on the Road*. New York: Harper & Row, 1978. Just Me! 62.

Lobel, Arnold. *The Man Who Took the Indoors Out*. New York: Harper & Row, 1974. Foolish Furniture, 79.

Lobel, Arnold. *Mouse Tales*. New York: Harper & Row, 1972. *See It! 23.

Lobel, Arnold. *The Rose in My Garden*; illus. by Anita Lobel. New York: Greenwillow, 1984. Habitat: the Garden, 3.

Lullabies Go Jazz by John Crosse. Sunland, CA: Jazz Cat Productions, 1985. Christmas Lullabies, 54.

Lullaby. 4 min. International Film Bureau, 1975. *Dream Time, 80.

Lund, Doris H. *Attic of the Wind*; illus. by Ati Forberg. New York: Parents', 1966. Wind Power, 12.

Mabey, Richard. *Oak & Company*; illus. by Clare Roberts. New York: Greenwillow, 1983. *Habitat: the Tree, 2.

MacDonald, Margaret. *When the Lights Go Out*. New York: H.W. Wilson, 1988. *Russian Winter, 89.; *Black Cats, 33.

Maestro, Betsy, and Giulio Maestro. *Harriet Goes to the Circus*; illus. by Giulio Maestro. New York: Crown, 1977. *Number Rhumba, 25.

Maestro, Betsy, and Giulio Maestro. *The Story of the Statue of Liberty*. New York: Lothrop, 1986. *Fourth of July Parade, 48.

Maestro, Betsy, and Giulio Maestro. *Where is My Friend?*; illus. by Giulio Maestro. New York: Crown, 1976. *Wheels and Gears, 14; *Classifying Chairs, 15; *Elephants, Babies, and Elephant Babies, 73; Be My Friend, 43.

Magee, Doug. *Trucks You Can Count On*. New York: Dodd, Mead, 1985. Take Me Ridin' in Your Car! 70.

Mahy, Margaret. *The Man Whose Mother Was a Pirate*; illus. Brian Froud. New York: Atheneum, 1972. Paste a Collage! 93.

Mander, Jerry, George Dippel, and Howard Gossage. *The Giant International Paper Airplane Book*. New York: Simon and Schuster, 1967. *But Will It Fly? 11.

Mari, Ielo, and Enzo Mari. *The Apple and the Moth*. New York: Pantheon, 1969. *Apple Day, 30; *Habitat: the Tree, 2.

Marshall, James. *George and Martha One Fine Day*. Boston: Houghton Mifflin, 1978. *Feeling Foolish, 46.

Marshall, James. *Yummers!* Boston: Houghton Mifflin, 1973. *Portly Pigs, 76.

Martin, Bill, Jr. *The Earthworm and the Underground*; illus. by Ted Rand. A Little Woodland Book. Chicago: Encyclopedia Britannica Educational Corp., 1979. *Meet a Worm, 8.

Martin, Bill, Jr. *Frogs in a Pond*; illus. by Colette Portal; guitar by Al Caiola. A Little Nature Book. Chicago: Encyclopedia Britannica Educational Corp., 1975. *Habitat: the Pond, 5.

Martin, Bill, Jr. *Germination*; illus. by Colette Portal; guitar by Al Caiola. A Little Nature Book. Chicago: Encyclopedia Britannica Educational Corp., 1975. *A Seed Grows, 7.

Martin, Bill, Jr. *Messenger Bee*; illus. by Colette Portal; guitar by Al Caiola. A Little Nature Book. Chicago: Encyclopedia Britannica Educational Corp., 1975. *Habitat: the Garden, 3.

Martin, Bill, Jr. *Moon Cycle*; illus. by Colette Portal; guitar by Al Caiola. A Little Nature Book. Chicago: Encyclopedia Britannica Educational Corp., 1975. *Harvest Moon, 31.

Martin, Bill, Jr. *A Mushroom is Growing*; illus. by Colette Portal; guitar by Al Caiola. A Little Nature Book. Chicago: Encyclopedia Britannica Educational Corp., 1975. *Lots of Rot, 10: *A Mushroom is Growing, 9.

Martin, Bill, Jr. *The Owl and the Mouse*; illus. by Ted Rand; guitar by Al Caiola. A Little Woodland Book. Chicago: Encyclopedia Britannica Educational Corp., 1979. Owls in the Night, 32.

Martin, Bill, Jr. *Poppies Afield*; illus. by Ray Barber; guitar by Al Caiola. A Little Nature Book. Chicago: Encyclopedia Britannica Educational Corp., 1975. *Habitat: the Field, 1.

Martin, Bill, Jr. *The Wild Turkey and Her Poults*; illus. by Laura Cornell; guitar by Al Caiola. A Little Woodland Book. Chicago: Encyclopedia Britannica Educational Corp., 1979. *Thanksgiving Turkeys, 52.

Martin, Rafe, and Ed Young. *Foolish Rabbit's Big Mistake*. New York: Putnam's, 1985. Feeling Foolish, 46.

Martin, Sarah Catharine. *Old Mother Hubbard and Her Dog*; illus. by Paul Galdone. New York: McGraw-Hill, 1960. *Problem Pups, 77.

Masha. *Three Little Kittens*; illus. by Masha. Racine, WI: Golden, 1942. Spring Kittens, 38.

Matsuno, Masako. *A Pair of Red Clogs*; illus. by Kazue Mizumura. New York: Collins, 1960. *New Shoes, 66.

Matrioska. 5 min. Filmmaker: Co Hoedeman. National Film Board of Canada, 1970. *Russian Winter, 89.

Mayer, Mercer. *A Boy, a Dog, and a Frog*. New York: Dial, 1967. *Frog Songs, 96.

Mayer, Mercer. *There's a Nightmare in My Closet*. New York: Dial, 1968. *Monster Bash! 85.

McCloskey, Robert. *Blueberries for Sal*. New York: Viking, 1948. *Blueberry, Strawberry, Jamberry! 87.

McCloskey, Robert. *Lentil*. New York: Viking, 1940. Fourth of July Parade, 48.

McGovern, Ann. *Too Much Noise*. Boston: Houghton Mifflin, 1967. *Hear It! 20.

McNulty, Faith. *How to Dig a Hole to the Other Side of the World*;

illus. by Marc Simont. New York: Harper & Row, 1979. *Volcanoes Erupt! 19.

McNulty, Faith. *The Lady and the Spider*; illus. by Bob Marstall. New York: Harper & Row, 1986. *Habitat: the Garden, 3.; The Caring Day, 61.

McPhail, David. *Pig Pig Rides*. New York: Dutton, 1982. *Portly Pigs, 76.

McPhail, David. *The Train*. Boston: Little, Brown, 1977. Here Comes the Train! 69.

Mellonie, Bryan and Robert Ingpen. *Lifetimes: The Beautiful Way to Explain Death to Children*. New York: Bantam, 1983. Lots of Rot, 10.

Mendoza, George. *And I Must Hurry for the Sea is Coming In*; photos by DeWayne Dalrymple. Englewood Cliffs, NJ: Prentice-Hall, 1969. *On the High Seas! 71.

Merriam, Eve. *The Birthday Cow*; illus. by Guy Mitchel. New York: Knopf, 1978. *Owls in the Night, 32.

Merrill, Jean, and Ronni Solbert. *The Elephant Who Liked to Smash Small Cars*. New York: Pantheon, 1967. *Feeling Mad, 59.

Merrill, Jean, and Ronni Solbert. *A Few Flies and I: Haiku by Issa*; illus. by Ronnie Solbert. New York: Pantheon, 1969. *Wonderful Words, 84.

Milgrowm, Harry. *Adventures With a String*; illus. by Tom Funk. New York: Dutton, 1965. *Tools Work for Us! 13.

Miller, Edna. *Mousekin's Golden House*. Englewood Cliffs, NJ: Prentice-Hall, 1964. *Pumpkin Magic, 49.

Milne, A. A. *The House at Pooh Corner*. New York: Dutton, 1928. *Snow Bears, 35.

Milne, A. A. *When We Were Very Young*. New York: Dutton, 1927. *The Rainy Day, 40.

Minarik, Else Holmelund. *Little Bear*; illus. Maurice Sendak. New York: Harper & Row, 1957. Freaky Food, 78.; Chicken Soup, 98.; *Feeling Glad, 58.; *Snow Bears, 35.; *Smell It! 24.; Happy Birthday to Me! 57.

Mizumura, Kazue. *I See the Winds*. New York: Crowell, 1966. Wind Power, 12.

Mole and the Car. 16 min. Phoenix, 1977. Take Me Ridin' in Your Car! 70.

Moncure, Jane Belk. *The Look Book*; illus. by Lois Axeman. Chicago: Children's Press, 1982. *See It! 23.

Moncure, Jane Belk. *A Tasting Party*. Chicago: Children's Press, 1982. Taste It! 21.

Monsell, Helen Albee. *Paddy's Christmas*; illus. by Kurt Wiese. New York: Knopf, 1942. *Here Comes Santa Claus, 56; Snow Bears, 35.

Moore, Clement. *The Night Before Christmas*; illus by Marvin Brenn; designed by Paul Taylor. New York: Random House, n.d. *Here Comes Santa Claus! 56.

Mooser, Stephen. *The Ghost With the Halloween Hiccups*; illus. by Tomie de Paola. New York: Watts, 1977. Trick or Treat, 51.

Murphy, Jill. *Peace at Last*. New York: Dial, 1980. Sleepy Storytime, 65; Hear It! 20.

Nelson, Esther L. *Dancing Games for Children of All Ages*. New York: Sterling, 1974. *Thanksgiving Turkeys, 52; Elephants, Babies, and Elephant Babies, 73.

Newton, James R. *Forest Log*; illus. by Irene Brady. New York: Crowell, 1980. Habitat: the Tree, 2; Lots of Rot, 10.

Nicoll, Helen, and Jan Pienkowski. *Meg's Eggs*; illus. by Jan Pienkowski. New York: Atheneum, 1972. *Dinosaurs, 17.

Nicoll, Helen, and Jan Pienkowski. *Meg and Mog*. New York: Atheneum, 1972. Black Cats, 33.

Niok. 29 min. Walt Disney, 1959. Elephants, Babies, and Elephant Babies, 73.

Noble, Trinka Hakes. *Apple Tree Christmas*. New York: Dial, 1984. Apple Day, 30.

Nodset, Joan L. *Go Away, Dog*; illus. by Crosby Bonsall. New York: Harper & Row, 1963. Problem Pups, 77.

Nodset, Joan L. *Who Took the Farmer's Hat?* New York: Harper & Row, 1963. *Wind Power, 12.

Numeroff, Laura Joffe. *If You Give a Mouse a Cookie*; illus. by Felicia Bond. New York: Harper & Row, 1985. *What Then? 28.

O'Hagan, Caroline. *It's Easy to Have a Snail Visit You*; illus. by Judith Allan. New York: Lothrop, 1980. Down in the Grass, 6.

O'Hagan, Caroline. *It's Easy to have a Worm Visit You*; illus. by Judith Allan. New York: Lothrop, 1980. *Meet a Worm, 8.

One Little Kitten. 3 min. Texture, 1981. *Spring Kittens, 38.

One Was Johnny. 3 min. Weston Woods, 1976. *Number Rhumba, 25.

Orbach, Ruth. *Apple Pigs*. New York: Collins-World, 1977. *Apple Day, 30.

Ormerod, Jan. *101 Things to Do With a Baby*. New York: Lothrop, 1984. The New Baby, 63.

Our Dinosaur Friends: For the intermediate years. Prod. Art Barduhn. Recording. Covina, CA: American Teaching Aids, 1978. *Dinosaurs, 17.

Oxenbury, Helen. *The Great Big Enormous Turnip*. From a story by Alexei Tolstoy. New York: Watts, 1968. *Feeling Glad! 58; Russian Winter, 89.

Oxford Scientific Films. *Common Frog*; photos by George Bernard. New York: Putnam's, 1979. Habitat: the Pond, 50.

Oxford Scientific Films. *Jellyfish and Other Sea Creatures*; illus. by Peter Parks. New York: Putnam's, 1982. Habitat: The Sea, 4.

Palacios, Argentina. See Joel Rothman.

Parish, Peggy. *Amelia Bedelia*; illus. by Fritz Siebel. New York: Harper & Row, 1963. Foolish Furniture, 79.

Parish, Peggy. *Dinosaur Time*; illus. by Arnold Lobel. New York: Harper & Row, 1974. Dinosaurs, 17.

Parish, Peggy. *No More Monsters!*; illus. by Marc Simont. New York: Harper & Row, 1981. *Monster Bash! 85.; *The Caring Day, 61.

Park, Ruth. *When the Wind Changed*; illus. by Deborah Niland. New York: Coward, 1980. *Making Faces, 64.

Parker, Nancy Winslow. *Poofy Loves Company*. New York: Dodd, Mead, 1980. *Problem Pups, 77.

Paterson, Diane. *Smile for Auntie*. New York: Dial, 1976. *The New Baby, 63.

Patrick, Gloria. *This is . . .* ; illus. by Joan Hanson. Minneapolis: Carolrhoda, 1970. *Rhyme, Rhyme, Rhyme, 83; Print It!, 91.

Peanut Butter and Jelly. 2 min. Filmmaker: Eliot Noyes, Unifilm, 1976.

Pedro. 9 min. Walt Disney, 1943. *Mailman, Mailman Bring Me a Letter, 44; But Will It Fly? 11.

Peet, Bill. *Randy's Dandy Lions*. New York: Houghton Mifflin, 1964. Happy Lions, 72.

Perkins, Al. *Hand, Hand, Fingers, Thumb*. New York: Random House, 1969. Drummer Hoff, 99.

Perkins, Al. *The Nose Book*; illus. by Roy McKie. New York: Random House, 1970. Smell It! 24.

Petersham, Maud, and Miska Petersham. *The Circus Baby*. New York: Macmillan, 1950. *Elephants, Babies, and Elephant Babies, 73.

Phillips, Joan. *Tiger is a Scaredy Cat*; illus. by Norman Gorbaty. New York: Random House, 1986. Don't Be Scared Storytime.

Piatti, Celestino. *The Happy Owls*. New York: Atheneum, 1964. *Owls in the Night, 32.

Pienkowski, Jan. See Helen Nicoll.

Pierre. 6 min. Weston Woods, 1976.

Pigs. 11 min. Churchill, 1967. Happy Lions, 72.

Pine, Tillie S., and Joseph Levine. *Simple Machines and How We Use Them*; illus. by Bernice Myers. New York: McGraw-Hill, 1965. *Tools Work for Us! 30.

Pinkwater, Daniel Manus. *The Big Orange Splot*. New York: Hastings House, 1977. Just Me! 62.

Piper, Watty. *The Little Engine That Could*; illus. by George and Doris Hauman. New York: Platt, 1961. *Here Comes the Train! 69.

Play Your Instruments and Make a Pretty Sound by Ella Jenkins. Recording. New York: Folkways, 1968.

Polis, Gloria Owens. *Resource Handbook for Early Learning*. Bellevue, WA: Bellevue Community College, 1978.

Polushkin, Maria. *Mama's Secret*; illus. by Felicia Bond. New York: Four Winds, 1984. Blueberry, Strawberry, Jamberry! 87

Pomerantz, Charlotte. *If I Had a Paka: Poems in Eleven Languages*; illus. by Nancy Tafuri. New York: Greenwillow, 1982. *Freaky Food, 78; *Blueberry, Strawberry, Jamberry! 87.

Pomerantz, Charlotte. *The Tamarindo Puppy*; illus. by Byron Barton. New York: Greenwillow, 1980. *The New Baby, 63.

Potter, Beatrix. *The Tale of Little Pig Robinson*. Warne, 1980. Portly Pigs, 76.

Potter, Beatrix. *The Tale of Mrs. Tittle-Mouse*. New York: Warne, 1910. Mice Are Nice, 75.

Potter, Beatrix. *The Tale of Pigling Bland*. New York: Warne, 1913, 1941. Portly Pigs, 76.

Potter, Beatrix. *The Tale of Two Bad Mice*. New York: Warne, 1904, 1934. Mice Are Nice, 75.

Prelutsky, Jack. *The Baby Uggs Are Hatching*; illus. by James Stevenson. New York: Greenwillow, 1981. *Monster Bash! 85.

Prelutsky, Jack. *Rainy Rainy Saturday*; illus. by Marylin Hafner. New York: Greenwillow, 1980. *Taste It! 26.

Prelutsky, Jack. *The Random House Book of Poetry for Children*; illus. by Arnold Lobel. New York: Random House, 1983. *The Rainy Day, 40; *Freaky Food, 78; *Happy Hanukkah, 53; *Crocodiles and Alligators, 74.; *Mice Are Nice, 75; *Black Cats, 33; *Feathered Babies, 37; *Wind Power, 12.; *Smell It! 24.; *A Mushroom Is Growing, 9.

Preston, Edna Mitchell. *One Dark Night*; illus. by Kurt Werth. New York: Viking, 1969. *Trick or Treat, 51.

Preston, Edna Mitchell. *Pop Corn and Ma Goodness*; illus. by

Robert Andrew Parker. New York: Viking, 1969. Rhyme, Rhyme, Rhyme, 83.

Preston, Edna Mitchell. *The Temper Tantrum Book*; illus. by Rainey Bennett. New York: Viking, 1969. *Feeling Mad, 59.

Provensen, Alice, and Martin Provensen. *The Glorious Flight Across the Channel With Louis Bleriot*. New York: Viking, 1983. Voici Paris! 90; *But Will It Fly? 11.

Puricelli, Luigi. See Ermanno Cristini.

Quackenbush, Robert M. *Clementine*. Philadelphia: Lippincott, 1974. Barnyard Dance, 97.

Quackenbush, Robert M. *She'll Be Comin' Round the Mountain*. Philadelphia: Lippincott, 1973. Barnyard Dance, 97.

Quackenbush, Robert M. *Skip to My Lou*. Philadephia: Lippincott, 1975. Barnyard Dance, 97.

Quigley, Lillian Fox. *The Blind Men and the Elephant*; illus. by Janice Holland. New York: Scribner's, 1959. Elephants, Babies, and Elephant Babies, 73.

Raffi, Rise and Shine; with Ken Whiteley. Willowdale, Ontario: Shoreline Records. *Number Rhumba, 25.

Rainy Day Dances, Rainy Day Songs by Patty Zeitlin and Marcia Berman, with Anne Lief Barlin. AR570. Freeport, NY: Educational Activities, 1975. *The Rainy Day, 40.

Really Rosie. 26 min. Weston Woods, 1976. *Chicken Soup, 98.

Really Rosie. The Broadway Cast Album of Maurice Sendak's *Really Rosie*. Caedmon, 1981.

The Red Balloon. 34 min. Filmmaker: Albert Lamorisse. Macmillan Films, 1956. *Voici Paris! 90.

Reiss, John. *Colors*. New York: Bradbury, 1969. *Color Me Red! 26.

Remarkable Riderless Runaway Tricycle. 11 min. Filmmaker: John Sturner and Gary Templeton. Phoenix, 1986. *Wheels and Gears, 14.

Rice, Eve. *New Blue Shoes*. New York: Macmillan, 1975. New Shoes, 66.

Rice, Eve. *Sam Who Never Forgets*. New York: Greenwillow, 1977. *The Caring Day, 63.

Rieger, Shay. *Our Family*. New York: Lothrop, 1972. Mold It! 94.

Robbins, Ken. *Building a House*. New York: Four Winds, 1984. My House, My Home, 68.

Robbins, Ken. *Tools*. New York: Four Winds, 1983. Tools Do Work for Us! 13.

Robbins, Ruth. *Baboushka and the Three Kings*; illus. by Nicolas

Sidjakov; verse by Edith R. Thomas; music by Mary Clement Sanks. New York: Parnassus, 1960. Russian Winter, 89.

Rockwell, Anne. *Cars*. New York: Dutton, 1984. Take Me Ridin' in Your Car, 70.

Rockwell, Anne. *First Comes Spring*. New York: Crowell, 1985. It's Spring! 36.

Rockwell, Anne. *In Our House*. New York: Crowell, 1985. My House, My Home, 68.

Rockwell, Anne. *Machines*. New York: Macmillan, 1971. *Tools Work for Us! 13; *Wheels and Gears, 14.

Rockwell, Anne. *Trucks*. New York: Dutton, 1984. Take Me Ridin' in Your Car! 70.

Rockwell, Anne, and Harlow Rockwell. *The Toolbox*. New York: Macmillan, 1971. *Tools Work for Us! 13.

Rockwell, Harlow. *The Compost Heap*. Garden City, NY: Doubleday, 1974. *Lots of Rot, 10.

Rojankovsky, Feodor. See John Langstaff.

Rose, Anne. *How Does a Czar Eat Potatoes?*; illus. by Janosch. New York: Lothrop, 1973. A Visit to the King and Queen, 86.

Rosetti, Christina. *What is Pink?*; illus. by Jose Aruego. New York: Macmillan, 1971. *Color Me Red! 26.

Rosie's Walk. 5 min. Filmmaker: Gene Deitch. Weston Woods, 1970. *Barnyard Dance, 97.

Ross, Tony. *I'm Coming to Get You*. New York: Dutton, 1984. *Monster Bash! 85.

Rothman, Joel, and Argentina Palacios. *This Can Lick a Lollipop: Body Riddles for Children; Esto Goza Chupando un Caramelo: Las Partes del Cuerpo en Adivinanaza Infantiles*. English by Joel Rothman; Spanish by Argentina Palacios; photos by Patricia Ruben. Garden City, NY: Doubleday, 1979. *Smell It! 24.

Rounds, Glen. *Sweet Betsy from Pike*. Chicago: Children's 1973. Barnyard Dance. 97.

Roy, Ronald. *Three Ducks Went Wandering*; illus. by Paul Galdone. New York: Seabury, 1979. Feathered Babies, 37.

Ryder, Joanne. *Inside a Turtle's Shell*; illus. by Susan Bonners. New York: Macmillan, 1985. *Down in the Grass, 6.

Ryder, Joanne. *Snail in the Woods*. Assisted by Harold S. Feinberg; illus. by Jo Polseno. New York: Harper & Row, 1979. Down in the Grass, 6.

Ryder, Joanne. *The Snail's Spell*; illus. by Lynne Cherny. New York: Warne, 1982. *Is It Fast, Is It Slow? 27; *Down in the Grass, 6.

Rylant, Cynthia. *Night in the Country*; illus. by Mary Zilagyi. New York: Bradbury, 1986. *Don't Be Scared Storytime, 60.

Rylant, Cynthia. *This Year's Garden*; illus. by Mary Zilagyi. Scarsdale, NY: Bradbury, 1984. Habitat: the Garden, 3.

The Sand Castle. 14 min. Filmmaker: Co Hoedeman. National Film Board of Canada, 1977. *Mold It! 94.

Sandburg, Carl. *Rootabaga Stories*. New York: Harcourt, 1922, 1951. Dancing Dolls, 100.

Sandburg, Carl. *The Wedding Procession of the Rag Doll and the Broom Handle and Who Was In It*; illus. by Harriet Pincus. New York: Harcourt, 1922, 1967. *Dancing Dolls, 100; *Be My Friend, 43.

Sasaki, Isao. *Snow*. New York: Viking, 1980. The Snowy Day, 34.

Sasek, M. *This is Paris*. New York: Macmillan, 1959. Voici Paris! 90.

Scarry, Huck. *Huck Scarry's Steam Train Journey*. New York: Collins-World, 1979. Here Comes the Train! 69.

Scarry, Richard. *Richard Scarry's Great Big Air Book*. New York: Random House, 1971. But Will It Fly? 11.

Scarry, Richard. *Richard Scarry's What Do People Do All Day?* New York: Random House, 1968, 1979. Mailman, Mailman, Bring Me a Letter, 44.

Scheer, Julian, and Marvin Bileck. *Rain Makes Applesauce*; illus. by Marvin Bileck. New York: Holiday House, 1964. *Apple Day, 30; *Wonderful Words, 84.; *The Rainy Day, 40.

Scheffler, Ursel. *A Walk in the Rain*; illus. by Ulises Wensell; trans. by Andrea Merman. New York: Putnam's, 1984, 1986. The Rainy Day, 40.

Schlein, Miriam. *Fast Is Not a Ladybug*; illus. by Leonard Kessler. New York: W.R. Scott, 1953. *Is It Fast? Is It Slow? 27.

Schwartz, Alvin. *Ten Copycats in a Boat and Other Riddles*; illus. by Marc Simont. New York: Harper & Row, 1980. *Copy Cats, 82.

Schwartz, David M. *How Much Is a Million?*; illus. by Steven Kellogg. New York: Lothrop, 1985. Number Rhumba, 25.

Scott, Ann Herbert. *On Mother's Lap*; illus. by Glo Coalson. New York: McGraw-Hill, 1972. *Christmas Lullabies, 54; *Feeling Glad! 58; *The New Baby, 63.

Seeger, Pete, and Charles Seeger. *The Foolish Frog*; illus. by Miloslav Jagr. New York: Macmillan, 1973. Chicken Soup, 98.

Seignobosc. See Françoise.

Selsam, Millicent E. *Greg's Microscope*. New York: Harper & Row, 1963. Take a Closer Look! 16.

Selsam, Millicent E. *Mushrooms*; photos by Jerome Wexler. New York: Morrow, 1986. A Mushroom Is Growing. 9.

Selsam, Millicent, and Jerome Wexler. *The Amazing Dandelion*. New York: Morrow, 1977. A Seed Grows, 7.

Selsam, Millicent, and Joyce Hunt. *A First Look at Rocks*; illus. by Harriet Springer. New York: Walker, 1984. Your Own Special Rock, 18.

Sendak, Maurice. *Alligators All Around: An Alphabet*. New York: Harper, & Row, 1962. *Crocodiles and Alligators, 74.

Sendak, Maurice. *Chicken Soup With Rice*. New York: Harper & Row, 1962. *Chicken Soup, 98.; *Thanksgiving Turkeys, 52.

Sendak, Maurice. *Hector Protector and As I Went Over the Water: Two Nursery Rhymes*. New York: Harper & Rwo, 1965. A Visit to the King and Queen, 86.

Sendak, Maurice. *In the Night Kitchen*. New York: Harper & Row, 1970. *Sleepy Storytime, 65; *Dream Time, 80.

Sendak, Maurice. *One Was Johnny*. New York: Harper & Row, 1962. *Number Rhumba, 25.

Sendak, Maurice. *Pierre*. New York: Harper & Row, 1962. *Happy Lions, 72.

Sendak, Maurice. *Where the Wild Things Are*. New York: Harper & Row, 1963. *Monster Bash! 85.

Seuss, Dr. *And To Think That I Saw It On Mulberry Street*. New York: Vanguard, 1937. Fourth of July Parade, 48.

Seuss, Dr. *The Foot Book*. New York: Random House, 1968. *New Shoes, 66.

Seuss, Dr. *Green Eggs and Ham*. New York: Random House, 1960. Freaky Foods, 78.

Seuss, Dr. *Happy Birthday to You!* New York: Random House, 1959. *Happy Birthday Me! 57.

Seuss, Dr. *Horton Hatches the Egg*. New York: Random House, 1940, 1968. *The Caring Day, 61.

Seuss, Dr. *How the Grinch Stole Christmas*. New York: Random House, 1957. *Here Comes Santa Claus! 56.

Sewall, Marcia. *The Wee Wee Mannie and the Big Big Coo: A Scottish Folk Tale*. Boston: Little, Brown, 1977. Highland Fling, 88.

Shannon, George. *Dance Away*; illus. by Jose Aruego and Ariane Dewey. New York: Greenwillow, 1982. *Is It Fast? Is It Slow? 27.

Showers, Paul. *A Book of Scary Things*; illus. by Susan Perl. Garden City, NY: Doubleday, 1977. *The Don't Be Scared Storytime, 60.

Showers, Paul. *The Listening Walk*. New York: Crowell, 1961. Hear It! 20.

Showers, Paul. *Look At Your Eyes*; illus. by Paul Galdone. New York: Crowell, 1962. *See It! 23.

Shulevitz, Uri. *Dawn*. New York: Farrar, 1974. *Sleepy Storytime, 65.

Shulevitz, Uri. *One Monday Morning*. New York: Scribner's, 1967. *A Visit to the King and Queen, 86.

Shulevitz, Uri. *Rain, Rain, Rivers*. New York: Farrar, 1969. *The Rainy Day, 40.

Silverstein, Shel. *The Missing Piece*. New York: Harper & Row, 1976. *Looking at a Line, 92.

Simon, Norma. *How Do I Feel?*; illus. by Joe Lasker. Chicago: Albert Whitman, 1979. Feeling Mad, 59.

Simon, Norma. *I Was So Mad!*; illus. by Dora Leder. Niles, IL: Albert Whitman, 1982. Spring Kittens, 38.

Simon, Norma. *Where Does My Cat Sleep?*; illus. by Dora Leder. Niles, IL: Albert Whitman, 1982. Spring Kittens, 38.

Simon, Seymour. *Let's-Try-It-Out Wet & Dry*; illus. by Angie Culfogienis. New York: McGraw-Hill, 1969. The Rainy Day, 40.

Skorpen, Lisel Moak. *We Were Tired of Living in a House*; illus. by Doris Burns. New York: Coward-McCann, 1969. My House, My Home, 68.

Skurzynski, Gloria. *The Magic Pumpkin*; illus. by Rocco Negri. New York: Four Winds, 1971. *Pumpkin Magic, 49.

Slobodkin, Louis. *One is Good But Two Are Better*. New York: Vanguard, 1956. Be My Friend, 43.

Slobodkina, Esphyr. *Caps For Sale*. New York: Addison-Wesley, 1940. *Copy Cats, 82.

Smile for Auntie. 4 min. Weston Woods, 1979. *The New Baby, 63.

Smith, Henry. *Amazing Air*. New York: Lothrop, 1982. But Will It Fly? 11.

Snowy Day. 6 min. Weston Woods, 1964. The Snowy Day, 34.

Sobol, Harriet Langsam. *Pete's House*; illus. by Patricia Agee. New York: Macmillan, 1978. My House, My Home, 68.

Solbert, Ronni. See Jean Merrill.

Spier, Peter. *Crash! Bang! Boom!* Garden City, NY: Doubleday, 1972. Fourth of July Parade, 48.

Spier, Peter. *A Fox Went Out on a Chilly Night*. Garden City, NY: Doubleday, 1961. *Harvest Moon, 31.

Spier, Peter. *Peter Spier's Christmas*. Garden City, NY: Doubleday, 1961. Here Comes Santa Claus! 56.

Spin, Spider, Spin by Patty Zeitlin and Marcia Berman. Activity Records, 1974. *Meet a Worm, 8.

Steig, William. *Sylvester and the Magic Pebble*. New York: Simon & Schuster, 1969. *Your Own Special Rock, 18.

Stein, Sara Bonnett. *Cat*; illus. by Manuel Garcia. New York: Harcourt, 1985. *Black Cats, 33.

Stein, Sara Bonnett. *Mouse*; illus. by Manuel Garcia. New York: Harcourt, 1985. *Mice Are Nice, 75.

Steiner, Charlotte. *My Bunny Feels Soft*. New York: Knopf, 1958. *Touch It! 22.

Strand, Mark. *The Night Book*; illus. by William Pene du Bois. New York: Clarkson N. Potter/Crown, 1985. *The Don't Be Scared Storytime, 60.

Suzie and the Little Blue Coupe. 8 min. Disney, 1952.

The Tender Tale of Cinderella Penguin. 10 min. Filmmaker: Janet Perlman. National Film Board of Canada, 1981. *A Visit to the King and Queen, 86.

This Old Man; illus. by Pam Adams. Restrop Manor, Purton Wilts, England: Child's Play, 1974. *Feeling Foolish, 46.

Titherington, Jeanne. *Pumpkin, Pumpkin*. New York: Greenwillow, 1986. *Pumpkin Magic, 49.

Todd, Kathleen. *Snow*. New York: Addison-Wesley, 1982. Touch It! 22.; The Snowy Day, 34.

Tolstoy, Alexei. See Helen Oxenbury.

Tompert, Ann. *Little Fox Goes to the End of the World*; illus. by John Wallner. New York: Crown, 1976. *On the High Seas! 71.

Tompert, Ann. *Nothing Sticks Like a Shadow*; illus. by Lynn Musinger. Boston: Houghton Mifflin, 1984. *Shadow Play, 42.

Toolbox Ballet. 8 min. Xerox Films, 1982. *Tools Work for Us! 113.

Toye, William. *How Summer Came to Canada*; illus. by Elizabeth Cleaver. New York: Lothrop, Lee & Shepard, 1951. Thanksgiving Turkeys, 52.

Tresselt, Alvin. *Autumn Harvest*; illus. by Roger Duvoisin. New York: Lotherop, Lee & Shepard, 1951. Thanksgiving Turkeys, 52.

Tresselt, Alvin. *Follow the Wind*. New York: Lothrop, 1950. *Wind Power, 12.

Tresselt, Alvin. *I Saw the Sea Come In*; illus. by Roger Duvoisin. New York: Lothrop, Lee & Shepard, 1954. *Habitat: The Sea, 40

Tresselt, Alvin. *Johnny Maple Leaf*; illus. Roger Duvoisin. New York: Lothrop, 1948. All Falling Down, 29.

Tresselt, Alvin. *The Mitten: An Old Ukrainian Folktale*; illus. by Yaroslava. New York: Lothrop, 1964. The Snowy Day, 34.

Tresselt, Alvin. *Rain Drop Splash*; illus. by Leonard Weisgard. New

York: Lothrop, Lee & Shepard, 1946. The Rainy Day, 40; *Russian Winter, 89.

Tudor, Tasha. *Pumpkin Moonshine*. New York: Oxford, 1936. Pumpkin Magic, 49.

Turkle, Brinton. *Thy Friend, Obadiah*. New York: Viking, 1969. The Caring Day, 61.

Tworkov, Jack. *The Camel Who Took a Walk*; illus. by Roger Duvoisin. New York: Dutton, 1951. *Wonderful Words, 84.

Udry, Janice May. *The Moon Jumpers*; illus. by Maurice Sendak. New York: Harper & Row, 1959. *Shadow Play, 42.

Udry, Janice May. *Oh No Cat!*; illus. by Mary Chalmers. New York: Coward, 1976. Spring Kittens, 38.

Udry, Janice May. *A Tree is Nice*; illus. by Marc Simont. New York: Harper & Row, 1956. *Habitat: the Tree, 2.

Ueno, Noriko. *Elephant Buttons*. New York: Harper & Row, 1973. Elephants, Babies, and Elephant Babies, 73; *Looking at a Line, 92; Button, Button, 67.

Ungerer, Tomi. *Cricter*. New York: Harper & Row, 1958. *Looking at a Line, 92.

Ungerer, Tomi. *The Hat*. New York: Parents', 1970. Spring Hats, 39.

Van Allsburg, Chris. *Ben's Dream*. Boston: Houghton Mifflin, 1982. Dream Time, 80.

Van Allsburg, Chris. *The Polar Express*. Boston: Houghton Mifflin, 1985. Christmas Bells, 55; Dream Time, 80.

Van Allsburg, Chris. *The Wreck of the Zephyr*. New York: Houghton Mifflin, 1983. On the High Seas, 71.

Vessel, Matthew F. See Herbert H. Wong.

Viorst, Judith. *Alexander and the Terrible, Horrible, No Good, Very Bad Day*; illus. by Ray Cruz. New York: Atheneum, 1984. *Feeling Mad, 59.

Viorst, Judith. *The Tenth Good Thing About Barney*; illus. by Erik Blegvad. New York: Atheneum, 1971. Lots of Rot, 10.

Vipont, Elfrida. *The Elephant and the Bad Baby*; illus. by Ramond Briggs. New York: Coward, 1969. *Elephants, Babies and Elephant Babies, 73; *Freaky Food, 78.

Vogel, Ilse-Margaret. *The Don't Be Scared Book*. New York: Atheneum, 1964. *The Don't Be Scared Storytime, 60.

Waber, Bernard. *Lyle, Lyle, Crocodile*. Boston: Houghton Mifflin, 1965. Crocodiles and Alligators, 74.

Waber, Bernard. *You Look Ridiculous Said the Rhinocerous to the Hippopotamus*. Boston: Houghton Mifflin, 1966. Just Me! 62.

Wadsworth, Olive A. *Over in the Meadow*; illus. by Mary Maki Rae. New York: Viking Kestrel, 1985. Number Rhumba, 25.

Wagner, Jenny. *John Brown, Rose, and the Midnight Cat*; illus. by Ron Brooks. New York: Bradbury, 1978. *The Caring Day, 61; *Black Cats, 33.

Wahl, Jan. *Cabbage Moon*; illus. by Adrienne Adams. New York: Holt, 1965. *Harvest Moon, 31.

Walter, Mildred Pitts. *My Mama Needs Me*; illus. by Pat Cummings. New York: Lothrop, Lee & Shepard, 1983. *The New Baby, 63.

Ward, Brian R. *The Ears and Hearing*. New York: Watts, 1982. Hear It! 20.

Ward, Brian R. *The Eye and Seeing*. New York: Watts, 1981. See It! 23.

Ward, Brian R. *Touch, Taste and Smell*. New York: Watts, 1982. Taste It! 21; Touch It! 22.

Ward, Lynd. *The Biggest Bear*. Boston: Houghton Mifflin, 1952. The Caring Day, 61.

Ward, Lynd. *The Silver Pony*. Boston: Houghton Mifflin, 1973. Dream Time, 80.

Watanabe, Shigeo. *How Do I Put It On?*; illus. by Yasuo Ohtomo. New York: Putnam's, 1979. New Shoes, 66.

Watanabe, Shigeo. *I Can Build a House!*; illus. by Yasuo Ohtomo. New York: Philomel, 1982. My House, My Home, 68.

Waterton, Betty. *A Salmon for Simon*; illus. by Ann Blades. New York: Atheneum, 1980. The Caring Day, 61.

Watson, Clyde. *Father Fox's Pennyrhymes*; illus. by Wendy Watson. New York: Crowell, 1971. Rhyme, Rhyme, Rhyme, 83.

Wegen, Ron. *Sand Castle*. New York: Greenwillow, 1977. *Mold It! 94.

Welber, Robert. *The Winter Picnic*; illus. by Deborah Ray. New York: Pantheon, 1970. *The Snowy Day, 34.

Westcott, Nadine Bernard. *The Giant Vegetable Garden*. Boston: Little, Brown, 1981. Freaky Food, 78.

Wheeler, Cindy. *Marmalade's Snowy Day*. New York: Knopf, 1982. The Snowy Day, 34.

Wheeler, Cindy. *Marmalade's Yellow Leaf*. New York: Knopf, 1982. *All Falling Down, 29.

Why'd the Beetle Cross the Road. 8 min. Filmmaker: Jan Skrentny. Pyramid, 1984. *Down in the Grass, 6.

Wildsmith, Brian. *Brian Wildsmith's 1, 2, 3*. New York: Watts, 1965. Number Rhumba, 25.

Wildsmith, Brian. *Goat's Trail*. New York: Knopf, 1986. Copy Cats, 82.

Willard, Nancy. *Night Story*; illus. by Ilse Plume. San Diego: Harcourt, 1981. *Dream Time, 80

Williams, Garth. *The Chicken Book: A Traditional Rhyme*. New York: Delacorte, 1970. *Number Rhumba, 25.

Williams, Terry Tempest. *Between Cattails*; illus. by Peter Parnall. New York: Scribner's, 1985. Habitat: the Pond, 5.

Williams, Vera B. *A Chair for My Mother*. New York: Greenwillow, 1982. Foolish Furniture, 79.

Winter, Jeanette. *Come Out to Play*. New York: Knopf, 1986. Dream Time, 80.

Withers, Carl. *Tale of a Black Cat*; illus. by Alan Cober. New York: Holt, 1969. *Black Cats, 33.

Wizard of Speed and Time. 3 min. Filmmaker: Mike Jitlov. Pyramid, 1980. *Is It Fast? Is It Slow? 27.

Wolff, Ashley. *The Bells of London*. New York: Dodd, Mead, 1985. Christmas Bells, 55.

Wolff, Ashley. *Only the Cat Saw*. New York: Dodd, Mead, 1985. The Don't Be Scared Storytime, 60.

Wong, Herbert H., and Matthew F. Vessel. *Pond Life: Watching Animals Grow Up*; illus. by Harold Berson. Reading, MA: Addison-Wesley, 1970. Habitat: the Pond, 5.

Wood, Don and Audrey Wood. *The Little Mouse, the Red Ripe Strawberry, and THE BIG HUNGRY BEAR*; illus. by Don Wood. Singapore: Child's Play, 1984. *Freaky Food, 78; *Blueberry, Strawberry, Jamberry! 87.

Woolley, Catharine. *The Horse With the Easter Bonnett*; illus. by Jay Hyde Barnum. New York: Morrow, 1952. Spring Hats, 39.

Worthington, Phoebe, and John Worthington. *Teddy Bear Gardener*. New York: Warne, 1983. Teddy Bears Go Dancing, 81.

Wright, Dare. *The Lonely Doll*. Garden City, NY: Doubleday, 1957. Dancing Dolls, 100.

Yashima, Mitsu. *Momo's Kittens*; illus. by Taro Yashima. New York: Viking, 1961. Spring Kittens, 38.

Yashima, Taro. *Umbrella*. New York: Viking, 1958. *The Rainy Day, 40.

Yashima, Taro. *The Village Tree*. New York: Viking, 1953. Habitat: the Tree, 2.

Yashima, Taro. *Youngest One*. New York: Viking, 1972. *Be My Friend, 43; Classifying Chairs, 15.

Ylla and Arthur S. Gregor. *The Little Elephant*; photos by Ylla. New

York: Harper & Row, 1956. Elephants, Babies, and Elephant Babies, 73.

Yulya. *Bears are Sleeping*; illus. by Nonny Hogrogian. New York: Scribner's, 1967. *Russian Winter, 89.; *Christmas Lullabies, 54; *Snow Bears, 35.

Zea. 5 min. 17 sec. Filmmaker: Andre LeDuc and Jean-Jacques LeDuc. National Film Board of Canada, 1981. *Take a Closer Look, 16.

Zemach, Harve. *The Judge: An Untrue Tale*; illus. by Margot Zemach. New York: Farrar, 1969. Monster Bash! 85.

Ziefert, Harriet. *Sarah's Questions*. New York: Lothrop, Lee & Shepard, 1986. Habitat: The Field, 1.

Zion, Gene. *Harry the Dirty Dog*; illus. by Margaret Bloy Graham. New York: Harper & Row, 1956. *Problem Pups, 77.

Zion, Gene. *The Plant Sitter*; illus. by Margaret Bloy Graham. New York: Harper & Row, 1959. The Caring Day, 61.

Zion, Gene. *Really Spring*; illus. by Margaret Bloy Graham. New York: Harper & Row, 1956. It's Spring! 36.

Zion, Gene, and Margaret Bloy Graham. *All Falling Down*. New York: Harper & Row, 1951. *All Falling Down, 29.

Zolotow, Charlotte. *Mr. Rabbit and the Lovely Present*; illus. by Maurice Sendak. New York: Harper & Row, 1961. *Color Me Red! 26; Easter Rabbit, 47.

Zolotow, Charlotte. *The Quarreling Book*; illus. by Arnold Lobel. New York: Harper & Row, 1963. Feeling Mad, 59.

Zolotow, Charlotte. *The Storm Book*; illus. Margaret Bloy Graham. New York: Harper & Row, 1952. The Rainy Day, 40.

Zolotow, Charlotte. *A Tiger Called Thomas*; illus. Kurt Werth. New York: Lothrop, 1962. Trick or Treat, 51.

Index of Films

Alexander and the Car with the Missing Headlights. Weston Woods, 1966. 13 min. *Take Me Ridin' in Your Car! 70.

Alligators All Around. Weston Woods, 1976. 2 min. *Crocodiles and Alligators, 74.

Angus Lost. John Sturner and Gary Templeton. Phoenix, 1987. 11 min. *Problem Pups, 77.

Bon Voyage, Charlie Brown. Paramount Home Video, 1980. 76 min. Voici Paris! 90.

A Boy, a Dog, and a Frog. John Sturner and Gary Templeton. Phoenix, 1980. 9 min. *Habitat: The Pond, 5; *Frog Songs, 96.

Captain Silas. Ron McAdow. Yellow Bison, 1977. 14 min. *On the High Seas! 71.

The Chairy Tale. Norman McLaren. International Film Board, 1957. 10 min. *Foolish Furniture, 79.

Charlie Needs a Cloak. Weston Woods, 1977. 7 min. *What Then? 28.

Chicken Soup with Rice. Weston Woods, 1976. 5 min. Chicken Soup, 98.

Colter's Hell. Robin Lehman. Phoenix, 1973. 14 min. Volcanoes Erupt! 19.

Dinosaur. Will Vinton. Pyramid, 1981. 14 min. *Dinosaurs, 17.

The Foolish Frog. Gene Deitch. Weston Woods, 1973. 8 min. *Frog Songs, 96.

The Happy Lion. Macmillan. 7 min. *Happy Lions, 72; Voici Paris! 90.

House Cats. Phoenix, 1986. 5 min. *Black Cats, 32.

Legend of Johnny Appleseed. Disney, 1948. 20 min. *Apple Day, 30.

Lullaby. International Film Bureau, 1975. 4 min. *Sleepy Story-time, 65; Dream Time, 80.

Matrioska. Co Hoedeman. National Film Board of Canada, 1979. 5 min. *Russian Winter, 89.

Mole and the Car. Phoenix, 1977. 16 min. Take Me Ridin' in Your Car! 70.

Niok. Walt Disney, 1959. 29 min. Elephants, Babies, and Elephant Babies, 73.

One Little Kitten. Texture, 1981. 2 min. *Spring Kittens, 38.

One Was Johnny. Weston Woods, 1976. 3 min. *Number Rhumba, 25.

Peanut Butter and Jelly. Eliot Noyes. Unifilms, 1976. 2 min. Freaky Food, 78.

Pedro. Walt Disney, 1943. 8 min. Mailman, Mailman, Bring Me a Letter, 44; But Will It Fly? 11.

Pierre. Weston Woods, 1976. 6 min. Happy Lions, 72.

The Red Balloon. Albert Lamorisse. Macmillan Films, 1956. 34 min. *Voici Paris! 90.

Really Rosie. Weston Woods, 1986. 26 min. Chicken Soup, 98.

Remarkable Riderless Runaway Tricycle. Phoenix, 1976. *Wheels and Gears, 14.

Rosie's Walk. Gene Deitch. Weston Woods, 1970. 5 min. *Barnyard Dance, 97.

The Sand Castle. Co Hoedeman. National Film Board of Canada, 1977. 14 min. *Mold It! 94.

Smile for Auntie. Weston Woods, 1974. 4 min. *The New Baby, 63.

The Snowy Day. Weston Woods, 1964. 6 min. The Snowy Day, 34.

Suzie the Little Blue Coup. Walt Disney, 1952. 8 min. Take Me Ridin' in Your Car! 70.

The Tender Tale of Cinderella Penguin. Janet Perlman. National Film Board of Canada, 1981. 10 min. *A Visit to the King and Queen, 86.

Toolbox Ballet. Xerox Films, 1972. 8 min. *Tools Work For Us!, 13.

Why'd the Beetle Cross the Road? Filmmaker Jan Skrentny. Pyramid, 1984. 8 min. *Down in the Grass, 6.

The Wizard of Speed and Time. Mike Jitlov. Pyramid, 1980. 3 min. *Is It Fast? Is It Slow, 27.

Zea. Andre LeDuc and Jean-Jacques LeDuc. National Film Board of Canada, 1981. 5 min., 17 secs. *Take a Closer Look, 16.

Appendix: Musical Notations for Songs

OPENING SONG: JENNY JENNY ARE YOU HERE?

CHILD ANSWERS

JEN-NY   JEN-NY   ARE YOU HERE?   YES YES   I AM HERE.

HELLO SONG: HELLO EVERYBODY.

HEL- LO EVERY BO-DY   YES IN-DEED.   YES IN-DEED. YES IN-DEED, HEL-

LO EVERY BO-DY   YES IN-DEED. YES IN-DEED MY   DAR-LING.

HELLO SONG: HELLO HELLO WE ARE GLAD TO MEET YOU.

HEL- LO   HEL- LO   WE ARE GLAD TO MEET YOU.

HEL- LO   HEL- LO   HEL-LO EVE RY   ONE.

CIRCLE TIME SONG: OLD BRASS WAGON.

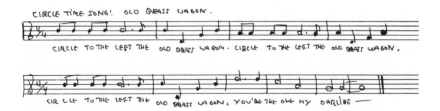

CIRCLE TO THE LEFT THE OLD BRASS WAGON. CIRCLE TO THE LEFT THE OLD BRASS WAGON,

CIR CLE TO THE LEFT THE OLD BRASS WAGON, YOU'RE THE ONE MY DARLING —

PROGRAM # 1. LITTLE ARABELLA MILLER.

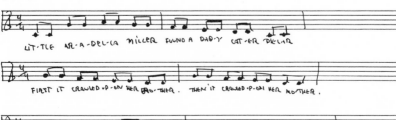

LIT-TLE AR-A-BEL-LA MILLER FOUND A BABY CAT-ER-PILLAR

FIRST IT CRAWLED UP ON HER BRO-THER.   THEN IT CRAWLED-UP-ON HER MOTHER.

THEY SAID AR-A-BEL-LA MIL-LER   TAKE A-WAY THAT CAT-ER-PIL-LAR !

PROGRAM #3. I'M BRINGING HOME A BABY BUMBLEBEE.

I'M BRINGING HOME A BABY BUMBLEBEE. WON'T MY MOMMY BE SO PROUD OF ME.

I'M BRINGING HOME A BAB-Y BUMBLE BEE   OUCH! HE STUNG ME!!

PROGRAM #3. THERE WAS A BEE-AI-EE-AI-EE.

THERE WAS A BEE-AI-EE-AI-EE SAT ON A WALL-AI-ALL-AI-ALL HE WENT A-

BUZZ-AI-UZ-AI-UZ AND THAT WAS ALL-AI-ALL-AI-ALL.

PROGRAM #4. ALL THE FISH ARE SWIMMING IN THE WATER.

ALL THE FISH ARE SWIMMING IN THE WAT-ER   ALL THE FISH ARE SWIMMING IN THE WA-TER.

ALL THE FISH ARE SWIMMING IN THE WATER   HI-HO ROLLDY-ROLLDY— DAY

PROGRAM #12. WIND POWER.

I WISH I WERE A WIND-MILL, A WIND-MILL, A WIND-MILL. AND

IF I WERE A WIND-MILL, I'D MOVE IN THE WIND LIKE THIS— ACTIONS~

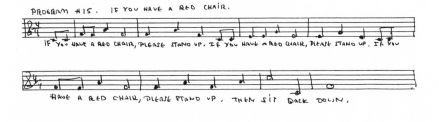

PROGRAM #15. IF YOU HAVE A RED CHAIR.

IF YOU HAVE A RED CHAIR, PLEASE STAND UP. IF YOU HAVE A RED CHAIR, PLEASE STAND UP. IF YOU

HAVE A RED CHAIR, PLEASE STAND UP, THEN SIT BACK DOWN.

PROGRAM #19. I'M A MOUNTAIN OH SO HIGH. *

I'M A MOUN-TAIN OH SO HIGH. WITH MY HEAD UP IN THE SKY.

I LOOK ROUND THE COUN-TRY-SIDE. DOWN MY SLOPES THE SKI-ERS SLIDE.

MOUN-TAIN MOVE MOUN-TAIN STOP! MOUN-TAIN MOUNTAIN BLOW YOUR TOP!

PROGRAM #21. PEANUT BUTTER.

PEA-NUT PEA-NUT BUT-TER... JELLY! PEA-NUT PEA-NUT BUT-TER... JELLY!

FIRST YOU TAKE THE PEA-NUTS AND YOU SQUISH 'EM YOU SQUISH 'EM YOU

SQUISH 'EM SQUISH 'EM SQUISH-EM SING-ING PEA-NUT PEA-NUT

BUT-TER... JELLY!

PROGRAM #24. NOW THE CHICKEN IS A-BOILING.

NOW THE CHI-CKEN IS A- BOIL-ING.

IN THE STEW-MY POT HE BUB-BLES.

OUT HE POPS HIS HEAD AND ASKS US

DON'T YOU KNOW I NEED SOME ON-IONS.

#24 PUT YOUR FINGER ON YOUR NOSE.

PUT YOUR FINGER ON YOUR NOSE ON YOUR NOSE. PUT YOUR FINGER ON YOUR NOSE ON YOUR NOSE. PUT YOUR

FINGER ON YOUR NOSE. YOU SMELL WITH YOUR NOSE. PUT YOUR FINGER ON YOUR NOSE ON YOUR NOSE.

PROGRAM #25. FIVE LITTLE BUNS.

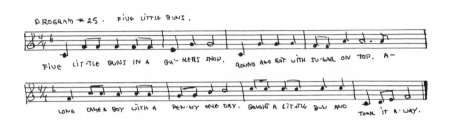

FIVE LIT-TLE BUNS IN A BA-KER'S SHOP, ROUND AND FAT WITH SUGAR ON TOP. A-

LONG CAME A BOY WITH A PEN-NY ONE DAY. BOUGHT A LIT-TLE BUN AND TOOK IT A-WAY.

PROGRAM #26. BLUEBIRD.

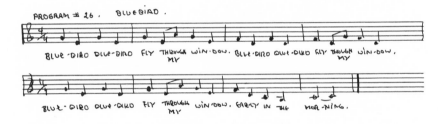

BLUE-BIRD BLUE-BIRD FLY THROUGH WIN-DOW. BLUE-BIRD BLUE-BIRD FLY THOUGH WIN-DOW,
MY   MY

BLUE-BIRD BLUE-BIRD FLY THROUGH WIN-DOW, EARLY IN THE MOR-NING.
MY

PROGRAM #29 AUTUMN LEAVES ARE FALLING DOWN. *

AUT-UMN LEAVES ARE FALL-ING DOWN. FALL-ING DOWN FALL-ING DOWN,

AUT-UMN LEAVES ARE FALL-ING DOWN. ALL O-VER TOWN.

PROGRAM #31. MISTER MOON.

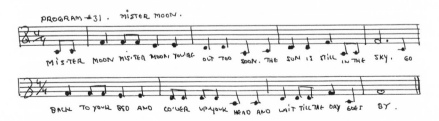

MIS-TER MOON MIS-TER MOON, YOU'RE OUT TOO SOON. THE SUN IS STILL IN THE SKY. GO

BACK TO YOUR BED AND CO-VER UP YOUR HEAD AND WAIT TILL THE DAY GOES BY.

PROGRAM # 43. SHAKE MY HAND AND YOU'LL BE MY FRIEND.

SHAKE MY HAND AND YOU'LL BE MY FRIEND. BE MY FRIEND. BE MY FRIEND.

SHAKE MY HAND AND YOU'LL BE MY FRIEND. WE'LL ALL BE FRIENDS.

PROGRAM # 44. MAILMAN MAILMAN BRING ME A LETTER.

MAIL MAN MAIL MAN BRING ME A LETTER

MAIL MAN MAIL MAN BRING ME A LETTER

I CAN HARDLY WAIT TO SEE WHAT IT IN YOUR BAG FOR ME.

PROGRAM # 47. EASTER BUNNY HOP HOP HOP! *

EASTER BUNNY HOP HOP HOP WRIGGLES HIS NOSE WHEN HE STOP STOP STOPS.

EASTER BUNNY HOP HOP HOP WRIGGLES HIS EARS WITH A FLIP FLIP FLOP.

EASTER BUNNY HOP HOP HOP WRIGGLES HIS TAIL WITH A DIP DIP DOP!

EASTER BUNNY HOP HOP HOP BRINGING US BASKETS FOR EASTER DAY.

PROGRAM # 47. HAPPY PETER PINK EARS.

HAP-PY PE-TER PINK EARS. HAPPY PE-TER PINK EARS.

HAP-PY PE-TER PINK EARS. HAP-PY PE-TER PINK-EAR

RUN RUN RUN RUN HOP HOP RUN RUN RUN RUN HOP HOP

RUN RUN RUN RUN HOP HOP RUN RUN RUN RUN HOP HOP!

PROGRAM # 50. WITCHES' POT *

HALL-O-WEEN HALL-O-WEEN. WIT-CHES STIR THEIR BIG BLACK POT.

HALL-O-WEEN HALL-O-WEEN WIT-CHES STIR THEIR BREW SO HOT.

OO-OO-OO-OO-OO-OO— OO-OO-OO-OO-OO-BOO!

PROGRAM # 52. THE TURKEY IS A FUNNY BIRD.

THE TUR-KEY IS A FUN-NY BIRD. GOBBLE-GOBBLE-GOBBLE, AND

ALL HE SAYS IS JUST ONE WORD. GOBBLE-GOBBLE-GOBBLE.

PROGRAM # 52. FIVE FAT TURKEYS ARE WE.

FIVE FAT TUR-KEYS ARE WE — WE SAT ALL NIGHT IN A TREE WHEN THE

COOK CAME A-ROUND, WE COULD-N'T BE FOUND. AND THAT'S WHY WE'RE HERE, DON'T YOU SEE!

GOBBLE GOBBLE GOBBLE GOBBLE GOBBLE

PROGRAM # 77. RAGS.

I'VE GOT A DOG HIS NAME IS RAGS, EATS SO MUCH THAT HIS TUM-MY SAGS.

EARS FLIP FLOP AND HIS TAIL BIG WAGS, AND WHEN HE WALKS HE ZIG ZIG ZAGS!

FLIP FLOP   FLIP FLOP   ZIG ZAG.

PROGRAM # 81. TEDDY BEARS GO DANCING.

TED-DY BEARS GO DANC—ING HOP HOP HOP.

SEE THE TED-DIES PRANC-ING HIPPITY HIPITY HOP.

NOW THEY STUMBLE NOW THEY FUMBLE NOW THEY TUMBLE IN A JUMBLE NOW THEY'RE GETTING UP A-GAIN

HIP-DI-TY HOP HIP-IN-TY HOP HIPPITY HIPPITY HOP HOP HOP

PROGRAM # 82. THE MONKEY STAMPS STAMPS STAMPS HIS FEET.

THE MONKEY CLAP CLAP CLAPS HIS HANDS. THE MONKEY CLAP CLAP CLAPS HIS HANDS.

MONKEY SEE AND MONKEY DO. MONKEY'S JUST THE SAME AS YOU.

PROGRAM # 83. JUMP JUMP JUMP. *

I WILL JUMP JUMP JUMP JUMP JUMP AND I'LL BUMP BUMP BUMP BUMP BUMP.

PROGRAM # 89. MATRIOSKA. *

MAT – RI – O - SKA MAT-RI-O-SKA MAT-RI-O-SKA DANCE DANCE.

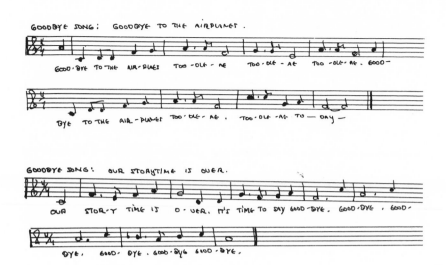

GOODBYE SONG: GOODBYE TO THE AIRPLANE.

GOOD-BYE TO THE AIR-PLANE TOO-DLE-AE TOO-DLE-AE TOO-DLE-AE. GOOD-

BYE TO THE AIR-PLANE TOO-DLE-AE. TOO-DLE-AE TO — DAY —

GOODBYE SONG: OUR STORYTIME IS OVER.

OUR STOR-Y TIME IS O-VER. IT'S TIME TO SAY GOOD-BYE. GOOD-BYE. GOOD-

BYE. GOOD-BYE. GOOD-BYE GOOD-BYE.

Subject Index

Numbers here correspond to program numbers, unless preceded by "p.", which designates "page."

Aerodynamics, 11. *See also* Wind
Afraid, feeling, 60, 85
African song, 16
Airplanes, 11, 27
Alligators, 74
Alphabet. *See* Letters of the alphabet
Anger, feeling, 59
Animals, fantasy, 32, 33, 35, 37, 38, 72–77, 96; real, 1–8, 17, 32
Apples, 2, 30, 78
Applesauce, 78
April Fool's Day, 46
Arbor Day, 2, 29, 30. *See also* Trees
Art, 58, 62, 91–94; use in storytime, p. 6–7. *See also* Crafts
Automobile. *See* Cars
Autumn, 29–33. *See also* Halloween, Thanksgiving

Babies, 73
Baby, new, 63
Bagpipes, 88
Bears, 35, 89. *See also* Teddy bears
Bedtime, 65. *See also* Lullabies, Night
Bees, 3
Beetles, 6
Bells, 55
Berries, 87
Bicycles, 14
Birthdays, 57
Boats, 71
Bonnets. *See* Hat
Bravery, 61
Bubbles, 12
Bugs. *See* Insects
Bulletin boards, 9, 47, 77

Bunnies. *See* Rabbits
Buttons, 67

Cake, 57
Candy, 56, 84
Caring, 61
Carpentry, 13
Cars, 14, 70
Caterpillars, 1
Cats, 33, 38, 75; Copy, 82
Celebrations, 43–57
Chairs, 15, 79
Chicken, 37, 97, 98
Christmas, 54–56
Classification, 15
Clay, 22, 59, 94
Collage, as illustration, 93; as craft, 1, 2, 22, 23, 25, 41, 43, 93. *See also* Mosaic
Colors, 26
Composition, musical, 95
Compost, 10
Concepts, basic, 25–28. *See also* Senses
Cookies, 27
Copy cats, 82
Costumes, 51
Counting, 25
Crafts, 8, 9, 17, 19, 24, 29, 30, 37, 55, 56, 58, 60–67, 69–77, 86–88, 90, 96, 99, 101. *See also* Art, Clay, Collage, Diorama, Drawing, Mosaic, Painting, Paper folding
Creative dramatics. *See* Dramatics, creative
Crocodiles, 74

Dancing, 50, 51, 81, 85, 97, 100, 101

Dark, 23, 60. *See also* Bedtime, Night
Death, 10
Dinosaurs, 17
Diorama, 17
Dogs, 77
Dolls, 89, 100. *See also* Teddy bears
Dramatics, creative, 4, 6, 8–10, 12, 19, 23, 24, 27, 29, 32, 35, 37, 40, 41, 43, 45–47, 49, 56, 58, 61, 64, 65, 67, 68, 71–73, 78, 89, 95, 97, 100; use in storytime, p. 9–10. *See also* Singing games, Dancing
Drawing story, 33
Drawings, as illustrations, 92
Dreams, 80
Dreidel, 53
Drums, 54, 99
Ducks, 36, 37

Ears, 20
Earth, interior, 19
Earthworms, 8
Easter, 47. *See also* 36, 37
Eggs, 37; Easter, 47
Elephants, 73
Emotions. *See* Feelings
Ethnic programs, 88–90
Expressions, facial, 64
Eyes, 23

Faces, making, 64
Fairy tale setting, 86
Fall. *See* Autumn
Famous people. *See* Van Leeunhoek, Schubert
Fantasy, 35, 69–87
Farm, 30, 37, 49, 76, 97
Fast, 26
Feelings, 20–24; anger, 59; bravery, 60; caring, 61; copying, 82; fear, 60, 85; foolish, 46; grumpiness, 59; happiness, 58; jealousy of new baby, 63; self-confidence, 62; showing, 64; sleepiness, 65
Feet, 66
Field, 1

Films, use in storytime, p. 8–9. *See also* Index of Films, p. 235–36.
Flags, 48
Flannel boards, 73, 83, 88; use in storytime, p. 11
Flowers, 1, 3, 6, 7, 24, 36, 101
Flying, 11
Food, 21, 98; food activities, 16, 21; freaky food, 78. *See also* Apples, Berries, Cake, Eggs, Jam, Peanut butter, Popcorn, Pumpkin, Soup, Strawberries, Turkey. *See also* Birthdays, Hanukkah, Thanksgiving
Fools, 46
Fourth of July, 48
France, 90
Friends, 43, 44, 61
Frogs, 5, 96
Furniture, 79. *See also* Chairs

Games: dreidel, 53; "Simon says," 82; "weather telling," 66. *See also* Singing games
Gardens, 3. *See also* Flowers
Gears, 14
Ghosts, 50, 51
Glad, feeling, 58
Grass, 1, 93
Grumpy, feeling, 59

Habitats, 1–6
Halloween, 49–51
Hanukkah, 53
Happy, feeling, 58
Harvest, 31, 58, 87
Hat, making, 38, 46, 86
Hearing, 20
Holidays, 43–57
Home, 68
House, 13, 68; furniture in, 79
Hunt, shamrocks, 45

Imagination, 69–87
Inchworms, 1
Insects, 1, 2, 3, 6
Instrument, stringed, 96
Inventors, 16
Ireland, 45

Jack-o-Lanterns, 49
Jam, 21, 87
Jungle, 72–74

Kilt, 86
King, 86
Kittens. *See* Cats

Lacing, 66, 67
Leaves, 29
Letters, 44
Letters of the alphabet, 92. *See also* Reading
Life cycle, 1, 2, 7, 10
Light, 23
Line drawing, as illustration, 92
Lions, 72
Listening, 20
Love, 43
Lullabies, 54. *See also* Bedtime, Night

Machines, simple, 13, 14
Mad, feeling, 59
Magic, 27
Magnifying glass, 16
Mail, 44
May Day, 101
May Pole, 101
Me, a celebration of, 62
Mice, 32, 33, 75
Microscopes, 16
Mirrors, 23
Mold, 10
Monkeys, 82
Monsters, 85. *See also* Ghosts, Witches
Moon, 31
Mosaic, 17
Movement. *See* Dancing. (Most programs include a movement segment, often an action song).
Mushrooms, 9, 10
Music, use in storytime, p. 4–6, p. 187–88
Musical programs, 96–101. (All programs include singing). *See also* Appendix: Musical Notations for Songs
Musicians, famous, 95

Nature. *See* Science
Night, 32, 60, 65, 80, 85. *See also* Bedtime, Dark
Noise, 20
Nonsense, 78–87
Nose, 24
Numbers, 25

Ocean. *See* Sea
Owls, 32

Painting, (craft), 34
Palace, 86
Paper airplanes, 11, 27
Paper cutting, 35
Paper folding, 32
Parades, 39, 43, 45, 48, 100
Parent involvement in storytime, p. 1–4
Paris, 90
Patriotism, 48, 99
Peanut butter, 21
People, famous. See Van Leeunhoek, Schubert
Piano, 95
Picnics, 1, 34, 81
Pigs, 76
Playdough. *See* Clay
Poetry, 3, 4, 9, 12, 37, 45, 54, 62, 77, 79; use in storytime, p. 4–5. (Most programs include poetry).
Poetry program, 78, 83, 84
Point of view, 23
Pond, 5
Popcorn, 16
Postman, 44
Predicting, 27
Prints, (craft), 82, 91
Prints, as illustration, 91
Pumpkins, 49
Puppets, 9, 45, 51, 85; use in storytime, p. 10–11
Puppies. *See* Dogs
Pussywillows, 38
Puzzle, 28, 31

Queen, 86

Rabbits, 47
Rain, 9, 40

256

Reading, 83
Rhymes, 83, 84
Rhythm instruments, 96–101; use in storytime, p. 5–6, p. 187–88
Rocks, 18
Rot, 10
Royalty, 86
Russia, 89

Sailing, 71
Sand castle, 94
Santa Claus, 56
Scared, feeling, 60, 85
Schubert, Franz, 95
Science, 1–31, 33, 42; use in storytime, p. 7–8
Science experiments, 3, 7, 8, 9, 11–14, 16, 20–24, 29, 42, 79
Scotland, 88
Sea, 4, 71
Season, 29–42. See also Celebrations
Seeds, 7
Seeing, 23
Self-esteem, 62
Senses, 20–24
Sequencing, 27
Shadows, 42
Shells, 4
Shoes, 66
Sight, 23
Singing games, 15, 32, 33, 35, 44, 50, 57, 66, 68, 73, 75, 98
Skin, sense of touch, 22
Sleep, 65, 80. See also Night
Slow, 26
Slugs, 6
Smell, 24
Snow, 34, 35
Sound, 20
Soup, 22, 98
Speed, 26
Spiders, 3
Spring, 36–40. See also April Fools' Day, Easter, May Day, Wind

Square dance, 97
St. Patrick's Day, 45
Storylines, predicting, 27
Strawberries, 87
Summer, 41, 42. See also 1–8
Sun, 41, 42

Taste, 21
Tartan, 88
Teddy bears, 81
Temper. See Feelings.
Thanksgiving, 52
Tools, 13
Touch, 22
Train, 69
Translucence, 23
Transparency, 23
Trees, 2, 10, 29, 30
Trick or treat, 51
Tricycles, 14
Turkeys, 52
Turtles, 5

Umbrellas, 40

Valentine's Day, 43
Van Leeunhoek, Anton, 16
Veterans' Day. See Patriotism
Volcanoes, 19

Walking, 2, 3, 6, 12, 18, 20, 22, 23
War, 99
Weather, 12, 34, 40–42, 66
Weddings, 43
Wheels, 14. See also Cars
Wind, 12
Winter, 34, 35; in Russia, 89. See also Thanksgiving, Hanukkah, Christmas, Valentine's Day
Witches, 50, 51
Woodblock, as illustration, 91
Words, playing with, 83, 84. See also Poetry
Worms, 8. See also Caterpillars

Zimbabwe, 66